*To Uncle Ben
With Best Wishes,
Loren Nicholson*

RAILS
ACROSS THE
RANCHOS

Centennial Edition Celebrating the
Southern Pacific Railroad Coastal Line
LIMITED TO 1500 COPIES

First passenger train arriving in Los Angeles from San Francisco.

RAILS ACROSS THE RANCHOS may be ordered directly from
    CALIFORNIA HERITAGE PUBLISHING
ASSOCIATES
    156 Del Norte Way
    San Luis Obispo, CA 93405
or directly through your bookstore.

This Centennial Issue is Limited to 1500 copies.

Library of Congress Catalog Number 80-50074.

ISBN 0-9623233-6-5

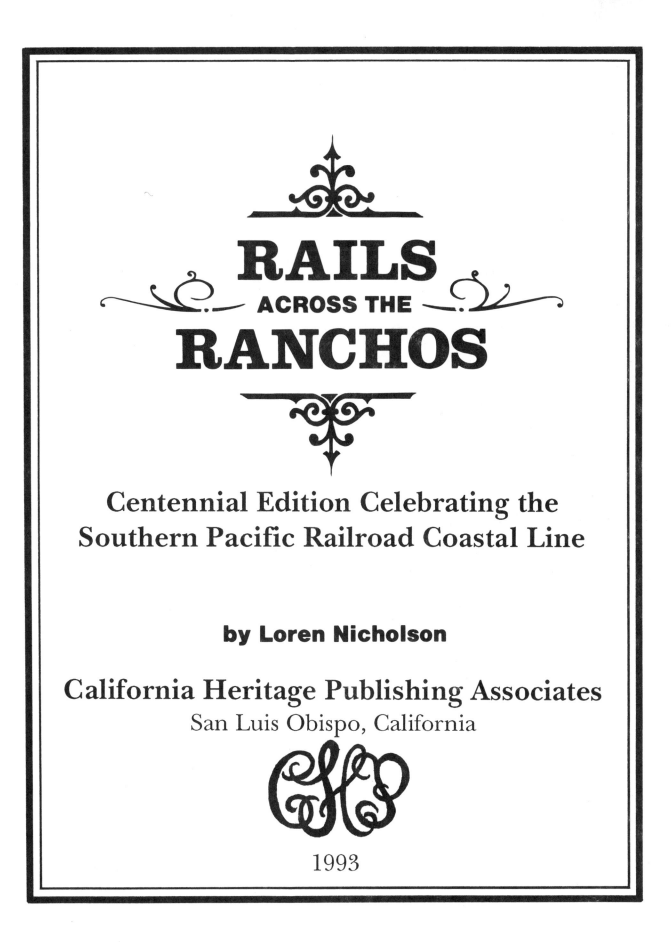

RAILS
ACROSS THE
RANCHOS

Centennial Edition Celebrating the
Southern Pacific Railroad Coastal Line

by Loren Nicholson

California Heritage Publishing Associates
San Luis Obispo, California

1993

Chronology of Southern Pacific Railroad Reaching These California Cities

* SAN FRANCISCO-SAN JOSE RAILROAD- (Name changed to Southern Pacific Railroad Dec. 2, 1865. Purchased by Central Pacific Railroad in 1868.).

*MAYFIELD- Oct. 10, 1863.

*SAN JOSE- Jan. 16, 1864.

*GILROY- Mar. 13, 1869.

*HOLLISTER- July 13,1871.

*GILROY TO PAJARO (Watsonville Junction)- Nov. 27, 1871.

*SALINAS- Nov. 1, 1872.

*TRES PINOS- Aug. 12, 1873.

*SOLEDAD- Aug. 12, 1873.

*KING CITY- July 20, 1886.

*SAN MIGUEL-Oct. 18, 1886.

*PASO ROBLES- Oct. 31, 1886.

*TEMPLETON- Nov. 16, 1886.

*SANTA BARBARA- A spur line was built from the California Central Valley mainline at Saugus. First passenger train arrived Aug. 26, 1887.

*SANTA MARGARITA- April 19, 1889.

*SAN LUIS OBISPO- May 5, 1894.

*PISMO BEACH- Jan. 14, 1895

*OCEANO- Jan. 27, 1895

*GUADALUPE- July 1, 1895

*SURF- 1897.

*SANTA BARBARA-SURF gap was closed. Coastal trains from the north began running to Los Angeles April 1, 1901.

*COASTAL RAILROAD traffic from San Francisco and points north were routed over a new line out of Santa Barbara by way of Oxnard and Burbank into Los Angeles beginning March 20, 1904.

*LATHROP- This was a new inland stop tying lines from both Sacramento and San Francisco Bay area with California's Central Valley. Established December 31, 1869.

*MODESTO- Nov. 8, 1970

*MERCED- Jan. 15, 1872

*FRESNO- May 28, 1872

*TULARE- July 25, 1872

*SUMMER- (EAST BAKERSFIELD)-Nov. 8, 1874

*THESE STOPS were followed by construction of 28 miles and eighteen tunnels through the Tehachapi Mountains requiring years before reaching Mohave.

*MOHAVE- Aug. 8, 1876

*LOS ANGELES- Sept. 5, 1876

*YUMA- May 23, 1977. Service began Sept. 30, 1877.

Table Of Contents

Acknowledgements   vii

Introduction   ix

I   The Grand Promise   1

II   Making Large Ranchos Into Smaller Ones   7

III   Tracks For San Miguel   19

IV   Passing El Paso De Robles   27

V   Fire, Tears and Music   35

VI   A New Town   45

VII   The Board Of Trade   51

VIII The Hotel Promoters   57

IX   Action On The Santa Margarita   65

X   New Towns To The South   77

XI   Two Great New Hotels   87

XII   Land Subscriptions   93

XIII Gathering New Hope   107

XIV The Search For Outside Support   113

XV   Railroad Work Really Begins   123

XVI Tunnel Building   133

XVII Work All Along The Line   151

XVIII Opening The Tunnels   159

XIX The Steel Bridge Across Stenner Creek   165

XX   The Train To San Luis Obispo   173

Epilogue   181

Notes   189

Index   193

Work train clears debri in Cuesta tunnel.

-DEDICATION-

This centennial edition celebrating the arrival of the Southern Pacific Railroad along the California coast is dedicated to RUSSELL CLAY GOODRICH, a lifelong book man with an avid interest in American railroads. Mr. Goodrich inspired this reprinting.

With Grateful Acknowledgements To:

Patricia Henley Nicholson, whose deep and abiding interest in California history awakened my own and whose research and copyreading have contributed generously to this book.

Margaret Price and Patricia Clark, whose kind and willing reference assistance at the San Luis Obispo Public Library over many years supported my desire to write about California.

Louisiana Clayton Dart, curator of the San Luis Obispo County Museum for 25 years, who shared her exceptional knowledge of the history and of the people of San Luis Obispo County during many fascinating discussions at the museum.

My wife, Dr. Bernice Loughran-Nicholson, who prepared the cover of this book and devoted long hours to organizing the index.

I am also grateful to the members of the San Luis Obispo County Historical Society, the South County Historical Society, the Atascadero Historical Society, the Santa Maria Historical Society and the Santa Barbara Historical Society for sharing so much information about California with me.

Hundreds of individuals may rightfully claim some contribution to this book, even though many will not recall how they helped.

With deepest thanks, I share my authorship with all of the above persons and groups.

Loren Nicholson

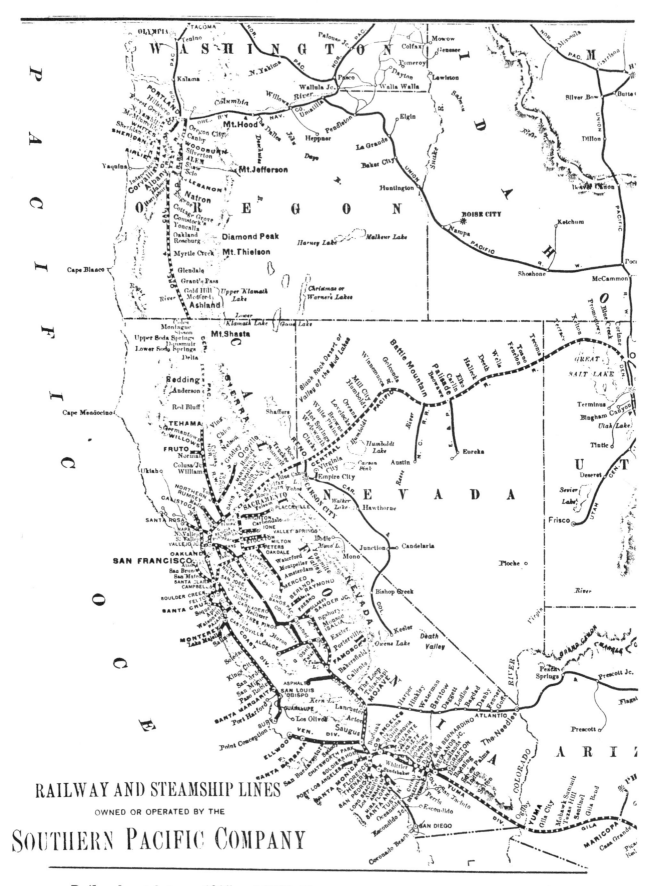

RAILWAY AND STEAMSHIP LINES

OWNED OR OPERATED BY THE

SOUTHERN PACIFIC COMPANY

Railroad map between 1895 and 1900. Note gap along coast between Surf and Ellwood.

Introduction:

"In the history of San Luis Obispo, when its next chapter shall be written, the page which will stand out in gold will be that devoted to the Fifth of May, 1894."
Benjamin Brooks, Editor
San Luis Obispo Tribune
May 5, 1894

Editor Brook's insightful projection referred to that day when the first Southern Pacific Railroad passenger train from San Francisco arrived in San Luis Obispo. It had taken him years of fretting, planning, complaining and cheer-leading to help make it happen.

During that last decade of the 19th century, this farwest rail line gradually stretched from both northern and southern California to eventually close an important railroad gap along the coast, opening the world to many appreciative communities of people.

So, now, 100 years later..during the last decade of our century..we write the next chapter to which Editor Brooks referred and celebrate the building of the railroad that made so much difference to the coastal people between San Francisco and Los Angeles. These were the rails across the great ranchos originally provided as land grants by the earlier Mexican governors to Mexican citizens who colonized the territory.

It took many years after American occupation of California in 1846 for the United States Land Commission to settle ownership claims of the Mexican grants. Most of the original owners had either sold their land or had disbursed it among family members by the time our story begins.

The coastal lands of San Luis Obispo and Santa Barbara counties remained isolated. Changes occurred slowly. It was the news about a possible coastal rail line reaching this area in 1885 that awakened everyone to new possibilities. Just the prospect had a striking effect upon both the land and the lives of the people who lived along what they called "the gap."

In the wake of railroad construction, large ranchos were subdivided, small towns grew larger and many new settlements came into existence...Templeton, Santa Margarita, Creston, Grover, Oceano...each with aspirations of becoming important places.

Upon open land across which all God's creatures once moved freely, new lines were drawn. There appeared fences blocking movement even across the fifty by one hundred foot lots in the settlements.

It is not a new story. It is a microcosm of a universal human movement...the division and subdivision of a beautiful natural unity that was once shared by all.

Myron Angel's book, the History of San Luis Obispo, brought this area's history up to 1883. Our story begins in 1885 and closes with the new twentieth century.

Loren Nicholson

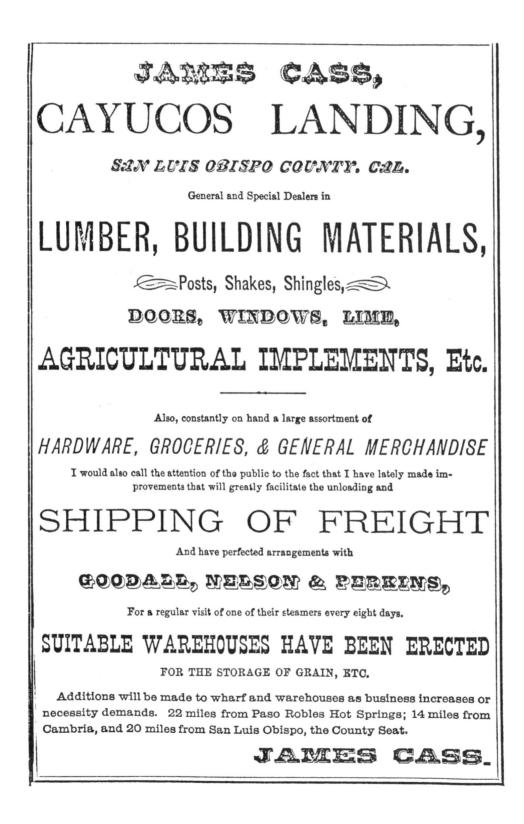

CHAPTER I

The Grand Promise

A MOST REMARKABLE EVENT occurred that Friday evening, July 3, 1885, in the remote little town of San Luis Obispo.

Folks from Nipomo, Santa Manuela, Arroyo Grande and other ranchos to the south slowly paraded their buckboards, wagons and fine carriages along rutted and dusty Monterey Street. Others arrived aboard the Pacific Coast narrow gauge railway. Coastal people from the San Miguelito, Los Osos and Cayucos ranchos had followed the wagon trails along the beaches from the north into town. From the other side of the Cuesta, people came through the rolling countryside of the El Paso de Robles, Asuncion, the Atascadero and the Santa Margarita.

They had all come to celebrate the opening of San Luis Obispo's first grand hotel—and more.

In their isolation from the rest of the world, they were sharing hope and a feeling of promise for the future.

The wondrous new Andrews Hotel, three stories high and towering above the town, stood at the corner of Monterey and Osos Streets, just two blocks from Mission San Luis Obispo de Tolosa.[1]

A local fire and brimstone preacher put into words the dreams that moved everyone: "I am listening," he said, "for the tramp of the coming multitudes . . . they are coming fifty thousand strong. Coming from their eastern homes to find this balmy atmosphere and to secure for themselves and for their children a future home . . . coming as the tide comes on the wave-bent shore; coming . . . as distant music on the air;

This architectural rendering of the hotel provided investors an opportunity to visualize the structure. There had never been a building of this magnitude in San Luis Obispo. It was located on the northwest corner of Monterey and Osos streets.

J. P. Andrews, the major investor and the man for whom the Andrews Hotel was named.

and those fifty thousand immigrants shall find shelter and a home." And with their coming, people hoped, a new prosperity would change life for the better.[2]

On this evening before Independence Day, a light breeze found its way through the Irish Hills, across Los Osos Valley and to the south side of San Luis Peak. It played about the cheeks of the arrivals at the hotel's covered archway. The men wore high stiff collars, vests with neatly rolled edges and long coats with wide lapels. The breeze ruffled the summer finery of the ladies as they stepped from the buggies. Delicate lace, bustles, ribbons and ankle-length dresses made the evening a Godey's Ladies' Book of summer fashion.

"The present condition (of the town) is that of steady progress," *Tribune* editor Myron Angel had modestly written a few years earlier. "Gas and water works have been constructed, a fire department organized, a military company equipped, a fine brick city hall erected . . . the Pacific Coast Railway is completed from Port Harford to Los Alamos." But Angel discreetly bypassed discussion of sewage, water and street conditions.

The pioneering firm of Goldtree Brothers, a general merchandising business, had indicated

its faith in the future of the town two years earlier by the construction of a fine two-story brick building at the corner of Chorro and Higuera Streets.

There were also two other recently built brick buildings in town. One was the San Luis Bank located just across Monterey Street from the hotel. The other was Loobliner's, a general store standing at the corner of Monterey and Court Streets in the same block with the bank. Beyond that, San Luis Obispo was a wooden town with its adobe past still in evidence here and there. There were bridges of a sort across the creeks at Mill, Court, Morro, Chorro, Nipomo and Broad Streets. The town claimed a population of about three thousand.

San Luis Obispo could be reached by steamship from other Pacific Coast ports. Ships landed passengers and cargo at the Port Harford Wharf in Avila, and the Pacific Coast Railway made regular runs between the port and San Luis Obispo.[3]

GRAND OPENING OF THE ANDREWS HOTEL
July 3, 1885

Board of Directors

J. P. Andrews, President	C. D. P. Jones
William Buckley	B. Sinsheimer
J. M. Fillmore	W. E. Stewart, Secretary

Committee on Arrangements

C. H. Phillips	W. Schwartz	C. H. Reed
Col. R. B. Treat	E. W. Steele	G. B. Staniford
W. L. Beebee	D. W. James	H. M. Warden

Stockholders

J. P. Andrews	C. D. P. Jones	J. D. Thompson
P. W. Murphy	Pacific Coast	Sinsheimer Brothers
Louis Marre	Steamship Company	L. M. Kaiser
	William Buckley	C. H. Phillips

Reception Committee

P. W. Murphy	W. M. Jeffreys	Morris Goldtree
L. M. Warden	C. H. Phillips	A. Redlasbrook
R. E. Jack	W. T. Lucas	C. R. Brumley
P. H. Dallidet, Jr.	Col. W. W. Hollister	Charles Maxwell
John Scott	J. M. Fillmore	J. H. Blackburn
James Cass	Dr. W. W. Hays	W. A. Gregg
Hon. J. H. Hollister	L. M. Kaiser	J. R. Patton
Joseph H. Hollister	Hon. Geo. Steele	W. H. Spencer
Arza Porter	Hon. H. Y. Stanley	B. Sinsheimer
J. F. Branch	J. C. Baker	R. M. Bean
H. A. Sperry	J. M. Jordon	J. P. Andrews
Myron Angel	L. Marre	E. Hatch
C. W. Merritt	L. Rockliffe	A. Phillips
McD. R. Venable	C. W. Dana	C. L. Russell

Members of the San Luis Obispo Military Band, along with several children and a few local dignitaries posed in front of the new hotel soon after it opened July 3, 1885. The street floor had a real estate office and a Wells Fargo and Company Express and Stage office. The center tower, the highest structure in town, housed a signal corps attachment.

All of these signs of progress were subjects for discussion as the sound of music by Professor McCoy and his little orchestra greeted the crowd and brightened the occasion. Professor McCoy would be busy the next day, too, leading the Independence Day parade. He always led the parades in town and occasionally conducted a military band concert at the Lytton Theater.

John Pinkney and Tennessee Amanda Andrews greeted all of the guests as they arrived. Andrews was principal stockholder in the new hotel venture, and at sixty-one years of age, he was at the pinnacle of his career. He had come to California in 1857 and settled in San Luis Obispo in 1859. Editor Angel described him as a "man of great force and iron will." Tireless industry certainly marked his career. He made his first money in ranching. In 1873 he organ-

ized the Bank of San Luis Obispo in partnership with several other prominent men including C. H. Phillips, R. G. Flint, John Biddle, Phillip Biddle and H. M. Warden. He continued a long period of bank ownership which also included the San Luis Obispo County bank and later the Andrews Bank. The latter eventually became the Commercial Bank.

Andrews donated the land for both the county courthouse, still in use in 1980 for that purpose, and the land for the Court Grammar School at the southwest corner of Palm and Santa Rosa Streets, where the City Recreation Building existed in 1980.[4]

After all the guests had been properly received in the vestibule and main hallway of the hotel, they spread and mingled throughout the rooms of the main floor. Old acquaintances from all parts of the county greeted each other.

Members of the San Luis Obispo Military Band, seated in front, left to right: Charles Knight, the mascot, and John Simas. Standing on left side: Joe Sullivan, Frank Rodriquez, and Manuel Marshall. Sitting, top row: Dale Wurch, Frank Boso, Frank Terry, Charles Denman, J. E. Van Schaick and Mat Shea. Standing on right: Fred Finney, John Shea and Professor Davis, who by the time this photo was made had replaced Professor McCoy as leader of the band.

It was a rare occasion for so many people from such distances to be assembled together.

The hotel lobby led directly from the Monterey Street entrance to the back doorway, looking out on a large undeveloped outdoor court which was to be developed into a garden for the pleasure of the hotel's guests. A carriageway in the court made it possible for guests to drive their buggies to this entrance from Osos Street. To the left and right of the hallway at this back entrance, wide stairways led to the upper floors.

The hotel was built in a large U-shape. The wing of the building facing Osos Street included a large ladies' reception room, a luxiously furnished and gaslighted reading room, several sample rooms to accommodate commercial travelers, toilet rooms and a large bar and billiard room. Tonight, some of these rooms were set up with tables for serving dinner.

The wing on the other side of the hotel beckoned most of the guests later in the evening. The main part of this west wing was the actual dining room, thirty-seven by sixty feet, reserved for dancing tonight. The wing also had two smaller rooms which could be opened to add to the dining accommodations or closed to take care of small dinner parties. Both rooms were open this evening. The kitchen, a large laundry, storerooms, pastry rooms and rooms for the Chinese help occupied the back portion of this wing.

Some of the out-of-town guests attending the grand opening dinner-dance had arrived early in the day and had taken accommodations at the Andrews. The hotel management had advertised in the *Tribune* that Pacific Coast Railway fares were reduced to half rates for persons attending the grand opening. Tickets to the opening included dinner and dancing and cost three dollars. Hotel rooms rented for two dollars and up per night.

On the second floor there were fifty-six rooms, many of them arranged as suites with parlors and bedrooms conveniently located near the public baths and toilets along the hall. Some suites included dining rooms connected to the downstairs by dumb waiters for receiving food from the kitchen.

One of the nicest suites in the hotel had been

Looking east from the mission down Monterey Street. Businesses in the foreground, left to right, are Goldtree Brothers' General Store and Sauer's Bakery. Note the condition of the street during rainy weather.

occupied a few evenings before the grand opening by a distinguished guest from New York City—none other than Whitelaw Reid, the editor of the *New York Tribune*. Even persons who had never heard of him knew of his newspaper. In earlier years, some of their forebears had been influenced by its first editor and publisher, Horace Greeley, whose editorials cried, "Go West, Young Man, Go West!" *Tribune* editor Myron Angel hosted Reid while he was in town. Those who met Reid could not know that four years later he would be appointed U.S. Minister to France (1889-92) and then later Ambassador to England (1905-12).

Second floor accommodations in each wing of the hotel were conveniently reached by a center hallway. Rooms were located on both sides of the hall with windows to the outside and "with very graceful and rich gas fixtures for artificial light. All accommodations include[d] hot and cold water, fireplaces and electric call bells."

The high roof with dormer windows formed an attic "almost the equivalent to a third story," and it contained thirty sleeping rooms. The center tower was already occupied as an observatory by the United States signal service, and it commanded a view of the city and surrounding country.

"The furniture throughout is the most elegant and luxurious that good taste could suggest or money could buy," the *Tribune* reported. Furnishings varied from room to room; some rooms were furnished in walnut, others in ash, and still others in cherry wood . . . "elaborate and highly polished. . . . Costly curtains, fine paintings in rich frames, soft velvet and Brussels carpets, grand mirrors and pleasant easy chairs adorn all."

The process of getting a whole hotel full of fine furniture to remote San Luis Obispo had required careful arrangements and planning. On May 22, 1885, J. P. Andrews and J. M. Fillmore returned from a trip to San Francisco on the steamer *Eureka*. While in San Francisco they had purchased furniture for 112 rooms and contracted the use of the steamer from the Pacific Coast Steamship Company to bring their cargo to San Luis Obispo. The two men debarked at Cayucos and traveled by stage for the rest of the trip. The furniture was unloaded at Port Harford and delivered to San Luis Obispo by the Pacific Coast Railway.

The dining room ceiling was high and unpainted. The natural wood, oiled and varnished, supported timbers and moldings which gave the room a massive lodge-like appearance. "The dining room tables [were] of ash with heavy central strands carved and polished." The tops were covered with felting over which the linen tablecloths were spread "thus relieving the chill and noise" when dishes were placed. Every piece of silverware was engraved with the name, "The Andrews."[5]

Dinner conversation reflected enthusiasm about the prospect of a new era in the county. After dinner, couples strolled in the direction of the soft strains of Professor McCoy's music in the dining room.

Perhaps the busiest person that evening was E. B. Morriss, the general manager of the Andrews. He had not only assumed the responsibility of the dinner-dance, but he was also chairman of the committee that had planned the next day's Independence Day celebration. The day would include a parade, contests, and fireworks in the evening. It would begin at sunrise with a thirty-eight gun salute and all of the church bells ringing.

Mr. Morriss was well-known to travelers who came regularly to San Luis Obispo. He had come to California in 1857 and to San Luis Obispo in 1860. Since then, except for a short

Higuera at Broad Street looking east during the 1880s. Wooden buildings, dirt streets, buckboards, wagons and teams of horses characterized San Luis Obispo during this time.

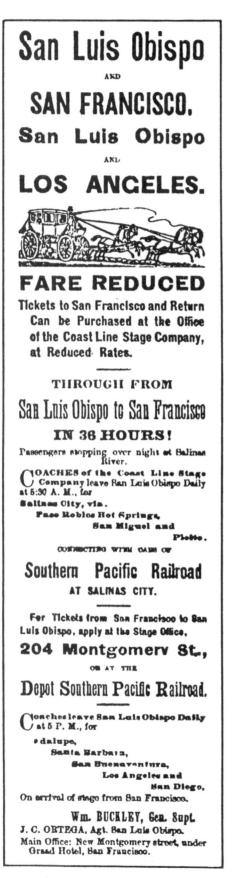

The stagecoach continued to be the principal mode of overland transportation along the California coast in the 1890s. This advertisement was first published in the San Luis Obispo Tribune November 13, 1875. Flint, Bixby and Company provided service at the time.

time when he sought his fortune in mining in Nevada, this city had been his home.

For many years, Morriss was the lessee and a partner in the Cosmopolitan Hotel with J. H. Blackburn. The Cosmopolitan Hotel had begun as "a small adobe with a good foundation, built by Juan Cappe for a saloon." A second story with additional rooms was added later. Other additions were made until the hotel was completed.

Blackburn and Morriss were the Cosmopolitan Hotel's first proprietors, and they continued as partners until 1880, when Morriss left the business. He returned as lessee in April 1883, then left again to become the manager of the Andrews.[6]

Some of the largest landowners in San Luis Obispo County attended this gala affair. A few of them had invested money in the hotel and for good reason—a hotel would dress up the town, reflect well upon the county, and help to attract prospective settlers and investors.

Many of the men in attendance that evening were to be influential in the changes that would take place in the county during the next ten years, and their names appear frequently in this book.

However, there was one man in the crowd who may have been sought out more that evening than some others—a man who was inspiring many to look anew at their county. He was Chauncey Hatch Phillips, a personable, highly charismatic, energetic man.

The glow of gaslights shone into the summer night from nearly every window in the hotel. The music of the orchestra reached across the blackness of the little town, and gay voices, laughter and dancing lasted into the night.

CHAPTER II

Making Large Ranchos Into Smaller Ones

Poorly developed wagon roads and the distance of San Luis Obispo County from both San Francisco and Los Angeles severely restricted the lives of those who found their way to this coastal area and settled.

But Chauncey Hatch Phillips was an uncommon man with uncommon drive. Phillips had succeeded in establishing rewarding contacts throughout San Luis Obispo County and north all the way to San Francisco. He was always ready to drive his horse and buggy in the direction of opportunity within the county, and for more distant contacts, he traveled aboard the Pacific Coast Steamship Company's vessels from Port Harford in Avila. Four ships made regular stops in 1885—the *Eureka*, the *Santa Rosa*, the *Los Angeles*, and the *Orizaba*. One of these ships anchored at Port Harford every two or three days to deliver and receive freight and passengers. Moving farm products overland to the wharf was an extreme hardship for farmers, and Phillips was among those who sought to make the task easier.[1]

Phillips had married a young woman named Jane Woods in Fond de Lac, Wisconsin in 1862. In 1864, at the age of twenty-seven, he traveled alone by steamer from the East Coast to California. Jane soon joined him. He worked for the United States Internal Revenue Department in Napa County, San Jose and San Francisco. Tall, lean, strong and commanding in appearance, he was unusually able in financial affairs, and he came into positions of leadership easily and quickly.

In 1871 Phillips traveled to San Luis Obispo looking for new opportunities. Soon after arrival, he met Horatio Moore Warden, and they joined forces to establish the county's first bank. After two years, they helped form a corporation and merged their operations with another new company, the Bank of San Luis Obispo. Phillips served as manager, cashier, and for a time, president, when Warden gave up that position.

During these years, Phillips also served as a prime mover in the development of a narrow-gauge railway line between Port Harford in Avila and the town of San Luis Obispo.[2] The town of Avila was laid out at the ocean at the mouth of San Luis Creek, and another community called Miles Station was planned above San Luis Creek near the location of the present-day Buddhist Temple above Highway 101. The local railway company constructed a line inland from Avila only as far as Miles Station in 1875, and then called upon the people of San Luis Obispo to subscribe to $25,000 worth of stock if they wanted the line to run further inland into town.

Phillips, along with another strong local leader, C. H. Johnson, promoted subscriptions for this stock. They raised $28,500, and in 1876 the line was extended inland into San Luis Obispo. The entire enterprise required less than fifteen miles of track, but it opened the way for moving farm products from the ranches of the county to ships docking at Port Harford.[3]

Phillips, having migrated to San Luis Obispo by way of San Jose and San Francisco, was undoubtedly aware of railroad activities in the north, but they were too remote at the time to affect San Luis Obispo.

A rail line had been laid between San Francisco and San Jose by a small company called the San Francisco and San Jose Railroad. It

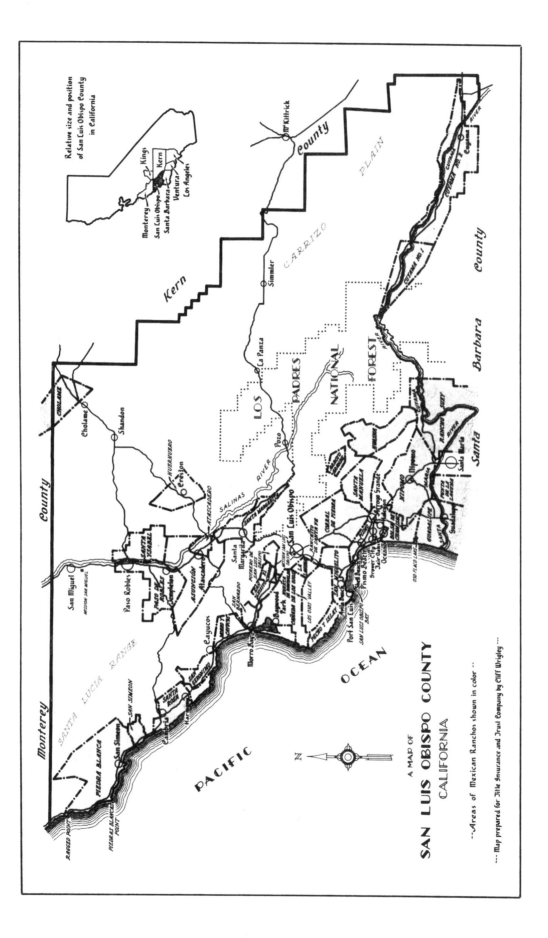

A MAP OF
SAN LUIS OBISPO COUNTY
CALIFORNIA

-- Areas of Mexican Ranchos shown in color --

---- Map prepared for Title Insurance and Trust Company by Cliff Wrigley ----

Relative size and position of San Luis Obispo County in California

provided passenger and freight service between these points beginning January 16, 1864.

In early December 1865, some of the founders reorganized the company and named it the Southern Pacific Railroad Company. They sought and received authorization from Congress to build a line through Santa Clara, San Benito and San Joaquin counties to Needles to connect with the Atlantic and Pacific (later named the Santa Fe) railroad.

In 1868 the "Big Four" bought the Southern Pacific Railroad and all of its rights. Leland Stanford was the company president; Collis Huntington was first vice president; Charles F. Crocker was second vice president; and Timothy Hopkins, foster son of Mark Hopkins, was treasurer. They brought to the new little company all of their accumulated experience as the builders of Central Pacific Railroad's transcontinental line.

The line from San Jose was extended southward very gradually. It took three years for it to reach the town of Hollister, service to that point beginning July 13, 1871. By November 27, 1871, the line had been extended to Pajaro Junction outside of Watsonville. It reached Salinas within another year, on November 1, 1872, and on August 12, 1873, was extended to Soledad. There it stopped for some years.[4]

Meanwhile, the Southern Pacific was much more active in the construction of line that could eventually meet the Atlantic and Pacific Railroad line at Needles. From San Francisco, they constructed line into the San Joaquin Valley and had begun service to Modesto by November 8, 1870. They had moved on to Merced by January 15, 1872, to Fresno by May 28, 1872, and to Tulare by July 25, 1872. This line was to become the Sunset Route. On November 8, 1874, the railroad reached Bakersfield; then began a difficult two-year struggle with building line through the Tehachapi Mountains, but by 1876 rail line was complete from San Francisco to Los Angeles by the valley route.

Also during 1876, the little narrow-gauge line between Avila and San Luis Obispo was completed.[5]

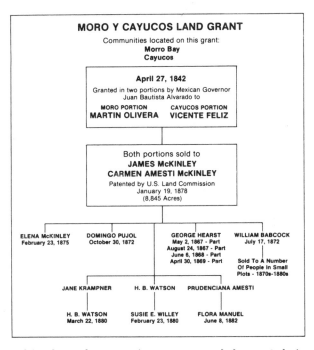

This chart shows major owners and dates of their acquisition of parts of this land grant as it was divided and sold through 1882. Not all dates were available.

In 1875 Phillips became interested in the Moro Y Cayucos Ranchos. This original Mexican grant was located between the present communities of Morro Bay and Cayucos and northward in San Luis Obispo County. To satisfy two applicants, it had been granted in two parts by Mexican Governor Juan Bautista Alvarado on April 27, 1842. The southern portion, identified as Moro, was granted to Martin Olivera. The northern part of the rancho, referred to as Cayucos, was granted to Vicente Feliz.

If the records are accurate, Olivera was sixty-two years old at the time he received the grant. He was married to Josepha Noriega. They had seven children and lived on the Sanizal Rancho in Monterey before receiving the Moro grant. Because of his age, it is not surprising to find that Olivera soon disposed of his interest in the grant.

Feliz, the owner of the Cayucos half of the rancho, was a soldier in the Mexican army, stationed in Santa Barbara during the early 1830s. By 1836 he was mayordomo at Buena Esperanza Rancho. He lost his wife, Felomena Valenzuela, when he was only twenty-six years old, but not before they had four children.

The entire Moro Y Cayucos property covered 8,845 acres stretching along the coast of San Luis Obispo County. Both portions of the grant soon came into the hands of James Mc-Kinley, a sometimes partner of Captain John Wilson and James Scott.

All three of these men were Scots and seamen who sailed the California coast during the Mexican period beginning in the 1830s. All had large land holdings in San Luis Obispo County. Often the Mexican land grantees lacked capital to stock the ranchos after they received them, and when they were offered cattle and other goods in exchange, they gave up the land.

McKinley became a Mexican citizen and married Carmen Amesti. As supercargo (business manager) on many coastal vessels, he became well known among rancho owners and tradesmen at every port.

When McKinley died, the title to Moro Y Cayucos remained unclear. This was common with the Mexican land grants. The boundaries were usually identified by landmarks that were indefinite or that changed over a period of time, and the papers specifying a change of ownership were often ambiguous. Nonetheless, Carmen McKinley and her offspring sold the rancho in a few large parcels.[6]

The father of William Randolph Hearst, George Hearst, an unusually successful miner and a successful politician who became United States Senator from California, bought three different parcels of land at the Cayucos end of the rancho between 1867 and 1869. By October 1872 Don Domingo Pujol was the owner of another large parcel. This brief description accounts for the sequence of ownership and division of the Moro Y Cayucos until the time Phillips became interested in it.[7]

Chauncey Phillips, with his experience in government, law, banking and land transfers, guided Don Domingo Pujol through a legal suit against McKinley heirs that had to be settled in the California Supreme Court. Finally, on January 19, 1878, title to the land was properly patented to McKinley heirs so the sales made by them became legal. All of this occurred many years after McKinley's death.

About this time, Phillips resigned from the bank and formed C. H. Phillips and Company, a real estate business. Young P. H. Dallidet joined him. (The Dallidet family adobe still stands in 1980, owned by the San Luis Obispo County Historical Society.)

Phillips arranged for the subdivision of Pujol's property into a number of farms suited for dairying, pasture land, and raising grain. Following the sale of this land, several successful dairy farms developed.[8]

Sometime after 1867, James Cass, an English seaman who tried unsuccessfully to become a farmer, established a lightering business near the location of the present town of Cayucos, transporting goods to and from coast steamers by means of surf boats. The steamers stopped off the coast to receive cargo from Cass's smaller craft and to unload cargo intended for delivery to farmers in that vicinity. The work was extremely hard and precarious. Sometimes everything was lost in a rough sea.

In partnership with a Captain Ingalls, Cass was able to build a 380-foot pier, a small store and a warehouse. Across the wagon road from the pier, he built a two-story home for his family. In 1980 the old home still stands, weather-beaten and uncertain.

In 1874, Cass, now called Captain Cass, entered into a partnership with William Beebee, John Hanford and L. Schwartz, three county businessmen, under the firm name of J. Cass & Company. They extended the wharf into deeper water, improved the warehouse facilities, and added a short railway for moving goods to and from ships and warehouse. Now steamers could dock at this location, and the hauling distance for farmers in the area was substantially reduced.[9]

Using the authority Pujol vested in him for the management and subdivision of Pujol's portions of Moro Y Cayucos Rancho, Phillips laid out town lots around the wharf. As these lots sold, a new coastal shipping settlement came into existence and enjoyed moderate success.[10]

The Moro Y Cayucos was Phillip's first major effort at subdividing the great Mexican land grants of San Luis Obispo County. Now, his reputation was established and his services were in demand. His need for success was probably intensified by the fact that he and Jane eventually had seven children, but he seemed to have a natural talent for constructing land deals that were lucrative for his clients and himself.

⚬❧⚬

In 1881 the Pacific Coast narrow-gauge railway line was extended south from San Luis Obispo to Arroyo Grande. In 1882 it was continued farther south to Santa Maria and Los Alamos, as landowners along the route made gifts of right-of-way land. Among these landowners were the Steele brothers.[11]

In 1882 Phillips began working with Edgar Willis Steele and George Steele in selling large parcels of land these men owned on four different Mexican land grants—the Arroyo Grande, the Bolsa de Chamisal, the Corral de Piedra, and El Pismo, all located in southern San Luis Obispo County and all contiguous. The value of these lands was now somewhat enhanced by the existence of the narrow-gauge railway that could move the products of the land to market.[12]

The Steele brothers had come a long way, worked hard, and made a variety of moves to reach this place in their lives.

They had migrated from New York to Ohio with their parents while still children. They came to California as young men, but not before gaining college educations and working as teachers. George and a cousin, Renseleur, led the way in 1855. The next year, Edgar, with his parents and two younger children, traveled by boat to the Isthmus of Panama, crossed by train, and boarded another boat for San Francisco. A little later, their brother Lewis joined them.

They had started life in California on a rented farm in Petaluma. Soon they had a few dairy cattle. They rented additional land at Point Reyes, accumulated more cattle, and raised other people's cattle on shares. They extended their business by leasing the 18,000-acre Pescadero Rancho in San Mateo County. Later they bought the Pescadero property.

When the lease expired on the Point Reyes property, the brothers visited southern San Luis Obispo County. Land values were depressed following the drought years of 1864 and 1865, and beginning in 1866 the Steele brothers bought 48,000 acres, at $1.10 an acre, on the four Mexican land grants mentioned. These grants had already been divided into a number of parcels owned by various people.

On their new lands, the Steele brothers continued their dairy operations as well as farming for some fifteen years before they began to sell their land.[13]

In 1872 George Steele was nominated for the state senate from San Luis Obispo County, but was defeated in that election. In 1880 he was again defeated in the election for assemblyman by Patrick Murphy of the Santa Margarita Rancho, but in 1882 he was elected state senator. He and his wife, Delia, lived in a big home on the Rancho Corral de Piedra.

⚬❧⚬

The Arroyo Grande Rancho had originally been granted to Zefarino Carlona, a native of Santa Barbara. The grant was approved April 25, 1842, while Juan Bautista Alvarado was governor, and consisted of 4,437 acres. Carlona brought cattle to the grant in 1841, and he may have built a house on the property.[14] His son-

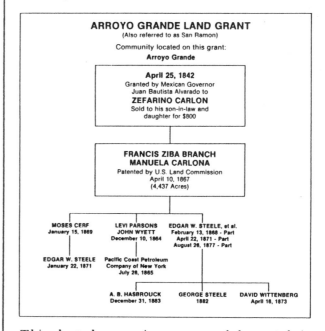

This chart shows major owners and dates of their acquisition of parts of this land grant as it was divided and sold through 1883. Not all dates were available.

in-law, Francis Branch, and his daughter, Manuela Carlona, owned the neighboring grant but built their home on the Arroyo Grande, where Branch was running cattle.

On April 12, 1843, Carlona turned the Arroyo Grande over to Branch and his daughter for $600, with the understanding that he could live on the property for the balance of his life, and that he could keep cattle. Branch received the patent from the United States Land Commission on April 10, 1867.[15]

Born in New York State in 1802, Branch had moved in steps across the country. From St. Louis, he had traveled with trading and trapping parties until he arrived in California in 1831, where he was first successful as a hunter, especially of sea otter for their valuable pelts. In time, he established a general store in Santa Barbara.

Branch became a Mexican citizen and became known as Francisco Branch. He was married to Dona Manuela Carlona in 1835. He was among the first of five foreigners to obtain Mexican land grants in what became San Luis Obispo County. In each case, the men married Mexican women. Branch named his 16,955-acre ranch the Santa Manuela, for his wife. In addition to

This two-story adobe was built for Ramon Branch on the Santa Manuela grant. This photo was taken during the early 1930s by Constance Van Harreveld, an enthusiastic local historian who sought to record extant adobe structures.

the Santa Manuela and later the Arroyo Grande, he also acquired the Pismo, the Huer Huero and parts of other land grants.

Francisco and Manuela had ten children and many grandchildren. Their wealth and well-being came slowly, and then they lost nearly all of their cattle during the great drought of 1864. They gradually recovered in part, but never completely. Branch died in 1874 at age seventy-two, but not before selling Edgar and George Steele, as well as others, large parcels of the Arroyo Grande Rancho.[16]

With help from Phillips, the Steele brothers subdivided their Arroyo Grande Rancho land into smaller farms and some lots along the Arroyo Grande Creek. The site of the town of Arroyo Grande on this ranch was first a Chumash Indian village. A natural town site, it was later the center for Mission San Luis Obispo gardens. The new lots along Arroyo Grande Creek now served to extend it and establish it as a community.[17]

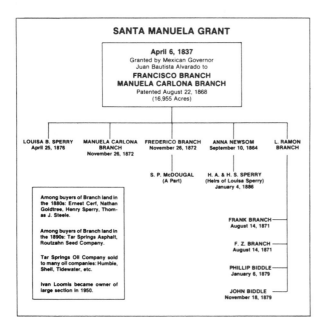

This chart shows major owners and dates of their acquisition of parts of this land grant as it was divided and sold through 1886. Not all dates were available.

❦

Phillips also promoted the sale of farms subdivided from that portion of Rancho Bolsa de Chamisal owned by the Steele brothers. The Bolsa de Chamisal had been granted originally to Francisco Quijada on May 11, 1837, by Governor Juan Bautista Alvarado and included 14,335 acres. By 1839 Quijada had constructed a

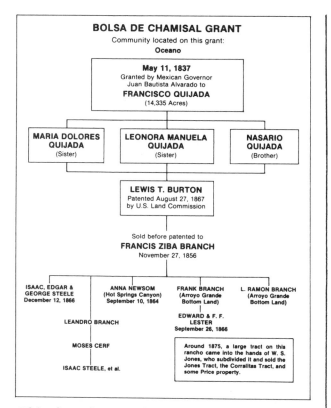

BOLSA DE CHAMISAL GRANT

Community located on this grant:
Oceano

May 11, 1837
Granted by Mexican Governor
Juan Bautista Alvarado to
FRANCISCO QUIJADA
(14,335 Acres)

| MARIA DOLORES QUIJADA (Sister) | LEONORA MANUELA QUIJADA (Sister) | NASARIO QUIJADA (Brother) |

LEWIS T. BURTON
Patented August 27, 1867
by U.S. Land Commission

Sold before patented to
FRANCIS ZIBA BRANCH
November 27, 1856

| ISAAC, EDGAR & GEORGE STEELE December 12, 1866 | ANNA NEWSOM (Hot Springs Canyon) September 10, 1864 | FRANK BRANCH (Arroyo Grande Bottom Land) | L. RAMON BRANCH (Arroyo Grande Bottom Land) |

LEANDRO BRANCH

EDWARD & F. F. LESTER
September 26, 1866

MOSES CERF

Around 1875, a large tract on this rancho came into the hands of W. S. Jones, who subdivided it and sold the Jones Tract, the Corralitas Tract, and some Price property.

ISAAC STEELE, et al.

This chart shows major owners and dates of their acquisition of parts of this land grant as it was divided and sold through about 1875. Not all dates were available.

small tule house and some corrals on his land and had begun to run horses and cattle.

Lewis T. Burton, a foreign businessman who became a Mexican citizen and married a Mexican girl in Santa Barbara during the Mexican period, agreed to construct a timber corral forty varas square on the rancho in exchange for one-half of the land grant. He paid for the survey dividing the land and shared the corral with Quijada.

Soon after this deal, Quijada died, leaving his share of the grant to his two sisters, Maria Dolores and Leonora Manuela, and a brother, Nasario, who then sold it to Burton.

The record shows that Francisco Branch bought this land from Burton on November 27, 1856. On December 12, 1866, Isaac C., Edgar W. and George Steele bought a large parcel of the rancho. Nearly all the rest of it came into the hands of various offspring of Francisco and Manuela Branch.[18]

❦

The Steele family had four different parcels of land on the Corral de Piedra Rancho which they offered for sale.

The Corral de Piedra, which included 30,911 acres, was granted to Jose Maria Villavicencio on May 28, 1846, by Governor Pio Pico. In December 1840, Villavicencio (Villa) had applied for land contiguous to a grant sought by his friend, Jose Ortega, who was seeking the Pismo grant. Villa was a native of California and a captain in the militia at Monterey.

Earlier, when another applicant sought this land, the neophyte Indians of Mission San Luis Obispo had complained that it was occupied by their people. But when Villa applied, the Prefect at the mission decided the land was unoccupied except for a few wild cattle and sent Villa's petition to Governor Alvarado, who signed the grant in favor of Villa on May 14, 1841.

In 1841 Villa built a house on his new land and began cultivating some of it. He also began to bring in cattle. There were some complications when the land was surveyed. It turned out

Originally located on the Corral de Piedra Rancho, this adobe was the home of the original grantee, Jose Maria Villavicencio. This adobe no longer exists. The photo was taken in 1931 by Constance Van Harreveld.

Doorway detail of Villavicencio adobe.

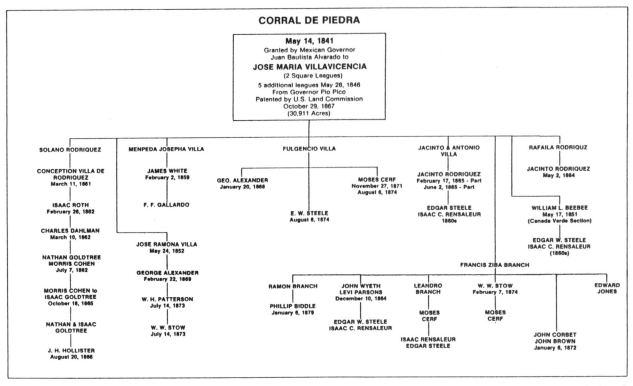

This chart shows major owners and dates of their acquisition of parts of this land grant as it was divided and sold through about 1880. Not all dates were available.

to be several thousand acres larger than Villa's petition showed. It was necessary to file a corrected petition which wasn't signed until 1846, at which time Pio Pico was governor.

Before Villa died, some of his children had built their homes and worked portions of the land on the Corral de Piedra. Francisco Branch eventually acquired three large parcels of land from the Villa family. The Steele brothers and their cousin Renseleur bought two of these parcels from Branch and a third from Jacinto Rodriguez who had acquired it from Jacinto and Antonio Villa, heirs of Jose Maria Villa. They bought a fourth parcel from William Beebee, who also had acquired it from Villa heirs.

Now, in 1882, the Steele brothers further subdivided these lands and offered them for sale through Phillips.[19]

❧

The fourth land grant on which the Steele brothers owned a large interest was El Pismo. This property stretched along the ocean and today includes the towns of Pismo Beach and Grover City.

Jose Ortega, a resident of Refugio Rancho, one of the earliest ranchos in Santa Barbara County, petitioned for the "place called Pismo," about two leagues south of Mission San Luis Obispo, on October 28, 1840. The "place" consisted of 8,839 acres stretching along the Pacific Ocean. Ortega stated in the petition that he and his wife had four children and that he would immediately utilize the land. He claimed that he owned 240 head of cattle, 50 mares, and 40 tame horses, and that he needed this land for grazing and keeping his stock.

He submitted his petition to the administrator of the mission, Juan Pablo Ayala. Ayala agreed to send the request to the governor providing that Ortega allow mission neophytes to gather the wild cattle on the land belonging to the mission. Interim Governor Manuel Jimeno granted Ortega's petition on November 18, 1840. Ortega constructed his home in 1841 and soon had more than one thousand head of cattle on the rancho.

Jose Mariano Bonilla was in charge of the mission by this time, and he was also district judge. He conducted the juridicial ceremony

Located on the El Pismo grant, this two-story adobe building still stands. It once served as a school house. Photo by Constance Van Harreveld, 1931.

Covered with clapboard, this adobe was the home of John Price and Dona Andrea Coloma Price. They raised thirteen children on the El Pismo grant. Photo by Constance Van Harreveld, 1931.

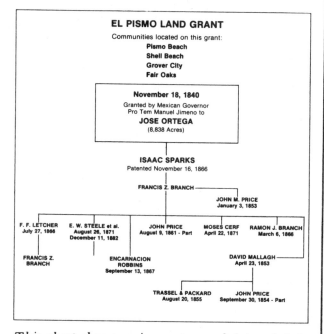

EL PISMO LAND GRANT

Communities located on this grant:
Pismo Beach
Shell Beach
Grover City
Fair Oaks

November 18, 1840
Granted by Mexican Governor
Pro Tem Manuel Jimeno to
JOSE ORTEGA
(8,838 Acres)

ISAAC SPARKS
Patented November 16, 1866

FRANCIS Z. BRANCH

JOHN M. PRICE
January 3, 1853

F. F. LETCHER July 27, 1866

E. W. STEELE et al. August 26, 1871 December 11, 1882

JOHN PRICE August 9, 1861 - Part

MOSES CERF April 22, 1871

RAMON J. BRANCH March 6, 1866

FRANCIS Z. BRANCH

ENCARNACION ROBBINS September 13, 1867

DAVID MALLAGH April 23, 1853

TRASSEL & PACKARD August 20, 1855

JOHN PRICE September 30, 1854 - Part

This chart shows major owners and dates of their acquisition of parts of this land grant as it was divided and sold through 1882.

for Ortega (a process for establishing boundaries and conferring new ownership) with surrounding landowners present as witnesses: Francisco Branch for the Santa Manuela, Francisco Quijada for the Bolsa de Chamisal, Jose Maria Villavicencio for the Corral de Piedra, and Miguel Avila for the San Miguelito.

Avila found fault with the boundaries between his rancho and the Pismo, but he was unable to convince the judge that his protest was valid. When the judge requested that Avila attend a survey of the land, he declined to do it, so Ortega received his grant.

But Ortega didn't keep the property long. On May 29, 1846, the Pismo Rancho was transferred to Isaac Sparks, who already owned the Huasna grant. Ortega traded the land with house, corrals and fences for 430 head of "black cattle, small and large" and $375 in goods whenever he wished them. Since Sparks owned a mercantile store, this was a convenient arrangement for both.[20]

Sparks was among those few Americans who made his home in California during the Mexican period. He was born in Maine in 1804. Later, his father constructed a flat boat and took him down the Ohio River and then to St. Louis. He grew up in Missouri, and as a young man traveled west with Jedediah Smith and Milton Sublet toward Santa Fe. There he joined a trapping expedition that brought him to California in 1832.

Here in this land belonging to Mexico, Isaac Sparks succeeded as a hunter of sea otter, starting near San Pedro. As time passed, he bought boats and hired men to help him. He continued successfully in this business until 1848 when he became a merchant in Santa Barbara and the town's first postmaster with the beginning of the American period. He had received the grant to the Huasna Rancho December 8, 1843, and the patent was cleared December 8, 1879. This grant consisted of 22,153 acres. At his death, the grant was bequeathed and divided among his daughters: Flora, who married Marcus Harloe; Rosa, who married Arza Porter; and Sally, who married Frederick Harkness.

Sparks didn't keep the Pismo Rancho very long. In 1853 he sold a portion of it to John M. Price, who also bought more of the same rancho from David Mallagh in 1854. Mallagh had had the only boat landing in the area on property now called Pirate's Cove. This was before wharves were constructed along the San Luis Obispo coast.[21]

In 1871, and again in 1882, the Steele family purchased land on the Pismo Rancho, and in 1882 Phillips began promoting its sale along with the other Steele property in southern San Luis Obispo County.

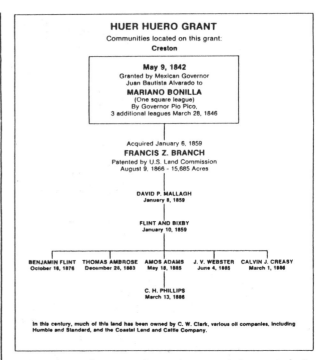

This chart shows major owners and dates of their acquisition of parts of this land grant as it was divided and sold through 1886.

These lands did not sell quickly—sales continued over a period of years—and Phillips certainly didn't handle all of the transactions, but the Steele properties were one of the major efforts in land promotion he had undertaken by the time strong anticipation of the arrival of the Southern Pacific Railroad in the county was beginning. Phillips must have already been thinking and planning for that day.

Up to this time, his efforts seemed to have been limited to the development of other people's property, but in 1886 he announced that he had bought the great Huer Huero Rancho, consisting of 46,000 acres, for $315,000. He must have begun seriously assessing his next moves in about 1885. There was activity by Southern Pacific south of Soledad for the first time in twelve years. It began to look as if Southern Pacific were interested in closing the coastal gap between San Francisco and Los Angeles.

If Phillips were to realize the success he desired, he would need large amounts of capital and land—how many times in a lifetime does opportunity knock so vigorously?—so, he wisely assumed full title to Huer Huero.

This rancho was located in one of the least accessible places in the northern part of the county. However, it had possibilities for farmers wanting inexpensive land within reach of the first likely entrance of the Southern Pacific Railroad into the county.

Near the center of the rancho, on a stretch of flatland generously covered by oak trees, Phillips laid out a small community center called Huer Huero, which later became the town of Creston. He had the rancho surveyed and subdivided into small farms and ranchos.[22]

The Huer Huero had been developed originally by Mission San Miguel. Then it was granted by Mexican Governor Juan Alvarado to Jose Mariano Bonilla on May 9, 1842. At that time it consisted of only one league of land.

Bonilla had been born in Mexico in 1807 and attended college there. He became a member of the bar in Mexico City before joining a group of

Mexican colonists coming to California in 1834. He served as a scribe to Governor Figueroa, and a little later was appointed a judge.

In 1837 Bonilla married one of the daughters of Don Inocente Garcia, then the administrator of Mission San Miguel. Bonilla served as his father-in-law's secretary.

He first occupied the Huer Huero land in 1839. The next year he built a house and corral. He brought in a herd of cattle from Rancho San Simeon, which belonged to his father-in-law, and also acquired about five hundred sheep and one hundred horses.

Bonilla didn't live on the rancho for long but instead put it in the charge of a mayordomo.

Far to the east of the mission settlements of the time, Huer Huero was as isolated then as in 1886 when Phillips acquired it, and in 1844 Tulare Indians attacked the rancho. They burned the house, destroyed the corrals and killed three vaqueros.

Bonilla tried again in 1845 to establish the land as an operating rancho. He had a new house and corral built and brought in more cattle. On March 28, 1846, he succeeded in adding two leagues of land to the rancho by an additional grant from Governor Pio Pico.

Again, the Indians attacked, taking the cattle. This time they killed his brother, Patricio. Bonilla was deeply discouraged, and some time after November 1847, he turned over the entire rancho to Francis Branch in exchange for 253 head of cattle.

After annexation of California to the United States, Bonilla held the position of sub-prefect and alcalde at San Luis Obispo under the American military government. He became the first judge of San Luis Obispo County after the state had a constitution, and later he served as district judge and San Luis Obispo County supervisor for several terms. He died March 19, 1878, when he was seventy-one years old.[23]

❦

It isn't clear how much use Francis Branch made of the Huer Huero, but in 1856 David P. Mallagh made a deal with Branch to acquire the ranch.

Mallagh wrote to Abel Stearns, a successful American businessman in San Pedro who had established himself during the Mexican period. He hoped Stearns might be interested in running cattle on the Huer Huero on shares. There is no record of Stearns' response, but Stearns' papers show other such requests directed to him from California men who had land and were hoping for a start in the cattle business.

Mallagh didn't keep the ranch long. In 1859 the large cattle company of Flint, Bixby and Company acquired the Huer Huero, and in 1885 and 1886 sold it to Tom Ambrose, J. V. Webster, Calvin J. Cressy and Amos Adams. These men were the ones with whom Phillips made his 1886 deal that brought the ranch under his control.

To the south and east of the Huer Huero Rancho, much government land had been opened for homesteading, but it was poor land and many settlers were having a desperate struggle trying to survive. With the development of Creston, some of them tried various businesses. Others who had some capital purchased Huer Huero land from Phillips because it was better land for farming than the land they had homesteaded.[24]

Phillips' next major undertaking was organization of the West Coast Land Company. Apparently, he made a proposal to the owners and principal officers of the Oregon Improvement Company, men who had both the vision and the resources that make big enterprise possible. They were responsive to Phillips' idea. Since 1882 this holding company had owned the Pacific Coast Railway, the narrow-gauge railway operating in San Luis Obispo and southern Santa Barbara counties. They also owned the Pacific Coast Steamship Company, with ships making regular stops at Port Harford in Avila.

George Perkins was an owner of the railway and steamship company, and he had political power. He had helped organize the Goodall, Nelson and Perkins Steamship Company in 1873, later merged with the Oregon Improvement Company. He had served as governor of California from January 8, 1880 to January 10, 1883. One day, he would be appointed United States Senator to fill the unexpired term caused by the death of Leland Stanford, and he would hold this office for twenty-one years. Perkins agreed to be a member of the board of directors of the new company proposed by Phillips.

John L. Howard, another principal officer in the Oregon Improvement Company, agreed to permit his name to be used as president of the new company. Isaac Goldtree, a large landowner and a member of a wealthy merchant family in San Luis Obispo, accepted the title of vice president. Robert E. Jack, a prominent banker, businessman and rancher, whose power was increasing each year, became treasurer. Phillips was secretary and manager of the company.

This combination of men with their capital, contacts, influence and business acumen made many things possible.

The West Coast Land Company was incorporated March 27, 1886. Its immediate objective was the purchase, development and sale of the land which comprised the ranchos El Paso de Robles, Santa Ysabel, and Eureka, and the unsold balance of the Huer Huero, a total of 64,000 acres.

Brochures were produced extolling the virtues of the county and listing farms for sale, and the company advertised far and wide. The Ionia, Michigan newspaper, which carried an advertisement, wrote: "Ionians who are con-

This chart shows major owners and dates of their acquisition of parts of this land grant as it was divided and sold through 1886. Less information about this grant was available during its earliest years than that available about others.

templating a change of climate and thinking of emigrating to the Pacific Coast will be interested in reading the advertisement of the West Coast Land Company. This company has recently placed on the market a valuable tract of land embracing 64,000 acres, and lying in the fertile San Luis Obispo valley. The reputation of the directors of the company is not confined to the limits of California, and is such as to ensure for the enterprise a successful issue. They are ex-Governor Perkins; John L. Howard, largely interested in steamship and railroad lines; C. H. Phillips, an energetic and sagacious businessman, to whom has been entrusted the management of the company's affairs and others equally distinguished in commercial circles."

Phillips' success attracted others into the land promotion business and created a sense of prosperity in the area. But all of this newborn activity was based upon one great expectation. Everyone was hoping and gambling upon the Southern Pacific Railroad's building a coastal line between San Francisco and Los Angeles that would run through San Luis Obispo County.

If that happened, Phillips' new land company was ready for a boom. If not, a bust was in store. However, Chauncey Phillips never operated blindly.[25]

This chart shows major owners and dates of their acquisition of parts of this land grant as it was divided and sold through 1886. Not all dates were available.

CHAPTER III

Tracks For San Miguel

The first local public notice that something was happening south of Soledad was a very short news item in the *San Luis Obispo Tribune* in May 1886.[1] The newspaper reported that 1,500 Chinese coolies were at work laying track. By July 20, 1886, the Southern Pacific had run a train to the King Ranch where the town of Kings (later Kings City) was laid out. At this point, Southern Pacific issued a supplementary timetable showing stops at Cholone and Coburns on signal or when a passenger wanted to debark. Kings was a telegraph stop. The fare from Salinas to Kings was two dollars.[2]

On October 1, 1886, a writer for the *San Luis Opispo Tribune* who lived in the Estrella District a few miles east of Mission San Miguel, reported that he and his neighbors could hear heavy blasting along the proposed route of Southern Pacific.

Soledad had been the terminus for the Southern Pacific Railroad for thirteen suffering years. Just the fact that a railroad was that close after so long, yet so far away, had caused both hope and despair in San Luis Obispo County. Raising crops or large herds of cattle or sheep was meaningless as long as it remained difficult—in fact nearly impossible—to get products to San Francisco and Los Angeles markets. A railroad could change lives and fortunes.

The big day occurred October 18, 1886. The first train came rolling into San Miguel, and people for miles around gathered to meet it. The *Tribune* reported "that the town is full, too full for utterance, hardly equal to the occasion." It was a great day for all three tavern keepers in the mission town.[3]

This drawing of Mission San Miguel appeared on a promotional brochure soon after the Southern Pacific Railroad constructed a line into the town on October 18, 1886.

San Miguel had its beginning in the summer of 1795. At the urging of the Church, Spanish Governor Diego Borica had ordered an expedition of soldiers sent out from Monterey in search of a site for construction of a mission about halfway between Missions San Antonio and San Luis Obispo. They were accompanied by Father Buenaventure Sitjar from Mission San Antonio.

Sitjar sought a location near resources capable of sustaining life—water, tillable soil, pasture land for cattle and sheep and horses, timber for firewood and for construction, rocks for building, and land that would accommodate trails for hauling materials to make roof tiles. At first the search was concentrated along both sides of the Nacimiento River, but finally a site next to the Salinas River was selected. Funds were granted for the mission, and Father Presidente Fermin de Lasuen came to the place to solemnize its beginning on July 25, 1797. He came directly from San Juan Bautista where he had conducted ceremonies for the establishment of that mission.

The site was dedicated in honor of the most glorious Prince of the Celestial Militia, Archangel St. Michael, "who fought the Dragon Lucifer and chased him out of paradise, who championed the cause of God's people, and who calls the faithful from this world to their Judgment to receive their reward."

Father Sitjar and the soldiers assigned to protect the new mission accompanied Father Lasuen, who reported to Governor Borica: "I blessed the water, the place and the great cross, which we venerated and raised." He named Father Sitjar and Antonio de la Conception Horra as San Miguel's first missionaries.

As Father Lasuen stood on the high ground above the river in the summer heat, he must have been pleased to discover that his presence and that of the others attracted a great number of Indians. They stood in awe as these white men clad like angels conducted their strange ceremony.

Then, as the story goes, under an arbor built for the occasion, a half naked Indian child came forward and dropped to his knees in the grass

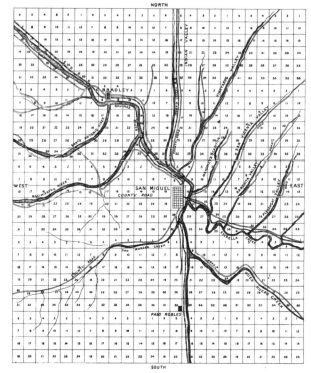

MAP OF SAN MIGUEL AND SURROUNDING COUNTRY.

An 1880s map showed San Miguel and the surrounding country with Southern Pacific Railroad track following the Salinas River and continuing beyond Paso Robles. The terminus at this time was Templeton. Note, too, the route of the planned Indian Valley Railroad, a narrow-gauge line that carried soft coal from the mines near Parkfield. The Bakersfield branch line paralleling Estrella Creek was never built.

before the great Father Presidente. It was a dramatic moment. The boy was the first person to be baptized at the site of the new mission, and the Christian name given him was Miguel Maria. There, in the dry summer heat, Father Lasuen baptized fifteen more children, and signed the baptismal book for future generations to witness.

With the help of Indians, construction of the mission began. By the end of 1797, an adobe building seventy-one feet long and seventeen feet wide had been built. An adobe chapel was also completed. The next year they built a somewhat more permanent church and a home for unmarried Indian girls.

On January 24, 1798, the church and the Indian neophytes celebrated another first at the mission. Timothy Sofar, an Indian, and his pagan mate had been living together as a family in keeping with their own customs. So had Jose Orra and Josepha. On this day, before Father Juan Martin, they "renewed before me their free and spontaneous consent, by words which they mutually pronounced before me." This joint ceremony was the first Christian marriage ceremony at the church.

There was continuous building during the next several years, including a house for the priests, a granary, and additions to various buildings. Forty-seven small adobe dwellings were constructed for Indian families working at the mission.

The early years of the mission were filled with hardship, but there was progress. Other missions, already established, made generous contributions of cattle, sheep, and other provisions.

But the mission scarcely reached a point of self-sufficiency before disaster struck. After dark on the night of August 25, 1806, there was a fire which not only destroyed buildings, but many of the tools and accumulated materials needed in the shops, and the church roof was partially destroyed.

In many ways, the priests of Mission San Miguel found themselves starting over. Once again they received help from the other missions in the form of food, tools, and looms. The buildings were gradually restored, corrals and additional dwellings for the Indians were built, and a tannery established.

In 1816 the stone foundation was laid for the final mission church. Tiles for the roof were made, and an enduring edifice came into being.

The Indians of San Miguel spoke in four different languages, depending upon the direction from which they came—whether from the San Antonio Mission area, the sea coast, the Tulares region to the east, or the south.

Indian families were close knit. Men and women loved each other and spoiled their children in ways that tried the patience of the Spanish priests. After seventeen years, Fathers Juan Martin and Juan Cabot reported that they had never found the Indians to exhibit any "aversion" toward either Europeans or Americans. They were impressed with the kindness and charity of the Indians among themselves and with outsiders. They readily offered food which they had prepared to all visitors.

In the fulfillment of their assignment, the fathers conducted catechism in the Indian languages of the area, even though it was not formally approved by the bishop. Little boys around the mission learned willingly to read the manuscripts provided by the church, both words and music, for the purpose of participating in the services.

In matters of health, the fathers learned some things from the mission Indians. The Indians used the hot springs at the place referred to as El Paso de Robles for rheumatic conditions, they used various roots, barks and leaves in treating illnesses, and they practiced bleeding and sucking of wounds as a way of treating infections.

They consumed a native drink which caused drunkenness, and in this state they often accidentally hurt themselves.

The fathers were impressed with the extent to which the Indians made promises and lived up to them, although they readily told lies. In fact, telling lies was one of their greatest weaknesses, the priests reported. But they were also disturbed by the general sensuality and idleness of both men and women.

The Indians coming from the plains to the east used beads for money and had a system of accumulative interest which could encumber borrowers for life. They lived communal lives, sharing ownership of nearly all belongings, and accumulating very little. An Indian woman could undertake a journey carrying everything the family owned. Their social system included practically no form of administering justice except wounding a wrongdoer with a dart in some way. Apparently, the wound did no permanent harm to the person chastised. There were no chiefs except in temporary situations such as a battle. All Indians were equal, and none served another.

In pre-missionary years the Indians' only musical instrument was a flute-like instrument. However, they enjoyed participation in singing and quickly learned to play the musical instruments provided by the mission.

After twenty years of work with California Indians, Fathers Martin and Cabot were still not sure whether the Indians had any real conception of the meaning of eternity, in spite of the fact that they readily confessed and participtate in Holy Communion. The Tulares had an elaborate burial ceremony. They tied a ball of *pelota* to the corpse and then danced at length around the body, weeping and moaning.

The fathers provided clothing for the mission Indians. The women wore cotton dresses and petticoats and blankets for coats. The men wore loose cotton and serge, covering enough of their bodies to "appear with decency." On the plains east of the mission, however, Indian women were content to wear a small apron of tules hanging down the front and back of their bodies. A belt around the waist supported this cover. A few wore tanned deer skins. The men wore about the same or less.

The fathers estimated that there were some nine thousand Tulares to the east of the mission, living on the plains in communal villages or rancherias, as the Spanish called them. The fathers had high hopes that they might be able to build an inland mission in order to bring these Indians into their fold.

In 1818 the new San Miguel Mission church was completed. Esteban Munras, a Spanish artist living in Monterey, left a lasting treasure in the interior decorations he designed for the new church. In 1821, with assistance from some of the Indians, he added bright colored designs to the stucco interior including a great blue all-seeing eye at the back of the altar. These decorations may still be seen in 1980.

Mission San Miguel, like other California missions, developed a number of outlying ranchos. No boundaries were established on its eastern side, and little use was made of the arid plains, but the mission claimed all the land between San Miguel and the ocean to the west. Using the labors of the Indians, the mission had about eight hundred head of cattle, a number of horses and some breeding mares on the coastal rancho which they called San Simeon.

To the south, Mission San Miguel occupied large amounts of land. At its Rancho de Santa Isabel, there was a vineyard. On Rancho San Antonio the Indians planted barley, and at Rancho El Paso de Robles, wheat. Some of these vast tracts of land were also used for raising sheep. At Ranchos El Paso de Robles and de la Ascuncion, adobe buildings were constructed and maintained for storing seed grain.

At times, lack of water resulted in such poor crops that Indians left the mission land to make their own way, eating such wild seed as they could harvest and such animals as they could hunt and kill. However, in 1827 Father Cabot reported that the mission had 2,130 head of cattle, 120 oxen, 7,904 sheep, and 62 pigs.

The great blow to the mission system in California occurred on January 6, 1831. Governor Echeandia issued a decree for the secularization of the missions, removing the power which the Church held over California lands and the Indians.

Jose Castro was appointed commissioner in charge of communicating with the Indians at Mission San Miguel. Along with three others, Juan B. Alvarado, Jose Maria Villavicencio and Jose Avila, he arrived at the mission in early January 1831 and assembled the Indians in front of the church.

Through Alvarado, who could talk to the Indians, Castro informed them of Governor Echeandia's proclamation setting them free. The next day, other Indians arrived at the mission, and Castro called another meeting. Alvarado talked to these Indians, too, seeking to make them understand the joyousness of the occasion. They were free! Now they could till soil and reap the benefits of their labors all for themselves. They could hunt and fish and raise domesticated animals and never again wait for a dole from the church!

Mission San Miguel had been in existence for less than forty years. It had brought hundreds of Indians into the fold of its Christian commune. All served the mission. In turn, all received both physical and spiritual sustenance from the mission. For most of the Indians, especially the young, the mission commune was the only way of life known to them. There was no other system to which they could now readily turn. They were socially and culturally bound to a way of life, and they lacked both sophistication and knowledge either as individuals or as a group to organize themselves or initiate another system that would assure their survival.

When Alvarado requested that all those Indians who wished to remain with the padre stand to the left and all those who preferred to be free stand to the right, nearly all moved to the left.

Mission San Miguel was not actually confiscated by decree until August 9, 1836, more than five years later.

Regardless of decrees, some semblance of mission life continued. In 1837 there were 525 Indians associated with the mission, and large numbers of cattle, sheep and horses were on the ranchos. Some young, unmarried girls continued to live in the apartments of the mission provided for that purpose. However, this ended abruptly in 1837 when a group of American men attacked the Indian girls in their apartments. Subsequently, Father Garcia sent the girls to their families, abolishing this system of schooling and training young women for work in the church.

In 1838 Father Moreno wrote about the mission's poverty and the disappearance of mission property.

In spite of hardship, the spiritual activities of the mission continued, though now clearly separated from the economic activities which were under the leadership of secular administrators. In October 1840 Father Moreno was replaced by Father Ramon Abella, the last of the Franciscans.

Missions San Miguel and San Luis Obispo were the first in Upper California to be transformed into regular parishes under the jurisdiction of the bishop of the diocese. In 1840 the Reverend Miguel Gomez, ordained at Santa Barbara shortly before, was put in charge of Mission San Luis Obispo with jurisdiction over San Miguel. But this did not help the deterioration occurring at San Miguel.

In 1841 Eugene de Mofras, the French writer and traveler in California, found Mission San Miguel "half dilapidated." He found less than thirty Indians there. Father Prefecto Duran reported on March 18, 1844 that "Mission Miguel, Archangel, is today without livestock and the neophytes are . . . dispersed for want of a priest to care for them."

Mexican Governor Pio Pico succeeded in a plan he had for renting and converting the missions into pueblos on May 28, 1845. The Indians, under the articles drawn up, could hold Mission San Miguel by returning to it within a month. It was not really anticipated that they would move back. In fact, it's doubtful they even knew of the governor's decree. In any case, the missions were then declared without owners.

Under the articles of this decree, Mission San Miguel was sold on July 4, 1846, only three days before California was taken by the United States. The mission was now under the private ownership of Petronillo Rios and William Reed. Apparently, Reed and his family had moved into the mission building in 1845. Petronillo Rios had an adobe house nearby. Perhaps he and his family had lived in the mission at one time, but Rios' interests and involvements made him at best a temporary or spasmodic tenant.[4]

The Rios adobe, later called the Caledonia, is now owned by San Luis Obispo County and it is cared for by an organization of residents called "Friends of the Adobe." It is visible from Highway 101.

The adobe rooms of the mission building, now serving as a museum and shop for the church, must forever recall as part of the mission's history one of the most horrible and bloody mass murders to occur in California history. Reed and his family lived in the mission for three years. His daughter, son-in-law, their three children and an Indian helper also lived there. Bancroft, Angel, Engelhardt and others provide varying interpretations of what occurred. Still another source is an unpublished autobiographical work titled, "The Life and Adventures of James P. Beckwourth." In this tale, the young man relates his shocking discovery.

Beckwourth, a young adventurer pursuing various ways of making a living, was working for an American government commission in Monterey in December 1848. "I was engaged," he said, "to carry dispatches [to and from] Captain Denny's ranch where I was met by another carrier. On my route lay the Mission of San Miguel owned by a Mr. Reed, an Englishman. As his family was a very interesting one, I generally made his home my resting place. On one of the visits, arriving about dusk, I entered the house as usual, but was surprised to see no one stirring."

At this time the mission buildings were crumbling and generally unkept. The trail which passed the mission was dusty. In the month of December, the mission appeared cold and gloomy, and when Beckwourth arrived it was getting dark.

He walked around, probably calling out, hoping to attract someone's attention. Finally he stepped into the kitchen. "On the floor I saw someone lying down, asleep, as I supposed. I attempted to arouse him with my foot, but he did not stir."

Beckwourth thought about the Indians of the vicinity and became frightened. He returned to his horse for his pistols. Then he lighted a candle and started a cautious search of the rooms. "In going along a passage," he records, "I stumbled over the body of a woman. I entered a room and found another, a murdered Indian woman who had been a domestic."

Beckwourth suddenly realized that the murderers of Reed's family could easily still be hidden in the mission. He quickly left the building, mounted his horse and rode as hard as he could to reach the headquarters of Rancho Paso de Robles. At the time, Petronillo Rios held this land grant, having acquired it from Pedro Narvaez, the officer in charge of port activities in Monterey when the Americans captured the pueblo.

According to Beckwourth's tale, fifteen Mexican and Indian vaqueros accompanied him back to the mission that same night. "On again

entering the house," he reported, "we found eleven bodies all thrown together in one pile . . . we found the murderers had set fire to the dwelling [mission] but the fire had died out."

They locked up the building and started back to El Paso de Robles Rancho. Beckwourth had ridden seventy-two miles that day and needed rest.

Word of the tragedy was sent to the alcalde at San Luis Obispo. Earlier in the year John Price had been appointed alcalde by Colonel R. B. Mason, First Dragoons, Governor of California. It is not clear whether he was still serving in this capacity in December. In any case, Price told the story somewhat differently.

Shortly before the murder of Reed and his family, Reed had been successful in mining gold in the north. As was Reed's custom at the mission, passersby were readily invited to join the family as guests. A group of sailors who had deserted ship at Monterey stopped at the mission on their way south. Reed entertained the men and spoke happily of his recent success in mining; in fact, he showed them his bountiful cache of gold dust worth several thousand dollars.

Price said that he and his brother-in-law, Francis Branch, stopped at the mission upon returning from a mining trip to Stanislaus County. They arrived at Mission San Miguel tired and expecting some welcoming signs from the Reed family. When no one appeared, they dismounted and entered the mission rooms.

They were shocked and partially overcome by the sight that met their eyes. A child had been brained by someone's beating its head against a pillar of the corridor. Every person in the family had been murdered.

Price said he and Branch rode as fast as their horses would carry them to Rancho El Paso de Robles. A party went from the rancho to the mission to bury the dead, and another party set out in pursuit of the murderers.

Beckwourth, who claims to have made the discovery of the murders before anyone else, says that after some rest, he joined the alcalde of San Luis Obispo. He says that forty men from San Luis Obispo, moving in small parties in different directions, combed the countryside.

"It was my fortune," the young man relates, "to find the trail and with my party of six men, I managed to head off the suspected murderers so as to come up with them in the road from directly the opposite direction . . ."

Beckwourth could not avoid conversation with them, but he kept it as casual as possible. His group then rode hard to Santa Barbara, got twenty additional men and rode back in pursuit of the murderers, he wrote.

The gang of murderers was found camping near the coast at Carpinteria. Both Beckwourth and Price say that a battle ensued. Price wrote that one of his party was killed and several were hurt, but all of the murderers were slain. One murderer rushed into the ocean hoping to escape, but he was shot. The bodies of the others were left where they fell as food for the vultures and coyotes.

Beckwourth reported that one man was murdered, one was captured without injury, and the others were wounded.[5]

Englehardt tells a still different story. He says that the murderers, five of them, were pursued by a force of men from Santa Barbara under Cesario Lataillade and overtaken on the coast near Ortega Rancho. One of the murderers, wounded in the battle, shot and killed Ramon Rodriquez, who had been rash in rushing upon the gang. Another desperado jumped into the ocean and was drowned. The other three, Joseph Lynch, Peter Remer (Raymond), and Peter Quinn, were captured and taken to Santa Barbara. These men were executed in Santa Barbara on December 28, 1841.[6]

It is easy to see that many men could claim a part in seeking justice in this case. Various men played leadership roles at various times—or at least claimed the role. It is difficult to decide whether the men were shot on the spot as Beckwourth said, or whether they were held, as the report to Governor Mason implies, for instructions before being executed.

Dempsey, the uninjured member of the gang of desperados, "turned state's evidence," Beckwourth said. " . . . On the night of the murder, his party stopped at Reeds' . . . Reed told them

that he had just returned from the mines, whereupon it was determined to kill the whole family and take his gold, which turned out to be the pitiful sum of one thousand dollars."

"After the confession of Dempsey," Beckwourth said, "we shot the murderers, along with the state's evidence, and thus ended the lives of two Americans, two Englishmen, and ten Irishmen, they having committed the most diabolical deed that ever disgraced the annals of frontier life."

Frontier justice had prevailed, but what had happened to the gold dust taken by the desperados? In effect, the governor agreed with a plan the men apparently suggested. Some of the gold dust was given to the family of Ramon Rodriguez, the Santa Barbara man in the citizens group who was killed. Some of it was used to provide aid to the injured, and some of it was used to replace weapons and personal property lost by the Santa Barbara posse in the fighting.

On May 3, 1859 the United States Land Commission made a lasting decision on behalf of the Catholic Church. Upon application by Joseph Alemany, Roman Catholic Bishop of the Diocese of Monterey, Mission San Miguel, along with all of the California missions, was returned to the Church. For San Miguel, this included some land around the buildings designated as orchards and vineyards.

Still, the mission remained deserted. From time to time, it was occupied by businesses

Forlorn and little used, Mission San Miguel attracted very little attention except from visitors who came to nearby Paso Robles for the hot springs and sulphur mud baths.

catering to travelers along the trail. During the 1860s, it was little more than "cover for wanderers, gamblers, drunkards, and outlaws," Englehart said. At one point, one of the rooms served as a saloon. Another was used as a sample room and agency for a business which sold sewing machines.

While the other buildings continued to fall into ruins, the church building held up remarkably well. It was respected and preserved, though unused.

In 1876 W. H. Menton leased the mission buildings for use as a hotel, and Jacob Althano had a shoemaking shop in one room. There were a few grazing ranches near town, and there were two small general stores in the settlement.

In 1878 a very young priest, the Reverend Philip Farrely, was sent to San Miguel as resident pastor, the first to be assigned in many years. When he arrived in the desolate settlement and saw the ruins of the original mission, the buildings occupied by saloons and a church filthy from years of neglect, he must have wondered what fate could possibly have brought him to such an existence so early in life.

He lacked both church facilities and people to use them, so he began a search for a congregation. By day, he traveled on horseback and camped wherever he happened to be at nightfall. He found a few people who needed spiritual guidance among those scattered in the territory. He was warmly received among the Mexicans, who called him Padre Felipe, but before the year was out, he was transferred to Mission Santa Ynez.

The Reverend Jose Mut, a Catalonian stationed at San Juan Capistrano, was assigned to San Miguel. Father Mut took a different approach to re-establishing the church. He saw that the rafters which held a heavy tile roof were decayed and collapse imminent, and he wanted to preserve the deteriorating row of buildings comprising the convents.

He sought contributions from people within the area, and over the years, succeeded in raising $3,000. With this money, he made a great part of the mission habitable again. Father Mut served the mission for over a decade and is the only priest buried in the mission cemetery.[7]

For a long time during the early American period, the land to the east of the mission was vaguely assumed by people of the county to be part of a Mexican land grant. It isn't known who deserves credit for discovering that all of this land belonged to the government and was open for settlement, but a migration of settlers began during the 1870s. Land along the Salinas River and along Estrella Creek was taken up first. There were soon enough people in the Estrella district to build a school and a protestant church. Three thousand acres of wheat and barley was sown upon the Estrella plains in 1879, but the results were poor. Even though some gave up, there were still forty families in the Estrella district in 1880. Similarly, there was a settlement along Los Tablas Creek, including churches and a school.

And in a few more years, the arrival of the railroad brought new hope and, for some, a new lease on life.

A flour mill and warehouse buildings were built in San Miguel after arrival of the railroad. Farmers brought grain to town for processing and for shipping to the San Francisco market. This photo was taken in about 1892.

CHAPTER IV

Passing El Paso De Robles

Within two weeks after the Southern Pacific Railroad reached San Miguel, the line was also completed to the El Paso de Robles Resort Hotel, ten miles farther south. The first train arrived October 31, 1886, and it followed so closely the arrival at San Miguel because large rail-building crews worked both north and south of San Miguel at the same time.[1]

El Paso de Robles had been a well-established stagecoach stop for many years, with a family-owned two-story resort hotel and cabins and a small store that doubled as a post office and Wells Fargo office. It was located on the El Paso de Robles Rancho near a natural hot springs. The Blackburn family and James family were the owners of the resort.

When Daniel D. and James H. Blackburn, along with Lazarus Godchaux, purchased the Paso de Robles Rancho in 1857, they found some decayed remains of logs in one place that formed a hot springs pool dating back to days when Mission San Miguel was a religious and economic center. It was these hot springs on the rancho that became the nucleus of an impressive stagecoach era resort and health center, and eventually, the site of the town of Paso Robles.

According to Myron Angel and other writers, the warm springs water at this spot was also a haven for at least one grizzly bear. "There was formerly a large cottonseed tree growing on the bank of the springs with a limb extending low over the water," Angel said. "A huge grizzly was in the habit of making nocturnal visits to the spring, plunging into the pool, and with his forepaws, grasping the limb, swinging himself up and down in the water, evidently enjoying both his swing and the pleasant sensation of his dips in warm water with unspeakable delight."

The Blackburn brothers had accumulated an

Paso Robles Hot Springs Hotel as it appeared in 1871. The springs reservoir is located in lower right corner. (Overland Monthly, October 1871)

exceptional combination of talents and skills, as well as capital, by the time they arrived in San Luis Obispo County, and their further success might well have been predicted.

They were born at Harper's Ferry, Jefferson County, in what is now West Virginia. Daniel was born April 8, 1816, and James came into the world September 8, 1820. Their father died in 1822, leaving his wife, Margaret, with six young children to find her own way. At this time, the family was living in Springfield, Ohio. In their struggle to live, they developed traits commonly associated with pioneer families—as Angel put it, "self-reliance, frugality, industry and forethought."

Daniel attended school in Springfield, and learned the carpentry trade. James lived and attended school for some time in Logan County, Virginia.

When he was twenty-one, Daniel moved to Oquawkee, Illinois and during that same year, 1837, James joined him. At seventeen, working with his brother, James also became a capable carpenter. During the winter months he attended school.

Later Daniel gave up carpenter work in favor of clerking. Then he became a partner in a pork packing business. Meantime, James also went into business, but the record does not clarify what type of business.

During the years between 1844 and 1849, Daniel and James, as well as other members of the family, were receiving regular letters from their older brother, William, who had gone to California, settling in Santa Cruz. The many opportunities which their brother described excited them.

In 1849 Daniel and James, another brother, Jacob; Captain Finley, a brother-in-law; Henry Seymour, one of Daniel's partners; and a friend named James Westerfield teamed up for the journey to California.

They outfitted three wagons with three yoke of oxen to each wagon, and they packed a two-year supply of provisions. They attached themselves to a wagon train led by Captain McCullough. One hundred and twenty men made up the party which crossed the Missouri River at Iowa Point on May 5, 1849, to begin the journey to California. Apparently, they did not experience unusual hardship. In little more than three months, they completed the overland journey. They arrived at Deer Creek on August 12, 1849, and intent on finding gold, they immediately started their search.

According to Angel, "At that time there was no sign that a white man had ever been in that neighborhood, and the Blackburns were the first to mine in the region since celebrated as Nevada City. The mines were very rich, and they took the gold out by handfuls."

They remained in that area until November. Then, their brother-in-law, Captain Finley, became sick. The family sold their teams and provisions, actually making money from the sale, and headed for Sacramento.

After a week or two in the Sacramento area, Daniel, James and Jacob, along with Henry Seymour, journeyed to Santa Cruz. Soon afterward Finley joined them. Each man had $3,000 as his share from the mining and the sale of their outfits.

During his years in California, their brother William had enjoyed both financial and political success. Soon after arriving in 1844, he had become active in American efforts to bring California under the United States flag. When General Fremont organized a force for the march to Los Angeles, William joined as a company lieutenant. After that experience, he returned to Santa Cruz to operate a retail store. He was appointed alcalde by Colonel Richard B. Mason, military governor.

William owned considerable land in Santa Cruz, and he invited his brothers to join him in various business ventures. Daniel raised potatoes and marketed them with great success. He farmed his brother's land on shares and leased other land in the area.

William had been constructing a sawmill in the nearby Santa Cruz Mountains. James took over this project. At the time, large amounts of the lumber being consumed in San Francisco were imported by ship from Chile or the Atlantic Coast. At times, lumber sold for as much as five hundred dollars per thousand feet in San Francisco, Angel says.

James completed the sawmill and began manufacturing lumber for shipment to San Francisco. He continued this business until 1853, when he had an opportunity to sell it. On August 1, 1853, he and Lazarus Godchaux formed a partnership. As a competent carpenter and successful lumber manufacturer, James, with his partner, constructed the first substantial building in Watsonville and established the Blackburn and Godchaux Mercantile.

Three years later they experienced a fire in the wooden building, but they succeeded in saving both the building and the merchandise.[2]

Meantime, both Daniel and James were interested in acquiring ranch land. Word reached them concerning the availability of the El Paso de Robles Rancho. This rancho was originally granted to Captain Pedro Narvaez by Governor Manuel Micheltorena on May 12, 1844.[3]

Captain Narvaez was in charge of port activities in Monterey for about ten years before the permanent hoisting of the American flag. He had come to Monterey from Mexico as a soldier in the service of his country. He was apparently responsible for general "policing" in Monterey, at least as far as the conduct of ships' crews on land was concerned.

Occasional letters from American crew members jailed in Monterey reached Thomas Larkin, consulate for the United States. Apparently, Captain Narvaez was not always attentive to the needs of his prisoners. One American prisoner claimed that he had been locked up for seven days without food.[4]

Nonetheless, Larkin described Narvaez as a quiet, unobtrusive man. His position gave him influence in Monterey and to a lesser extent, throughout California. He was married and he accumulated land, cattle, and some money. Larkin said he showed little interest in political activities.[5]

When Commodore John Drake Sloat took Monterey for the United States in 1846, General Jose Castro escaped the settlement with an entourage of Mexican troops. Captain Narvaez apparently felt compelled to accompany Castro, but he and several other officers soon returned to their families in Monterey. Narvaez then sent word to Larkin that he and a group of his men would surrender themselves upon assurances from Commodore Sloat of safety for themselves and their families.[6]

Narvaez stocked cattle on the El Paso de Robles and operated it through a majordomo, but Indian raids of the cattle prevented the ranch from becoming a financial success.

Petronillo Rios, spelled Petronilos Rios on family photo. He served as county superintendent of schools in San Luis Obispo in 1857, the year that eight men passed the honor from one to the other. Rios built the adobe below on the El Paso de Robles rancho as well as the Rios-Caledonia adobe in San Miguel.

El Paso de Robles Rancho, consisting of 25,993 acres, came into the hands of Petronillo Rios, and on July 20, 1866, he received a patent for it from the United States Land Commission. In the meantime, however, he had sold his right to the rancho to the Blackburns.[7]

This same Rios, mentioned earlier along with William Reed, had also purchased Mission San Miguel, but their claim to it was later invalidated by the United States. Rios and his family also built and lived in what is now identified as the Caledonia Adobe in San Miguel.

Rios had arrived in California from Mexico as an artillery man in the Mexican Army in either 1824 or 1825. In 1827 he was an artillery sergeant in San Francisco. He remained at this

Petronillo Rios adobe at Templeton. This is the original home built on the Rancho Paso de Robles by Petronillo Rios. James Blackburn occupied the adobe between 1857 and 1872, then built a new home about two hundred yards to the north, bringing his lumber by team from Port Harford. This adobe was located about one mile south of Templeton on El Camino Real. All traces of the venerable building were removed when Highway 101 was constructed through the land.

post for many years. He married a lovely California girl named Catarina Avila. In 1834, they had a child whom they named Jose Camilo. The next year, Maria Lina was born, and in 1836 Jose Simon was born.

Rios was released from military duty in about 1840 and remained in California. In 1842 he was granted land in Monterey County.

Rios still lived in San Luis Obispo County in 1860. In 1877 his wife, Catarina, provided Bancroft a record of the Reed family murders at Mission San Miguel.[8]

∽

Angel reports that in July 1857 the Blackburn brothers and Lazarus Godchaux acquired El Paso de Robles Rancho for $8,000. Daniel moved to the rancho soon after the purchase. James remained in Watsonville for a while longer until he and Godchaux sold their mercantile store.

Almost immediately Daniel was drawn into county activities, beginning with participation in a vigilante committee. A crime wave was threatening the well-being of all. During the year before Daniel's arrival in the county, a murder had been committed in the vicinity of his ranch. The wagon and stagecoach trail through the county was very primitive and strangers traveling in the area were fair game to lawless marauders who moved in gangs. Men herding cattle from the southern part of the state to San Francisco were in constant danger of being robbed and murdered. In December of the year Daniel moved to the ranch, two more men were murdered nearby. They had purchased cattle at Santa Margarita Rancho and at Paso Robles Rancho, according to an article written by Walter Murray for the *San Francisco Bulletin*. The latter purchase may have been from Blackburn himself.

For the protection of their families and themselves, residents of the county formed a vigilante committee which took legal matters into their own hands. For a time, Daniel Blackburn was "sheriff" among the committee members. Angel credits him with making "many arrests of desperados and driving the infamous Jack Powers out of the state."

James joined his brother at the rancho in 1859. The next year the brothers divided the property. Daniel took as his share one league of land, including the warm springs area. James and his partner owned the balance of the ranch,

including the original Rios adobe ranch house dating from the early Mexican period. James constructed a steam-powered sawmill near his ranch house which could cut 6,000 feet of lumber a day.[9]

A sketch of the Paso Robles Hot Springs Hotel by Edward Vischer in 1864 shows a two-story wooden hotel and a one-story building which probably served various business purposes including the overland stage stop. It appears that a great deal was achieved during the first seven years after Daniel's arrival in the area.[10]

Senator Chris Jesperson traced bits of information about the Hot Springs through the *Bancroft Scraps*, a collection of newspaper clippings. For example, he found a clipping by a writer for the *San Francisco Bulletin* who traveled by McLaughlin and Manns stagecoaches to the Hot Springs during the same year that Vischer made his visit. The writer noted that the Hot Springs was the first place he had seen any life since leaving San Jose. Here, he said, "life appears badly crippled, walking on crutches and hobbling about with canes."

The *Bulletin* correspondent further wrote that a new hotel was being built at the time of his visit and the old one was being arranged for use as a hospital. The monthly charge was nine dollars for room, board, and use of the baths.

Four years later a San Francisco newspaper reported that accommodations were two dollars per day and from twelve to fourteen dollars per week. By this time, a house had been built around the hot springs pool. The pool was two feet by eight feet in size and four or five feet deep. Private bathrooms with tubs, and mud baths, were also available to guests.

The visiting correspondent of that year reported guests from Oregon, Idaho, Nevada, and Alabama.[11]

The Blackburn brothers pursued life with vigor, and their economic progress seemed continuously better. The record indicates that at age forty-six James was still a bachelor, and as Daniel approached fifty, so was he, but then he became interested in a young lady living in San Luis Obispo. Her name was Cecelia Dunn, and she was the daughter of Patrick and Mary Ann Dunn. They were Irish, but had come from

Australia.[12] An 1870 map of San Luis Obispo shows that Dunn owned a large piece of land along the south side of Monterey Street between Santa Rosa and Osos streets. He served in various civic positions including superintendent of schools.[13]

While Daniel courted Cecelia, another north county man, Drury Woodson James, age forty, was showing a keen interest in Louisa Dunn, Cecelia's sister. The men proposed, and the two couples were married in a double wedding ceremony on September 15, 1866. The Reverend Father Sastre performed the ceremony in the San Luis Obispo Mission Church.

Daniel and Cecelia had ten children. Drury and Louisa had seven children. It appears that the brothers-in-law, Daniel and Drury, were good friends, and they, along with their wives, frequently socialized. In 1869 Drury bought half interest in the hotel and hot springs property for $11,000.

Born November 14, 1826, at Whippoorwill River, Logan County, Kentucky, Drury James had come a long way both in distance and well-being when he joined Daniel as a partner in the Paso Robles Hot Springs property.

Very soon after his birth, his mother died. Within a year, his father also passed away, leaving three daughters and four sons. Drury's older sister, Mary, and her husband assumed responsibility for the family, and Drury grew up working on their farm and attending school.

Later he served in the war with Mexico. His time in the army and away from his family aroused in him a spirit of adventure. Before long he found himself in contact with other young men who were stirred by the stories of finding gold in California. In 1849 he joined an overland company which gathered at Fort Kearny, Nebraska. It included men from Ohio, Kentucky and Missouri. They crossed the Platte River on April 1, 1849, to begin their journey to California.

Four months later they set up camp at Hangtown, California (later Placerville) and began their search for gold on Weber and Hangtown creeks. Drury remained there during the winter months.

During the spring of 1850 he went to Santa Clara County and bought some cattle at twenty dollars per head. He drove them to Hangtown and sold them for sixty cents per pound on the hoof. Beef which he slaughtered himself sold for one dollar per pound in the Hangtown Market.

At twenty-four years of age, he had discovered a profitable and adventuresome way of life. During the next year he extended his buying trip to Los Angeles. Here, he could buy cattle at fifteen and twenty dollars per head. By driving them north, he could sell them for forty dollars per head.

He soon worked out a system of buying which proved highly profitable. He would move a herd of cattle from Los Angeles during the month of March. Later in the season he would buy closer to his market—San Luis Obispo, Monterey and Santa Clara counties. In this way, he could make three good drives each year with between five hundred and seven hundred head of cattle. He made one drive from Los Angeles with fifteen hundred cattle.

During these years of driving cattle from south to north, Drury became aware of the hot springs on the Paso Robles Ranch. It is probable that he even met Daniel Blackburn. He and his drovers used the hot springs to wash off the trail dust and to relax saddle-weary muscles.

With money accumulated from the droving business, Drury James and his partner, John D. Thompson, bought ten thousand acres of land in the La Panza area in 1860. The going price at that time was a dollar and twenty-five cents per acre. They soon had twenty-five hundred head of cattle on the range. By 1863 they had accumulated five thousand head. The years of 1863 and 1864 were the years of the drought and they were threatened with losing all of their stock, as were all farmers and cattlemen in the county. One advantage they had was the knowledge of how to move large herds for long distances. Another advantage was a good knowledge of California geography. Drury and his hands rounded up their herd and drove them—crying, hoof-sore and weak—to Tulare and Buena Vista lakes. They remained in this area until conditions were suitable for selling the cattle and returning home.

With his marriage to Louisa, Drury settled down. For the former Dunn sisters, Cecelia and

Louisa, as they raised their large families, the partnership and friendship of their husbands must have seemed a blessing.

In 1870, thirteen years after the Blackburn brothers and Godchaux purchased the ranch, the health resort was showing continuing progress. The *San Luis Obispo Tribune* described the property: "The place which nearest approaches to the dignity of a town or village in this county after San Luis Obispo and Cambria

Waiting stagecoach at the hotel. The old hotel was left standing for some time after the magnificent new Hotel El Paso de Robles was finished and ready to serve its fashionable clientele.

is the hot springs situated on the stage road, 34 miles from the town of San Luis Obispo, where there is an establishment for the accommodation of invalids who come to taste the sulphur water and be cured.

"Here, there is never a less number than 50 persons and often a much larger one. These springs are much celebrated for their medicinal qualities and are justly famous for the cures they had wrought in rheumatism, cutaneous disorders and syphilis. Invalids have come thither for relief from very distant parts, as Oregon and the eastern states."

We gain a somewhat better description of Paso de Robles Hot Springs in 1871 from a writer for *Overland Monthly Magazine* who came into the county from the north by stage. She described the surrounding country as she approached it.

"Toward the Paso Robles Hot Springs and beyond it, the level country may truly be likened to an English park, so clean is the sward and so luxuriantly do the trees . . . white oak and live oak . . . grow here.

"Before reaching the hotel at the springs, my fellow travelers pointed out to me a little redwood building which covered the far-famed hot mud bath of the Paso Robles.

"While the horses were being changed, I made my way to the main spring, eager to quaff a goblet of the health-giving fountain.

"I looked with profound pity on the men who had gathered around the dark looking waters . . . the place looked like the pool of Siloam where the angel was expected to stir its waters.

"Here, the angel seems ever present, for men turn away after drinking the horrid stuff as though they felt sure of being one step nearer to the health they are in pursuit of. Of the healing power of this bad-tasting water, in cases of rheumatism, neuralgia and gout, there can be no doubt.

"Not only those of our own time and generation who have tried its virtues speak enthusiastically of it, but what speaks equally loud in its favor is the fact that clear-sighted padres of the mission regime and the old Indians and Californians held it in high esteem."

An *Alta* correspondent of the same period, enroute from Northern California, provided these notes about his stop at the Hot Springs Hotel: "After a pleasant drive through a rolling country, we reached Paso Robles, or the Hot Springs of San Luis Obispo, in time for an excellent lunch, and we were offered an opportunity of looking about this favorite resort for invalids . . . the buildings are neat and comfortable and the grounds well arranged.

"The value of the baths for curative purposes . . . is . . . well known, and the fact that although it was early in the season, there were yet some 30 or 40 boarders, shows the appreciation in which they are held.

"They are easily reached by steamer from San Francisco as well as by stage route. The charges are moderate, and the proprietors seem only anxious that no want of their guests shall be unsupplied."

That year, Drury and Louisa built a fine home near the hotel. In 1873 Daniel sold a one-quarter interest in the hotel to his brother, James, who had moved from the original Rios adobe ranch house into a new home at the same site. It was located six miles south of the hot springs and the hotel. Angel described the property:

"In front of the house is a flourishing garden of flowers and grassy lawn and near is a large and thrifty orchard of many varieties of fruits and vines.

"A windmill raises water for domestic purposes for irrigating the garden, but not the trees, which do not need it.

"Nearby, he cultivates about 500 acres in wheat, barley and oats, but the rancho is chiefly devoted to grazing sheep. Of these, he has 7,000 head which yield an average of seven pounds of wool per head each year.

"Were the rancho, comprising 22,000 acres, fully fenced, it would support 10,000 head of sheep. There are also on it from thirty to forty head of horses and as many cows for the necessities of the farm. A steam sawmill is also one of the conveniences of the rancho, used in sawing lumber for fences, bridges and other purposes, the forests of oak furnishing the material."

With regular freight service provided by the railroad, new markets for grain developed. These thirty-horse teams pulling harvesting equipment became common on the Carrisa Plains outside Paso Robles.

In the early years after buying the rancho, Blackburn and Godchaux ran large herds of cattle on their portion of it, but they were caught unprepared for the drought in 1863-64 and lost three thousand head. Luckily, they had financial strength which made it possible to withstand their loss, and in 1865 they again stocked the ranch with cattle at eight dollars per head and with sheep at fifty cents each. God-

chaux moved to San Francisco and established a butchering business while James operated the ranch. Their partnership continued and with Godchaux at the marketing end of the meat business, it is likely that the partners were always assured of ready sales at the best prices for their stock.

The early bathhouse for the El Paso de Robles Hotel was located a mile north of town. Guests were provided regular coach service to and from the baths.

By 1883 El Paso de Robles Hotel and Hot Springs had developed into a privately-owned village with a two-story wooden resort hotel at its center. The hotel was surrounded by small wooden cottages accommodating guests paying first class rates.

Angel said they were "furnished with special care, and no where can be found more luxurious beds, finer blankets and bedding or more comfortable house equipments than in the cottages at Paso Robles."

There were two dining rooms—one for first class guests and the other for second class guests. Other buildings contained a store, billiard saloon, express, telegraph and post office, reading room, barber shop and a physician's residence and office.

By the main spring, across the wagon and stage road, was a long double row of bathrooms. The bathrooms were fed by a reservoir of sulphur water constructed by the Blackburns to collect the fast flowing spring waters.

"There were two plunge baths," Angel said, "one exclusively for ladies, through which the water is continuously running, thus insuring perfect cleanliness and equal temperature."

However, the resort's unique claim to fame was its mud baths. A building had been built around the thick muddy area that made up the mud spring. A raised platform ran through its center. "On one side of this [platform] is a plunge bath of tepid gas and sulphur impregnated water; on the other [side] is the famous mud bath."

A patient could submerge himself into the warm mud up to his neck, remaining from fifteen to thirty minutes. Then he could shift to the hot sulphur water on the opposite side of the platform to wash himself clean. After this experience, he could wrap himself in heavy blankets until he was perspiring profusely. Apparently, persons with rheumatism and other afflictions involving aches and pains in the joints enjoyed relief within a few days.

The mud bath was available to the ladies on Mondays, Wednesdays and Fridays; gentlemen used it on Tuesdays, Thursdays and Saturdays. Since the mud bath was located at quite some distance from the resort complex, the hotel provided carriage service to and from it.

In addition to the main spring and the mud baths, several other springs existed near the resort, including a sand bath, a soda spring and another sulphur spring.

A pamphlet advertising the resort at that time reported that mail left the resort twice daily and the complex of conveniences around the hotel included a Wells Fargo agency. The Wells Fargo agent was P. H. Dunn, the brother-in-law of Blackburn and James, who also operated the general store and served as postmaster.

Until 1886, people coming to the Paso Robles resort from the north found it necessary to leave

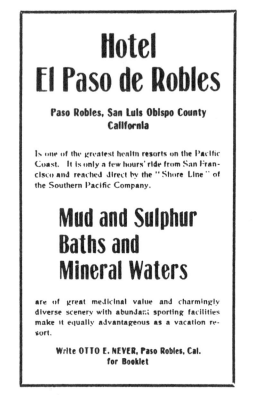

Among the publications used for advertising by the El Paso de Robles Hotel was Sunset Magazine. This advertisement appeared on the inside back cover in August 1899. At this time, the magazine was owned by Southern Pacific Railroad Company.

the train at Soledad and travel eighty-four miles by stagecoach.[14] But with the Southern Pacific Railroad now running trains through Paso Robles and making regular stops, the hotel would soon be ready for further expansion of its facilities.

This horse-drawn streetcar met passengers arriving by train in Paso Robles and took them to the hotel. Track along Spring Street also provided passage by streetcar between the health resort hotel and the elaborate bathhouse north of town.

CHAPTER V

Fire, Tears And Music

For a time after the opening of the Andrews Hotel in San Luis Obispo in 1885, optimism prevailed in local business and governmental matters.

Within the same month that the Andrews opened for business, a Colonel A. M. Gray, an architect and builder of theaters, visited San Luis Obispo. He was in town to submit plans to key people in the community for the construction of an opera house at the corner of Higuera and Broad streets on land owned by Mr. E.

Krebs. Krebs had been among the first men to purchase land in the early mission gardens when the mission offered it for sale. Gray presented several incomplete designs to influential people in town. He proposed a building that would seat seven hundred people. Gray's papers indicated that he had built "nearly all the best theaters in the state." This building was never constructed, but planning of many kinds persisted, maintaining an air of excitement.[1]

For several weeks during that year, Sins-

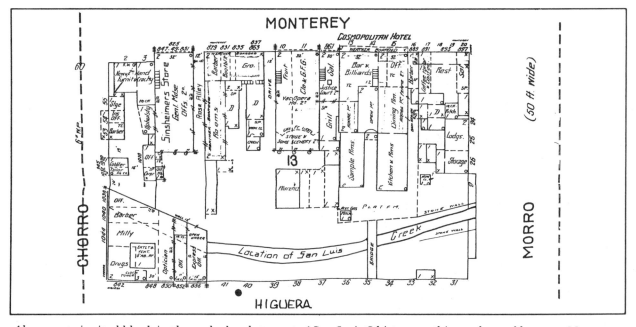

Always a principal block in the early development of San Luis Obispo was this one located between Monterey, Higuera, Chorro and Morro, immediately west of Mission San Luis Obispo. Here, Sinsheimers moved into their new brick building with the iron front in 1885. Alongside it, Rose Alley is visible. When in town, farmers watered their horses at this location because of its easy access to San Luis Obispo Creek. Gradually buildings were constructed over the creek so that it now runs under the business district for several blocks. Note that the Cosmopolitan Hotel occupied a large part of the block at the time. This map not only shows most of the rooms on the first floor of the hotel but also the location of some of the early adobe walls of the original bar and hotel of Juan Cappe constructed at a much earlier time. In our time, this block is occupied by at least a third layer of human occupation.

heimer Brothers General Store advertised that they had moved into their new brick building on Monterey Street at Rose Alley. In 1980 this structure still stands.[2]

The Andrews Hotel provided a certain style to both social and business activities in the area. The hotel became a meeting place for many groups. For example, when it was decided by some men of the county that a horticultural organization was needed to promote community interests, the meeting was called at the hotel.

The announcement of the meeting read: "We, the undersigned residents of San Luis Obispo County, being desirous of promoting our vitacultural and vinicultural interests, hereby agree to meet at the Andrews Hotel, Saturday, October 17, 1885, at 3 p.m. for the purpose of organizing a horticultural society for this county." For the most part, the names of the signers of the notice were familiar. They were important landowners and interested promoters of the area, including: C. H. Phillips, E. Krebs, Edward Ballard, P. H. Dallidet, Jr., H. M. Warden. W. W. Hays, J. P. Andrews, L. M. Kaiser, Arza Potter, J. F. Beckett, George Steele, E. A. Atwood, Stephenson Brothers, B. F. Pettit and J. H. Orcutt.[3]

On September 4 of that year, a news story in the *Tribune* announced still another advance in the business structures in the community. The "Ah Lui" (Ah Louis) brick building at the corner of Chorro and Palm streets was approaching completion, and "Mr. Lui" would soon again be able to accommodate his many past customers. Ah Louis was a leader among the Chinese who lived in San Luis Obispo. Some of the other Chinese also operated businesses along Palm Street between Chorro and Morro streets. They operated wash houses and gambling dens, worked as kitchen help in some of the hotels, and served as cooks and hired help on several ranches in the county. Ah Louis operated a small hiring agency. He would secure Chinese employees for anyone needing laborers. Many of the Chinese living in San Luis Obispo had been recruited by Ah Louis as laborers in the construction of the narrow-gauge railway between Avila, San Luis Obispo and points south to Los Alamos.

"The building is an ornament to that part of

Ah Louis, pioneer Chinese leader in San Luis Obispo County, provided the Chinese labor for construction of early railroads, regional mining operations, and county road building. His store served as a center for Chinese economic activities during the latter half of the nineteenth century. He died December 16, 1936 when he was ninety-eight years old. His children continue a family tradition of leadership and active participation in community affairs.

the city," the *Tribune* said, "as it would be to any part, and shows the proprietor to be an enterprising, competent businessman.

"The building is of brick fronting 26 feet on Palm Street by 42 feet on Chorro, two stories in height, the front stuccoed and having an iron rail piazza over the Palm Street front.

"The main room on the lower floor was designed and furnished with shelving, drawers, counters, etc. for a store, another good-sized room for storage of goods, another for a private room and office and a hallway across the building in the rear. The upstairs is divided into six rooms for sleeping apartments. The partitions are of alternate strips of dark and light redwood, oiled and varnished, giving a very pleasant effect."[4]

In 1980 this building is used as a gift shop under the management of Howard Louis, and is marked as a state historical site.

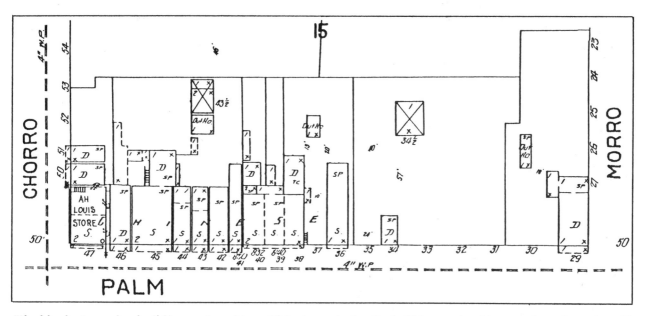

The block of wooden buildings referred to as Chinatown in San Luis Obispo existed into modern times, but all were eventually removed except for the brick building of the Ah Louis Store at the corner of Chorro and Palm, diagonally across from the mission. It is now a California Historic Landmark, operated as a gift shop by the Louis family.

For all of the improvements taking place in town that year, occasional difficulties also arose. For example, in October 1885, community leaders were concerned because a recently opened street was getting very little use. It was the street which was later known as Santa Barbara Street, running from Broad to where it met Osos Street. At that time, Santa Barbara and Osos streets apparently were not considered as two separate streets. This street cut across town from the Pacific Coast Railroad crossing on Broad Street to the courthouse and the Andrews Hotel on Monterey.

"Although open and fenced, its existence does not appear to be generally recognized," the newspaper reported. "Otherwise, it seems it would be more generally used in driving stock, as it is quite a cut off and outside the thickly built part of town." But for some time to come, drovers continued to herd their cattle past the mission and through the main streets of town.[5]

❧

The biggest social event in San Luis Obispo since the grand opening of the hotel occurred on Saturday night, October 16, 1885. It was called the "Andrews Hop." It not only attracted

This photo illustrates the early map shown on this page. These buildings were removed in modern times to make room for a large city parking lot. The Ah Louis building is visible at the far left.

a number of well-known married couples, but also many young single people.

Before the dancing started, Professor W. J. McCoy gathered his military band on the second floor balcony of the hotel overlooking Monterey Street and provided a musical program for the entire city. People gathered from all around the vicinity, sitting in their buggies with lap blankets and leaning against the Bank of San Luis Obispo and the other buildings

Gon Ying, the beautiful wife of Ah Louis, poses in full costume beside a Victorian marble-top table with early hand-wound calendar clock. Ah Louis disappeared from San Luis Obispo in 1887 and did not return for two years. In May 1899 he reappeared with his young wife. They had eight children in the years that followed.

across the street. Others crowded the hall and vestibule of the hotel in order to hear the music.

After the outdoor concert, the band switched to dance music in keeping with the "hop" theme. A canvas was stretched across the carpet in the reading room for dancing. Among the pretty single young ladies on the dance floor were the Misses Livingston, T. Staniford, S. and E. Leland, L. Johnston, A. Mallagh, E. Barnett and La Tourette.

Young gentlemen swinging their partners included the Mssrs. H. A. Vachell, A. H. Vachell, Frank Lewis, Leslie Bainbridge, Samuel Harris, E. B. Ballard, J. C. Morrison, J. L. Chamblin, P. H. Dallidet, Jr., L. M. Noah, A. M. Easton, J. D. Grant, William Warden, and Oscar Dowe.

Doing a good job as chaperones and also dancing were Mr. and Mrs. J. M. Fillmore, Mr. and Mrs. C. H. Phillips, Mr. and Mrs. R. B. Treat, Mr. and Mrs. E. B. Morriss, Mr. and Mrs. R. E. Jack, Mr. and Mrs. Staniford, Mr. and Mrs. L. M. Kaiser, Mr. and Mrs. G. B. Nichols, and Dr. W. W. Hays.

It was a memorable evening. For some young couples it may have lasted well beyond the eleven o'clock hour when the music stopped, and the horses pulling the buggies reluctantly allowed themselves to be led the long way home.[6]

Another party occurred the next month. Though not as large, and though it did not take place at the Andrews Hotel, it marked a significant change in the operation of the new hotel.

Public notice of the change appeared in a short item in the November 20, 1885 issue of the *Tribune*: "The management of The Andrews has passed into the hands of Mssrs. Sharp Brothers, late of the Ormsby House, Carson City, Nevada. The gentlemen are experienced hotel men, and they will undoubtedly keep The Andrews up to the very best standard. Mr. J. W. Sharp, the father of the sons, accompanies them, as does the family of Mr. H. W. Sharp, the eldest son, all of whom will be a welcome addition to our social circles."

In the same column of local events, another notice appeared: "The friends of E. B. Morriss tendered a serenade last Saturday evening upon the event of his resuming management of the Cosmopolitan Hotel. Anvils were fired, and McCoy's band of twelve pieces dispensed music for a couple of hours. Toasts were drunk to the old time proprietor and a happy time was had by all, showing the esteem in which Mr. Morriss is held."

After Mr. Morriss had left the Andrews Hotel and returned to the Cosmopolitan, the *Tribune* continued to carry an advertisement for the Andrews, but there seemed to be fewer social events occurring there.[7]

At the time the Sharp brothers assumed management of the Andrews, business was apparently very slow. It was quietly expressed among some citizens of San Luis Obispo that the

AH LUIS'
CHINESE
LABOR AGENCY
&
STORE!

Dry Goods,

   Black Teas,

      Sugars,

         Rice,

And all kinds of

Chinese Provisions.

Chinese Labor contracted for on short notice.

Satisfaction Guaranteed in all Business Transactions.

Orrice:—On Palm street, San Lui: Obispo.
326-6m.

AH LUIS' STORE.
——
Chinese and Japanese Ware
Of all Kinds.
Just the things for Holiday Presents !
——

 The only place in San Luis Obispo where Japanese goods can be found.

By 1881, Ah Louis' Store offered a line of imported gift merchandise. Today the store provides a wide range of oriental items.

During 1875, Ah Louis promoted his Chinese labor agency. The Pacific Coast Railway and various regional mining operations, as well as local hotels and other businesses, sought assistance from Ah Louis in hiring Chinese workers.

Andrews Hotel had turned out to be a big white elephant on the main street. There simple wasn't enough business activity to support such a magnificent structure.

Henry Sharp, the lessor, later said, "We took the hotel on the fifteenth of November [1885]. On the seventeenth came the great flood which swept away the railroad [narrow-gauge], and we lost considerable in our customers by it." A "great flood which swept away the railroad" occurred every time the rains were heavy and San Luis Obispo Creek overflowed, and Mr. Sharp may have been exaggerating a little, although it was a real concern. However, the hotel enjoyed patronage from people in the county and the Sharp brothers later reported that they succeeded in gradually raising the receipts from $1,800 to $3,000 a month.

Other events taking place attest to progress in town. On January 6, 1886 there was an announcement of completion of construction of the Mission School building, located at the 1980 site of Emerson Elementary School on Nipomo Street.[8]

On March 5, Professor McCoy's Military Band gave a concert at the Lytton Theater.[9]

Then came the fateful day of April 18, 1886.

The newspaper had reported little activity at the hotel during the preceding weeks. Encouraging word about the prospects of the Southern Pacific Railroad's running track all the way between Los Angeles and San Francisco was still occasionally heard. It was generally believed that this move by the railroad would make San Luis Obispo more prosperous.

Meantime, it was said that the hotel was doing enough business to justify its existence. When visiting town, people from around the county usually stayed overnight rather than make a one-day round trip by horse and buggy. Any visitors from out of the county were likely to stay in the hotel for several days at a time. So, the Andrews was succeeding up to the time of the tragedy.

Word reached most of the people in town around 5:15 P.M. that quiet Sunday afternoon when the bell at City Hall began ringing. There was always a feeling of dread when the bell rang in this way because it was a call for volunteer firemen to turn out.

As to the location, the *Tribune* reported that "there was no need of inquiring nor a second look. From the high roof of The Andrews a dense volume of smoke was seen ascending into the air, and the lurid flames soon bursting forth in various parts at once gave conviction that the noble structure, the pride of the city, was doomed to destruction."

Volunteer firemen with fire wagons rushed to the scene. Dozens of citizens saddled horses and rode to the hotel to help.

Although in recent years the city had made major additions to its fire fighting equipment, the feeble stream of water from the hoses could not touch the flames raging at the top of the building. The men handling the hoses attempted to hold the fire by concentrating their water on the front of the building. Then they turned to wetting the buildings on the opposite side of the street.

The effect seemed negligible, but eventually the heat became less intense, and dozens of men were able to get in and out of the bottom floor of the hotel, dragging and carrying out expensive furnishings.

Then just across Osos Street, smoke was sighted on the roof of the courthouse. Firefighters turned from the seemingly lost hotel to the county building. Ladders were put up, and firemen scaled them uncertainly, finally succeeding in getting both themselves and their hoses onto the roof. Men poured into the building to carry out the valuable county books and documents.

"That handsome structure was saved with but trifling damage," the report later read.

Steele and Wheelan's Flour Mill, located on the southeast corner of Monterey and Osos streets, was threatened by the continuous sparks that covered the entire neighborhood. Wheelan and a party of men climbed to the roof of the mill with a hose and kept a stream of water pouring over the top and along the sides. Flames broke out in various places but they succeeded in drowning them quickly, and the mill was saved.

Firefighters were less successful in salvaging the buildings directly across Monterey Street from the Andrews. "The great plate glass windows in the San Luis Obispo Bank at the

Corner of Monterey and Court gave way before the heat and soon the interior of the bank was in flames." The wooden building alongside the bank also caught fire. By this time, the water pressure was so low that little could be done to save this building. However, because the bank was a brick building, it and Loobliner's Store, also brick, established a firebreak beyond which the fire could not spread to the south.

Within two and a half hours "The Andrews was only a pile of burning cinders; the wooden buildings across the street were but beds of ashes, and the flames left nothing of the interior of the brick bank building. In that brief time, $160,000 of value had been destroyed, and the grand pride and ornament of the city swept from existence!" the newspaper said.

While the fire raged, all of the buildings on Monterey Street between Court and Morro streets were in great danger. Business owners loaded merchandise on wagons and hauled it to safety.

When the fire was over and people had time to consider how it had occurred, a number of facts about the construction of the hotel came to light. The fire had started in the attic, spreading inside the roof before suddenly appearing in several places at once across the top of the building. The cause of the fire was finally attributed to a defective flue.[10]

The *Tribune* spoke out with vigor about the fire and the construction of the hotel: "The flues of the hotel were of terra cotta pipes with frequent joints and very carelessly put up. The defects had been noticed and repairs made [at an earlier date] ... but with shabby treatment, safety seemed to have been an impossibility." After the fire, people spoke of the disjointed and open areas in the flue construction found by local repairmen. These men had also found the woodwork smoky and charred around the flues.

The *Tribune* said, "The building has been in constant danger, and its destruction by fire a certainty.

"The construction of the building was most shamefully slighted, the foundation settling, the walls cracking and the joints opening. The architect and contractors were guilty of neglect of duty and should be exposed and punished."

The *Tribune* had been critical of the contractors even at the time the foundation was laid. Editor Angel found himself very unpopular with the out-of-town contractors, and they had stopped work to repair foundation faults he described in the newspaper.[11]

This tragedy might have been a time for tears and utterances of hopelessness in town, but social conditions of the time scarcely permitted it. The very next afternoon, even while the ruins of the hotel still smouldered, a most amazing set of events occurred, providing insight into the social attitudes and personal courage of nineteenth century Americans.

On Monday afternoon, April 19, 1886, at 3:00 P.M., a mass meeting was called on the steps of the county courthouse, just across the street from the hotel. As the saddened crowd gathered, all looking for words to comfort one another—and looking up the steps expectantly toward J. P. Andrews, C. H. Phillips, and some of the other leaders of the community—they suddenly heard music in the distance. As they turned in the direction of the devastated hotel and other gutted buildings on Monterey Street, here came Professor McCoy and his military band. Every man in the group was playing his heart out.

Past the smoking, char-ridden and fallen buildings between Court and Osos streets, past the gutted brick shell of the San Luis Obispo Bank and Loobliner's Store, and finally in sight of the crowd before the sickening piles of black rubbish where only the evening before had stood the Andrews, San Luis Obispo's grand promise, the band marched, filling the dismal air with "inspiriting airs" and stepping onto the courthouse grounds amidst resounding applause. There, the people continued to gather, and the courthouse steps served as a stage.

Chauncey Phillips, the county's great land promoter, called the meeting to order. On the spot, Judge George Steele was elected chairman of the day and the Honorable Charles W. Dana was elected secretary.

Steele moved up the stairs where he could better see the crowd, and they could see him. "Fellow citizens of San Luis Obispo," he said, "we are assembled here today under circumstances that draw out the mettle men are made of. We are here in the sight of the ruins of the Andrews, that magnificent hotel which was the boast of our city and the pride of our county so far as hotels are concerned.

"Yesterday, it loomed up in all its splendor and brilliancy before us, and we admired it. We were so nicely treated by the hotel that we admired it all the more when we thought what were the prospects of our county on account of the hotel. We knew how it would draw a great number of people from abroad to our city.

"The establishment of the hotel was an impetus to progress in this community and county, but alas, the fire fiend has reduced it to ashes. I believe today there are men in our midst with the pluck, stamina and spirit in them not only to build the hotel but to run it successfully and show the people of the country and this city the stuff they are made of. Now, fellow citizens, we want to think this matter over and take some method to build this hotel, to reconstruct the prosperity of this city.

"Not alone to reconstruct but to increase it and to build a more magnificent hotel, if possible, than before, and to give a new impetus to the business of this county. We have great resources here. We have ability and pluck and all that is necessary to manifest it. By raising this hotel again, we can do it. If we only say it, it is done already. There is no difficulty about it whatever, and I say that the business shall prosper if we only put our shoulders to the wheel and move along. A plan will be laid for you for aid. We want every man to contribute his mite, if only two bits. Let every man and woman assist to raise it again, and we shall have it erected in a short time."

While the crowd cheered Steele's words, he brought Henry Sharp, one of the lessees and manager of the hotel, before the group. He was introduced and called upon to speak.

As the crowd quieted, Sharp said: "Fellow citizens of San Luis Obispo, when we came here and leased the Andrews Hotel, we did it under adverse circumstances. Everyone said that we never could make it pay—that it would be a failure. We told the gentlemen who gave us such advice to hold on and let us see what could be done."

There was long exuberant applause. Sharp continued, "We did show the people who said it would be a failure. We showed them in plain figures that we had made a little money and made it a success. It is true we did not possess much capital. What little we had, we put into the property and the building.

"I think it is to the benefit of this community and the county at large to reconstruct this building. Not in wood, but in brick, if possible, which can be done at less cost. I now think about $90,000. The hotel had hardly become known and with all that, the prospects were grand for this summer for filling the hotel to its utmost capacity, and I feel sure that the citizens of this community will rebuild the structure if they put their hands in their pockets." Again, there was applause and cheering.

From the talks given by these men, we cannot help but be aware of the strength of character and determination that moved them in their efforts. They refused to feel sorry for themselves. In this town meeting, they took strength from one another and found new fortitude. They offered solace and support to J. P. Andrews and others who were seriously hurt by the tragedy. They were tough and vital.

The next speaker was the Reverend Cox, a relatively new member of the community. "Mr. Chairman and fellow citizens," he started, "I am proud to meet so many of you and know that you are interested in the event which has called us here this afternoon. I am glad to meet my friend, Judge Steele, the presiding officer who gave us such a bright picture of the future outlook and said that you had the means and that you were of the right mettle, and I endorse his statements.

"There is no better metal for tenacity than steel, and I know he has a way of stealing our affections and our sympathies and our interests, and he has a way of keeping them and multiplying them and giving them back with his words of wisdom.

"Let us, today, ascend as it were, the mountains and take a retrospect of what we passed through. We all feel that the loss of the enterprise and treasure invested in that splendid hotel is a great calamity. I envy not the man his feelings; I envy no man his condition of character and heart who does not sympathize with the gentlemen most interested in this calamity and which has been inflicted upon this city and

county. This hotel, as Mr. Steele properly remarked, was our pride and rejoicing. Here came the pilgrim on his way seeking for rest and a pure, bright atmosphere and a secure dwelling place. He came to the Andrews Hotel. It was our pride when our friends came to town to take them and show them this hotel which had been and was the first in all this southern country. I have traveled through a large portion of the United States of America and been entertained at many hotels, but better attendance, more genteel and polite attentions and better provisions, I have met with nowhere in all the continent of America outside the largest cities. Sir, this city had the best in Southern California. [Applause]

"I am among the last of our citizens, but I have been here long enough to climb yonder hills and stand and look down in admiration as I gazed on yon distant mountains and I pictured the future of this county and this city, if you will. I saw a splendid progress and a grand future, and I mused on your glorious destiny.

"The adjoining counties in the south have had their period of prosperity. A wonderful tide of immigration has poured into them, and aided by the railroad traffic and aided and assisted by enterprising men, a most wonderful increase has been made in their population and a large advance had been made in the wealth of those respective counties. San Luis Obispo, during most of this time, has been laying quietly on the foundations of the coming days.

"Of course, our loss is great. Let me, if you please, review the situation while yet the smouldering embers are in our view. The large hotel cost $75,000; furniture, $25,000; the bank building on the opposite corner, $25,000; the adjoining buildings, $6,000; personal losses including Mr. Kurtz, the druggist, $4,000; the Sharp Brothers, estimated loss $5,000; Mr. Eaton, $500; other losses estimated in round numbers, $5,000; total loss about $145,000. Insurance, $12,500; total loss $133,000.

"Now, we admit this is a great calamity, but we thank God the fire fiend did not sweep along and burn us out of house and home. We still have our wives and children and homes untouched and unconsumed in which we can plot and contrive the ways and methods and plans

687 — COURT HOUSE, SAN LUIS OBISPO, CALIFORNIA.

Located at Monterey and Osos streets across from the Andrews Hotel, the San Luis Obispo County Courthouse was also threatened by the disastrous fire that occurred April 18, 1886. It was saved by the quick action of the volunteer fire department, and its steps became the location for a town meeting the next morning as citizens rallied around J. P. Andrews and offered financial aid for the construction of a new hotel. This postcard was originally sent by Lillie Muscio of San Luis Obispo to Irene Storni of Cayucos.

by which we can recuperate our energies and bring back the days of our prosperity.

"Our manhood and self respect remains and the enterprise of the people and the conditions of success are within our reach. Now, what is the outlook for this county? The men are out surveying the road for the extension of the Pacific Coast Railroad eastward, and the Southern Pacific Railroad officially authorized the statement that their railroad will be extended from Soledad to Newhall and shall pass through the city as well as the county of San Luis Obispo. [Applause] And more than this, the work has already begun, and soon you shall listen to the tramp of the railroad horse; and we shall take off our hats and give three cheers for the progress of San Luis Obispo, city and county. [Loud applause]

"Such is the outlook, with the prospect of the extension of this road through our city eastward so as to give opportunity for the coming of immigrants to find their way to our city and neighborhood. With the other line to and from Los Angeles passing through this way, with our fertile regions . . .

"Now, we are here for the purpose of expressing our resolution that this hotel (so great a loss to our city) has not burned out our energies, nor has it relaxed our will or our enterprise. We are here for the purpose of contributing, so far as in us lie, to the prosperity of this city.

"An organization has been recently formed, officered in your midst, by which fifty thousand acres of land has been pruchased which is to be cut up and subdivided and sold. Those purchasers and settlers will contribute to our wealth. Now, this hotel is a perfect necessity of the times in which we live, and the question to be decided today is whether we have the energy and the ability to say that this hotel or a grander one, if you please, one of more solid materials, one of as large proportions as that was, of as delicate outline shall be built in its stead. And we are here to express our sympathy with those who have suffered losses, some more heavily than others."

"We want, if you please," the Reverend Cox said, "to call upon you for subscriptions, and we will show you how it can be done."

Then Mr. Steele resumed the rostrum and called for subscriptions. J. P. Andrews immediately responded with a subscription of $10,000. Luigi Marre guaranteed $2,000, later raised it to $3,000. A. Tognazzini subscribed $3,000. C. H. Phillips, George Steele, and Blockman and Son offered $1,000. Dozens of people subscribed to $100 and $200 worth of stock. While the fire still smouldered, subscriptions totaling more than $30,000 were received for the construction of another hotel.[12]

The corner of Osos and Monterey never saw a hotel such as the first Andrews Hotel again, but the people of San Luis Obispo found courage to live with the loss of their first grand hotel while rallying together on the steps of their courthouse.

Eventually, J. P. Andrews constructed a complex of brick buildings in that block including the Andrews Bank (the building still stands in 1980) and a much less pretentious Andrews Hotel which later became a living residence for Cal Poly students called Hewson House.

But the pressure for another fine hotel in San Luis Obispo did not die.

CHAPTER VI

A New Town

It soon became apparent to everyone why the Southern Pacific Railroad Company had constructed line past Mission San Miguel and El Paso de Robles Hot Springs Hotel without pausing.

Somehow, Chauncey Hatch Phillips and members of the West Coast Land Company had successfully persuaded the Southern Pacific to run line south across that portion of the El Paso de Robles Rancho owned by them to a new town they planned. There doesn't seem to be any way of knowing how this arrangement transpired, but it brought all the variables together in Phillips' favor.

On Monday morning, September 13, 1886, R. R. Harris, surveyor and mapmaker, set up camp on the land which is now the town of Templeton. C. H. Phillips had instructed him to lay out 160 acres of business and residential lots for a town he intended to call Crocker in honor of Charles Crocker, the vice president of the Southern Pacific. However, the name was soon changed to Templeton. Phillips had apparently known for some time that the railroad would run track to this point.[1]

The *San Francisco Call* and other California newspapers gave Phillips and the West Coast Land Company enviable editorial support. "The West Coast Land Company has entered upon a great work for themselves in San Luis Obispo County," the *Call* reported. "It involves the settlement in its borders of at least 10,000 persons. From the character of the enterprise and the reputation of the gentlemen who are to conduct it, a brilliant and ample success must certainly follow."

Templeton was laid out in town lots. The area immediately around it consisted of plots

Although passenger trains no longer stop in Paso Robles, the original depot stands and remains a center around which residents sometimes celebrate their city's heritage.

referred to at that time as villa lots ranging in size from five to twelve acres. The balance of the land was subdivided into farms and ranches ranging in size from forty to four thousand acres.

Phillips advertised terms requiring one-third down with the balance payable in four equal payments over two, three, four and five years. Interest rates on unpaid balances were established at a flat six percent.

The Paso Robles and San Luis Obispo newspapers provided readers a regular accounting of land sold by Phillips, lot by lot and buyer by buyer. In keeping with the times, there was a great deal of speculation and exaggeration about progress.[2]

The November 5, 1886 issue of the *Tribune* announced the arrival of a Southern Pacific construction train at the new town site of Templeton. Track had been completed to Templeton on October 30, the same date that it reached Paso Robles. The news item predicted a permanent connection with the mainline from San Francisco beginning November 10, 1886. Erle Heath, in his booklet, *Seventy-Five Years of Progress,* wrote that the railroad finally reached Templeton on November 16, 1886.

Speculation about Templeton as a boom town started months ahead of laying out the town and before the railroad arrived. A variety of news items had appeared in the *San Luis Obispo Tribune* in August and September of 1886. For example:

"A wealthy citizen of San Luis Obispo has secured privileges for construction of large brick warehouses which are to be put up at once upon the approach of the railroad, and locations are already secured for a livery stable, hardware store, blacksmith shop and hotel . . ." said one news item.

" . . . A postmaster has been designated for Crocker [Templeton] and arrangements have been made for the building . . ."

"Mr. Phillips has been notified that the maps and catalogues of the Paso Robles Ranch will be delivered to the West Coast Land Company on next Thursday. There will be 5000 maps and the same number of catalogues. Wrappers have been prepared to send out 1500 of each on that day to answer letters of inquiry."

Chauncey Hatch Phillips placed advertisements in the local Tribune as well as newspapers in San Francisco, Los Angeles, and some midwestern cities. Although this advertisement does not specify terms, Phillips normally sought one-third down with the balance payable over a period of one to five years at six percent interest.

The Big Four were the promoters of first the western portion of the transcontinental line and later, the developers of the Southern Pacific Company lines. From left to right: Collis P. Huntington, Leland Stanford, Charles Crocker, and Mark Hopkins.

"Crocker [Templeton], being the last town before ascending the grade to Morro Bay, will very likely have machine shops and work shops of the Southern Pacific Railroad."

"A butcher shop is going up in Crocker [Templeton]." "A lumber yard is soon to be established in Crocker [Templeton]."

"A gentleman in this town [San Luis Obispo] has applied for the agency of Wells Fargo and Company at Crocker [Templeton]."

"Ten lots have been sold in the town of Crocker [Templeton]. Those on Main Street bring $2500 each."

The West Coast Land Company brochure noted that "with the opening of the railroad to Templeton . . . when the first passenger train arrived, its occupants found the nucleus of the . . . Templeton Hotel and several other buildings in course of construction." In December 1886 the unfinished Templeton Hotel announced its intention of having a grand ball at the earliest possible date.

"Every day witnesses the sale of from two to ten ranch subdivisions to persons whose purpose is to cultivate the soil they purchase," the brochure said.

"A large colony of Swedes has located two miles north of the town; a similar negotiation is pending which will require 5000 acres in another direction and within four miles." This group constructed the Templeton Lutheran Church which still stands in 1980.

The brochure described the town of Templeton within a few months after the arrival of the railroad. Readers were accustomed to allowing for promotional puffery, and the description adds somewhat to our knowledge of the way people thought at that time:

"Starting from nothing a little over 90 days ago, Templeton now contains one extensive and two smaller but quite respectable hotels, three general merchandise stores and two more in immediate prospect, a handsome and well-stocked drug store, a very neat structure for the office of the West Coast Land Company, a well-supplied meat market, a shoe shop, two blacksmith shops, five saloons, a billiard saloon, a large lumber yard, a sash and blind shop, several buildings and a paint establishment, two barber shops, a public hall, a post office with daily mail service and probably 25 to 30 dwelling houses."

A Mr. Bronson and a Mr. Haley started construction of a printing office and soon established the *Templeton Times*. It immediately became a continuous promotional voice for the development of the area.

Among Phillips' dreams for his new town was the Templeton Institute. He fully expected to start a private educational institution that would provide education from primary school through college. The "institute" did become a reality, but the college portion of it was never realized.

A depot and a freight warehouse were constructed and Southern Pacific proceeded to build both a turntable and a roundhouse in Templeton.

College Hotel, Santa Ynez, built with expectation that Southern Pacific Railroad would lay line through settlement. The community was by-passed.

Almost immediately Templeton had a Presbyterian clergyman. A few people also started a Sunday School at the local school house (referred to as the "primary department" of the Templeton Institute).

Within the coming year, a news item in the *Tribune* estimated Templeton's population at four hundred people. For some time, activity in Templeton was devoted to catching up to the claims already made for it by its promoters.[3]

❦

Land sales were conducted through auctions promoted in newspapers all along the railroad route beginning in San Francisco. Successes were reported within a month after the railroad arrived. At Paso Robles, the auction brought in $35,000 in sales. Sales at Templeton aggregated $121,254 in eighty days. Purchasers were largely interested in farm lands rather than town lots.

A reporter announced that the El Paso de Robles Hotel was overrun with visitors, many considering land purchases. One real estate firm successfully making sales around Paso Robles was called the Southern California Immigration Company. It operated out of what some local people felt were rather plush quarters.

Southern Pacific began construction of a depot in Paso Robles about the middle of December 1886, and this further added to the excitement in the county.[4]

That same month Phillips ran an ad in the *Tribune* providing rates for students at the Templeton Institute. J. D. E. Summers had been named principal. The Institute offered schooling at four levels: primary, high school, academic, and collegiate. The tuition for five months ranged from $12.50 to $25.00.

On December 24, 1886, a small announcement appeared in the *Tribune* which, at the time, didn't seem to attract enough attention. It read:

"Mr. Griffith, engineer of the Southern Pacific Railway, in charge of the survey between San Luis Obispo and Santa Barbara has received orders to report his force at once to San Francisco, and he expects to receive instructions there to proceed with work at Los Angeles. It is possible that this means an unexpected and perhaps serious delay in the construction of the road beyond Templeton."

In the same issue, there was a large listing of land sales by the West Coast Land Company.[5]

Templeton's sudden appearance and progress as a railroad town brought a few unexpected problems. The railroad brought itinerant workers, gamblers and thieves, but the town was without a law enforcement agency. Try as they might, local citizens just getting to know each other were not succeeding in getting assistance from the county.

"Here is a town," wrote one visitor, "without a judge or a constable, exposed to the predatory inclinations of these gentry, who are delighted to find so elegant an opportunity."

There were robberies, attacks on older people and a variety of other crimes. The terminal point for the railroad, this little boom town, attracted both hobos and misfits.

Nonetheless, soon after the beginning of the new year, 1887, Mrs. Phillips and several of her children accompanied her husband to Templeton to look at home sites. Phillips soon started construction of a large two-story Victorian house at the edge of town, and people took faith in the fact that he planned to move his gentle wife and many children to Templeton. This house still remains in 1980. In January, he sold their fine big home and twenty-six acres in San Luis Obispo to the Callendar family for $15,000. In 1980 this house is located on Johnson Avenue.

In April 1887, the West Coast Land Company announced plans for another huge land auction. They established only one limitation on bidders. Their offers had to be at least sixty percent of the company's catalog price. The experienced San Francisco auction firm of Easton and Eldridge was hired to conduct the bidding. The Southern Pacific Company offered an excursion rate of six dollars per person

Modern four-lane highway bridge crosses tracks before tunnels begin across the Cuesta into San Luis Obispo.

The new Southern Pacific Railroad depot at Los Angeles was built across from the Old Pueblo, the site of the original Spanish settlement. The building was a marvel of spacious waiting rooms marking its place as a transcontinental destination.

for round trip tickets from San Francisco and promised to keep Pullman cars in Templeton for travelers unable to get accommodations.

The West Coast Land Company announced that they fully expected two thousand visitors for three days beginning April 13, 1887. "The occasion will be a mammoth picnic such as California has never before witnessed," the promotional literature reported.

When the great days arrived, there were probably about a thousand people on hand to enjoy the barbecue and the excitement. Certainly people from all over the county were there. Visitors were provided free trips by wagon teams to view the surrounding country, and a barbecue was offered each day. Beef from

the herds of the Santa Margarita Rancho were slaughtered for the event. While people ate, a band provided music. It was an exhilarating occasion in remote San Luis Obispo County.

People gathered at the auctioneer's stand at high noon each day. Wendell Easton from the firm handling the auction said a few words referring to the good character of the promoters and the value of the lands for sale. Then George C. Ludington, the auctioneer, began offering parcels and taking bids. His work was continuous, hour after hour.

When the three-day auction ended, the West Coast Land Company announced that its sales had amounted to one-half million dollars since subdividing the great ranches.[6]

For a time during the early part of the 20th century an abalone processing plant operated on and alongside the wharf in the beach community of Cayucos. This postcard depicts racks of shells laid out to dry.

CHAPTER VII

The Board Of Trade

In San Luis Obispo, businessmen and landowners with all kinds of plans related to Southern Pacific Railroad activities were caught in a dilemma of uncertainty.

If Templeton should become a long-term terminal for the railroad, many men in San Luis Obispo with money tied up in land and plans for expanding their businesses were going to be financially hurt.

There was also other disillusioning talk. From time to time, there would be a rumor about the possibility that the Southern Pacific might cut through the Santa Lucia Mountains to the coast from Templeton to avoid the expense of tunneling across the Cuesta. If this happened, the coastal line would bypass San Luis Obispo, and Morro Bay would reap the benefits of being on the mainline.

In October 1886 some of the landmen called a meeting at the Cosmopolitan Hotel in San Luis Obispo. General Pat Murphy of the Santa Margarita Rancho gave a resume of subsidies provided the railroad while he was senator. Now, he told the gathering, the railroad would be coming this way, but unless San Luis Obispo could offer worthwhile inducements, it was likely that the town would be bypassed and a depot would be located nearer the coast.

Murphy had recently been in San Francisco and talked at length with Southern Pacific Railroad officials. He feared they would bypass his property, the Santa Margarita Rancho, just south of Templeton. He offered a fifteen-mile right-of-way through his ranch, but railroad officials seemed indifferent.

At the meeting in San Luis Obispo, he suggested that the businessmen should purchase twenty to twenty-five acres within the city and present it as a gift to the railroad for use as a depot and shops. C. H. Phillips supported Murphy's suggestion. Nothing was resolved at this meeting, but a new idea had been planted, and it had to lie dormant until its time was more pressing.[1]

Some optimistic planning for the future of the town continued. If trains should start running through San Luis Obispo, there was going to be a need for public transportation within the town limits. There was discussion about the need for it even now. When people traveled by steamship to Avila and then came into San Luis Obispo on the Pacific Coast narrow-gauge line, they needed a way to get around town.

So, the town Board of Trustees called for petitions for the establishment of a horse-drawn streetcar route. In January 1887, three men filed separately. The petitioners were L. M. Kaiser, Willard Kimball, and Thomas Sandercock. Someone else filed an application with the City Trustees to establish electric lights. No immediate action was taken on any of these petitions.[2]

On Monday, February 7, 1887, a group of men sent out an informal notice to a large group of local people requesting their attendance at another public meeting to be held in the courthouse. They thought it was time to form an association to promote immigration and, not incidentally, to promote land sales in the county.

The names of the signers of the notice were very familiar: Isaac Goldtree, J. P. Andrews, Benjamin Sinsheimer, J. A. Goodrich, L. M. Kaiser, W. L. Beebee, and R. E. Jack. Two names were conspicuously missing—C. H. Phillips and Pat Murphy. This meeting was intended to be "free from any suggestion of preconcerted plan or selfish motive." However, both Phillips and Murphy were present on the evening of the meeting.

There was a good turnout in the courtroom. Judge Frederick Adams was asked to serve as chairman. L. M. Kaiser and several others discussed the actions of community promotional associations in Santa Cruz, San Jose, Kern, Ventura, and Los Angeles. They were organized to promote the growth and welfare of their respective communities.

The men talked about the need of building a progressive city. With the destruction of the Andrews Hotel there was now need for another hotel, they agreed. The town was also in need of improvements if it hoped to attract settlers.

The new editor of the *San Luis Obispo Tribune*, Benjamin Brooks, moved that a Board of Trade for the city and county of San Luis Obispo be formed and suggested that it should consist of one hundred members. C. J. Russell, the real estate man, moved that a committee of ten be appointed to draw up a list of one hundred men in the county who would be asked to constitute the San Luis Obispo Board of Trade.

As criteria of membership, it was suggested that these men should not be mere ornament, but must be sympathetic to this effort and be willing to work.

So, a committee of ten was appointed by the chairman, Adams: C. J. Russell, Myron Angel, Isaac Goldtree, Benjamin Brooks, L. M. Kaiser, G. B. Nichols, Levi Rackliffe, J. P. Andrews, H. H. Dayle, and M. Egan; and Adams was also added to the committee.

Someone talked at length about the need to solicit funds to publish materials related to local resources and distribute them where they would do the most good in attracting visitors. Someone else urged planning for a decent, up-to-date hotel. At present, the town could not accommodate any type of excursion group. Myron Angel said that they should not be too quick to depreciate local hotels. While they were not luxurious, he said, they offered reasonable accommodations.

A committee was appointed to raise funds for the purpose of employing agents to secure immigration to the area. The group agreed to another informal meeting the following Saturday evening.[3]

The Committee of Ten met a few evenings later to decide the best way of drawing up a membership list for the Board of Trade. They decided to send out a circular to prominent men in the county who could be counted on to serve if appointed. Three hundred circulars were later prepared and mailed.

The Committee on Subscriptions immediately started making calls on businessmen and farmers in the area to raise funds to employ agents to promote immigration to San Luis Obispo. In one day, they reported subscriptions amounting to a total of $391 per month.

Ben Brooks was very excited about the action of the committees. "At no time in the history of San Luis has there been exhibited more general and enthusiastic interest in the public welfare," he wrote.

Some of the men in the county who received the mailing were confused about the object of the association, and a number of them frankly declined membership, preferring to wait and see how this Board of Trade idea developed. But within the week, one hundred men had expressed their willingness to be a part of the new promotional organization.

At the next meeting, Jasper Brown made a motion that the organization of one hundred now become permanent. Russell and Kaiser urged waiting another week. There were many prominent citizens, Russell said, who had not been heard from yet, and their interest could add much to the organization's success.

Chairman Adams appointed a Constitution and Bylaws Committee which included Benjamin Brooks, Edwin Unangst, L. M. Kaiser, and E. W. Steele, as well as himself.

There was a great deal of worry among members about who would be elected permanent officers. Some believed that if the wrong officers were chosen, that is, people who had a great deal to gain, the association would fail to serve the common good.

The name of the organization as proposed by the Constitution Committee was Board of Trade of San Luis Obispo County. The committee established that the group's principal objective should be "the consideration of all subjects pertaining to the interests of the city and the county and tending toward the advancement of the same."

The first officers elected were E. W. Steele, president; Jasper Turner, first vice president; Frederick Adams, second vice president; Dr. H. Cox, secretary; and R. E. Jack, treasurer. Now, they were ready for business.[4]

In late February 1887, Ben Brooks went into the newspaper back shop, picked up his type stick, and set type urging a rallying of the people in the county to work together. "The work of the past year is bearing fruit," he wrote. "The almost complete absorption of all available government land, the subdivision of the Paso Robles and adjoining ranches and the rapid melting away of those great tracts... [the] extension of the Southern Pacific to Templeton and its certain connection... [to] Santa Barbara are potent reasons for the immediate growth of the county."

At the same time, hopes were also high for assistance from the federal government in the construction of the breakwater and the erection of a lighthouse at Port San Luis, and there was still encouraging talk about construction of a large hotel in town.

Although the future seemed to offer many good things, there was a great deal of conflict among business interests in the county. Differences and jealousies existed among the businessmen both within and between communities. Real estate men represented their own interests to prospective customers and sent them away rather than recommend their competitors.

"If we would succeed as a county and individually, we must stand together and support each other and reserve our jealousies and rivalries for a more fit occasion," Brooks urged.

As the weeks went by the Board of Trade served as a valuable catalyst. It succeeded in getting jobs done and gave recognition to hard workers.[5]

On Monday evening, March 7, 1887, the committee on advertising asked members of the Board of Trade for permission to prepare and publish five thousand copies of a promotional pamphlet discussing the resources of the coun-

ty. This request was readily granted. All committees of the board were called upon to prepare and submit articles about the resources of the county within the jurisdiction of their committee for use in the promotional literature.

W. F. Sauer, the owner of the Lytton Theater, gave the board a receipted bill for two months' use of the theater for exhibition of local resources. The Pacific Coast Railway and the stage lines of the county agreed to transport without charge all goods sent to town for exhibition purposes. While Judge Adams was in San Francisco, he talked to the agent for the Pacific Coast Steamship Company about exhibiting San Luis Obispo products in the company's windows, and they agreed.

Representatives of the *Journal of Commerce* in San Francisco proposed at one meeting in March that with financial support from the board, they could put out a special issue or section of their publication devoted to promoting San Luis Obispo County resources. Although it meant taking advertising dollars that the *Tribune* would have liked, Brooks encouraged the acceptance of the proposition.[6]

Meantime, Brooks began preparing articles for the *Tribune* which were obviously intended for readers in other areas. In the March 18, 1887 issue of the *Tribune*, he carried a column-length story headlined "The Boom." This line was stacked over six subheadings, including "Double Prices in a Single Week," "Heavy Transfer of Real Estate to Capitalists," and "All Our Real Estate Men Crowded With Customers."

Among other things, Brooks wrote, "... the purchase by a syndicate of capitalists of $150,000 worth of real estate embracing the Graves, Abbott, Hays, Goldtree, Andrews, Herrera, Ingleside and adjoining properties definitely settles the vexed question in favor of a new and fine hotel.... The ostensible buyer being Mr. Ed Goodall of San Francisco, [but] current gossip insists upon locating the real parties in interest... The presence of Mr. Williard V. Huntington connected the sales at once with the Southern Pacific, but Mr. Huntington assured us that his flying visit here was entirely without reference to San Luis property or the railroad, but related solely to certain possible

investments of his own in the vicinity of Ysabel Ranch." The story dwelled on outside "capitalists" arriving from all over California exploring investment opportunities throughout San Luis Obispo County.[7]

It wasn't difficult for local people to separate truth from fiction.

In their own limited travel, some members of the Board of Trade discovered that most Californians outside the area scarcely realized that San Luis Obispo existed. In making several trips to San Francisco by steamer, a Mr. Kwitz discovered that most of his fellow passengers thought the single building in Avila they saw from the ship was San Luis Obispo. He hoped the board would put up some signs at the wharf giving directions into town, and he expressed hope that the Pacific Coast Railway would shuttle ships' passengers into town for a visit while docked.

The board talked about all kinds of needs in San Luis Obispo, but it had difficulty establishing an effective course of action. A few hardworking members complained that many of the committees were not functioning actively.

At one point on April 8, a very unpopular proposal was made at a board meeting by Mr. Hazen. He suggested that bonds for $100,000 be issued for the general improvement of the city, but absolutely no one responded. To say the least, it was thought to be an ill-considered proposal. C. H. Johnson finally urged a more

---

ABOVE, LEFT: *The San Luis Obispo Board of Trade is the forebear of the present-day Chamber of Commerce. At times during the eighties and nineties, it almost died, but as a cause would arise, the organization would again come to life. This advertisement appeared in Sunset Magazine, April 1902. At this time, the West Coast Land Company was still active and was participating in the development of Shandon, another community. The magazine was owned by the Southern Pacific Company at the time. It was used to promote immigration and passenger service from eastern cities.*

BELOW, LEFT: *During the 1880s and early '90s, the Pacific Coast Steamship Company continued to be the most comfortable way for California coastal people to travel. Ships made stops at three San Luis Obispo County wharves—Port Harford (Avila), Cayucos, and San Simeon. This advertisement was published in the April 1902 Sunset Magazine.*

business-like approach. Dr. Hathway, Myron Angel, and Col. Treat agreed that the city needed a sewer system, a cistern system for getting water, some improved bridges along San Luis Creek, and many other things, but they did not favor huge indebtedness.

It was resolved to take before the City Trustees a proposition for getting estimates of the costs for some of these improvements, and through either direct taxation or a responsible bond issue, to get these jobs done.[8]

At the meeting of the board on April 15, 1887, the Committee on Advertising reported that the printers were now setting type for 25,000 booklets, and that the first special promotional edition of the *Tribune* would soon be distributed to a list of people in other areas. This list was made up of names submitted to the Correspondence Committee by people throughout the county.[9]

At another meeting of the board in April, an Agricultural Association was organized. E. W. Steele was elected president; C. O. King, secretary; and R. E. Jack, treasurer. Their first order of business was to draw up a list of farmers to be solicited for membership.

A company in Los Angeles was reported to be interested in the bituminous rock in the vicinity for making street paving, and there was a report about finding gold along Arroyo San Carpojoro near San Simeon. The latter report came to nothing, but at that time of promise for the future, everything seemed possible.

The most tangible evidence of the Board of Trade's progress as a promotional organization appeared in the form of a booklet and as a special edition of the *San Luis Obispo Tribune* in May 1887.

At this time, E. W. Steele was president; J. N. Turner, vice president; Frederick Adams, second vice president; R. E. Jack, treasurer; and J. H. Barrett, secretary.

The booklet reported that visitors from San Francisco could easily travel through San Luis Obispo County. They could board the train in San Francisco at 8:30 A.M. and reach Templeton by 5:00 P.M. At 5:30 P.M. they could take a comfortable six-horse Concord Coach Stage "over fine road for 24 miles and be in San Luis Obispo by 9 P.M."

If they wished to take a side jaunt along the coast to the north, they could travel on a local four-horse stage leaving San Luis Obispo at 8:00 A.M. The stage went through the Chorro Valley to Morro Bay, along the beach to Cayucos and continued to Cambria, arriving about 3:00 P.M.

A traveler could continue his journey to Southern California by boarding the narrow-gauge railroad which went through Arroyo Grande, Nipomo, Santa Maria, and Los Alamos. From there, a waiting stage took travelers to Santa Barbara.

The front page of the special *Tribune* section featured a half-page map of the county and surrounding country. Pages one and two included an early history of the county.

A large article discussed the resources and progress of the area. There were special ads from Pacific Coast Steamship Company, Pacific Coast Railway Company, Hotel Marre at Avila, West Coast Land Company, and a number of real estate agents. Things were off to a good start, and the *Tribune* had made some extra money. Extra copies of the issue were printed and mailed to a long list of prospective settlers.[10]

Another special edition of the *Tribune* appeared July 1, 1887. Again the large county map was on the front page. This edition told the story of development in San Miguel, Templeton, and Paso Robles, and included articles promoting the prospects of the surrounding country as agricultural land.[11]

Later in July, still another special edition included one article discussing the ranchos of San Luis Obispo County. A reader could easily have believed that land was available on nearly all of the original twenty-one Mexican land grants in the county. This may have been almost true.[12]

The following week, on July 22, Brooks issued still another special section. A large amount of news space was devoted to stock-raising and its historical place in the county. In all of these special editions, which continued through August and were mailed far and wide, local businesses faithfully placed their advertisements.

By the end of 1887, the finance committee of the Board of Trade announced that contributions amounted to $3,296, and they had spent $2,684, all for promotion of the county.

The board had published 25,000 brochures, sponsored 10,000 or more copies of the San Francisco *Journal of Commerce* with feature articles about San Luis Obispo County, paid for 36,000 copies of the *Tribune*, distributed 25,000 copies of a thirty-eight page booklet, and sent an exhibit of products to various fairs. It had established contact with a representative in Kansas City who regularly distributed pamphlets and other material to prospective immigrants arriving at that point.

At the end of 1887, Brooks discussed the effect of all the promotion: "There has been no wild flood of excitement, no great boom has swept over the community, and there have been many disappointed ones whose schemes were laid with reference to a magic change of circumstance."

There had been no new track laid since the Southern Pacific stopped building at Templeton. San Luis Obispo had not experienced any great tide of immigration. But Brooks wrote, "Several great ranchos, magnificent tracts of land hitherto practically unutilized have been subdivided..." He referred primarily to the lands of the West Coast Land Company development.

Actually, the town of San Luis Obispo had not changed in any identifiable way. One investor in business property in San Luis Obispo told Brooks he regretted his action. "There is no energy or life in the place," he said.

CHAPTER VIII

The Hotel Promoters

From the time of the great fire that burned the Andrews Hotel in 1886, *Tribune* editor Benjamin Brooks and leaders affiliated with the promotion of San Luis Obispo clamored for another resort hotel.[1]

Envisioning, as they did, a great influx of new people with the eventual arrival of the railroad, active members of the Board of Trade and other businessmen were much aware of the town's shortcomings. Such hotels as existed were old and badly run-down, the town lacked any form of sewage system, and its streets were bogs of mud during the rainy season and eyesores thick with dust when dry.

They had talked about these conditions for years. Now it was time to do something about them. Both the big landmen and businessmen saw the arrival of the railroad as their opportunity to make the town prosperous and, in some cases, for individuals to become very rich.

The Board of Trade had dealings with various out-of-towners who expressed interest in constructing a hotel. The town offered to donate property valued at between $15,000 and $20,000, a large sum of money at that time and place, to anyone who would erect a "handsome hotel." One of the better prospects "dallied over the proposition" for months, then suddenly announced that he must hurry east on business, and suspended negotiations.

In March 1887, Brooks wrote a promotional editorial intended for readers in other areas. It was an exaggeration beyond all honest expectations. "It is certainly a curious state of affairs—the Southern Pacific Railroad is within 20 miles of the city. Before another rainy season sets in, the railroad will traverse it. There are ample grounds for believing that the Atchison, Topeka and Santa Fe road will reach here perhaps as soon. No one hotel would be adequate to accommodate the traveler when either road reaches San Luis."

Brooks urged local businessmen and landmen to take on this investment themselves. "If the capitalists of other cities, with tons of money idly accumulating in their vaults, cannot see the opportunity, let us go ahead ourselves."

One week in the middle of April 1887, a Captain Johnson of the Pacific Coast Steamship Company appeared in town. His company, it was known, had recently purchased land near the city for development purposes. Now, Captain Johnson was talking to local businessmen known to have capital, proposing the formation of a corporation for the erection of a hotel with a capital stock of $150,000 in ten-dollar shares. He found a few men immediately interested in subscribing: the Goldtree brothers were willing to subscribe $10,000; Pacific Coast Railway and Steamship Company (the company that employed him), $10,000; and the owners of the land where Johnson proposed to build would trade their land equity for $12,500.

Johnson proposed constructing the hotel on a city block between Higuera and Marsh streets facing Essex Street (now Johnson Avenue). He anticipated that the Southern Pacific Railroad would pass directly in back of the hotel and make regular stops.

At least two active members of San Luis Obispo's Board of Trade, R. E. Jack and E. W. Steele, both with large vested interests related to the growth of the town and the extension of the Southern Pacific, subscribed to $2,000 in stock each. Others who had long spoken favorably

This is the architect's rendering of the exterior of the hotel which Edwin Goodall proposed to local investors in San Luis Obispo on Tuesday evening, Septeber 27, 1887. Goodall and some of the others who subscribed to stock had already purchased a large tract of land around the proposed site of the hotel which they planned to subdivide and sell. They did not decide on a name for the hotel at the time.

about the need for a hotel now balked at making investments in the enterprise because it would not benefit them directly.

Capt. Johnson proposed to the city trustees that the new corporation be given the franchise for the horse-drawn streetcar route running from the Pacific Coast Railway Company's depot in town to the hotel. Since no action had been taken on earlier petitions seeking a street-car franchise, this suggestion was attractive to the trustees.

Johnson requested the franchise in the name of Edwin Goodall, principal owner of the Pacific Coast Steamship and Railway Company, and proposed construction of tracks across the town along Higuera, Marsh, Monterey and Palm streets, with cross lines over Broad, Osos and Chorro streets. He made some reassuring guarantees to the city fathers that work would begin within three months, and that the company would construct at least one mile of line within six months, and offered to support his promises with a $20,000 surety bond.

Brooks said, "Nothing can be urged against it unless the idea is seriously entertained that outside capital ought not to be permitted, and that all opportunities ought to be reserved for our own old residents.

"We are glad to help old friends," he added, "but we trust none of them will be so ill-advised as to bulk a prospect which is so much for the benefit of the whole community." Most people agreed with Brooks. There was no great money in a street railway unless affiliated with other ventures. Other petitioners were not ready or able to make such firm commitments.[3]

In early June 1887, Charles Goodall, president of Pacific Coast Railway, arrived in San Luis Obispo, and this started a real flurry of excitement. He talked to various local people, and told them that plans for the hotel were being prepared by a top hotel architect. He expected the hotel to cost about $60,000, and he intended to build it in sections as customer demand required.

Goodall soon had a crew surveying town streets for construction of streetcar tracks.[4] In

As a direct result of expecting Southern Pacific Company to build track into the City of San Luis Obispo, a large hotel and several blocks of residential lots were laid out by investors. Essex Street eventually became Johnson Avenue. Subdividers did not anticipate that Southern Pacific would insist upon running its line through their property, so changes resulted in their subdivision layout.

July a Pacific Coast steamer brought in some materials for the project, but steel rails due from Portland were delayed.

Capt. Johnson expressed apprehension about locating a labor force for construction of the new hotel when he was ready to go, but townspeople assured him that as soon as summer harvesting was finished, he would have no trouble. When people asked him what the company planned to name the hotel, he said he favored the name Hotel del Montezuma, but this was not settled.

The first construction problem for the new hotel would be a sewer system. Brooks thought the town itself needed a sewage system, and he wrote about it regularly.

A Through Railroad is now an Assured Fact.

The gap in the Southern Pacific Rail Line, between Templeton and Santa Barbara, will be completed at an early day.

This Line will be the MAIN LINE of the Southern Pacific Co., between San Francisco and Los Angeles and the East, and will run directly through this city, thus giving rail and ocean competition to the County.

The Advantages and Natural Resources of San Luis Obispo Co. are Unsurpassed.

The fact that this county borders the ocean, and possesses one of the best harbors on the Coast, and that ocean and rail competition is thereby assured, — that the city is now the center of a local railroad system, — that magnificent passenger and freight steamers call daily carrying the unrivalled production of this, to less favored counties:

The fact that the County is thoroughly and abundantly watered, needing no irrigation—that the finest fruits, vegetables, and cereals are raised here—that it stands unrivaled as a producer of the choicest butter, cheese, and other dairy products—that it possesses mountains of bituminous rock, sufficient to pave the streets of the whole country—and vast beds of asphaltum, and extensive mines of iron and other ore—sulphur wells and mineral springs, the medicinal virtues of which are known as well in Europe as in America, as well in Boston as in San Francisco or San Luis Obispo—that the climate is the finest in the State, neither too hot nor too cold; the possession of these, and other wonderful and magnificent natural resources, must make it apparent to the most casual observer that San Luis Obispo is bound to be the most sought after and popular, as it is one of the best and richest counties in the State, and that the beautifully located city of San Luis Obispo is destined to be one of the largest and most important on the coast

EXPORTS—SAN LUIS OBISPO.

There was shipped via Port Harford alone last year, by the steamers of the Pacific Coast S. S. Co.— not to mention shipments by other conveyance and from other landing— the following:

Asphaltum and Bituminous Rock	3,350,000 lbs.
Butter	1,990,000 "
Cheese	358,000 "
Wheat	13,466,000 "
Barley	18,100,000 "
Beans	8,072,000 "
Ore	4,110,000 "
Hogs	1,280,000 "
Sundries	9,584,000 "
Total,	60,316,000 "

573 Steamers, representing a tonnage of 656,260 tons, entered the harbor of San Luis Obispo (Port Harford), during 1887, besides a large fleet of sailing vessels and steam schooners.

The **Lumber** imported into San Luis Obispo, via Port Harford, alone in 1887 amounted to the Grand Total of 8,837,700 feet.

"Strangers approach the county seat, the principal town of the county, with large expectations," he said. "They cast reproaches at her [dirt] streets, primitive bridges, country hotels and lack of sewerage.

"'Where are your theatres, fine churches and parks? We see no evidence of wealth, progress and prosperity,'" Brooks paraphrased. When asked these questions, he said, all townspeople could do was "refer to an indefinite future in which all things are to be bettered."

"Her sister towns take a malicious pleasure in goading her, sneering at her pretentions, looking askance at her efforts, holding aloof from her Board of Trade and Agricultural Associations and celebrations," he wrote sadly.

In another issue of the newspaper, Brooks noted that San Luis Obispo was in the hands of many non-residents or others who felt no interest in her good name, who viewed the town and its immediate surroundings as a speculative investment. He reflected the view of many of the local people when he said, "The men of San Luis, her sons and lovers, are by no means blind to the interests and fair fame of their city, but they have generally but scanty means, and must limit their expenditure, and it might also be said that they are not too anxious to work for the benefit of speculative outsiders, the harpies who would fatten on such efforts."

Many local people were now feeling that all of the longed-for prosperity expected in the near future was not really for them. It was for "insiders" from the "outside" who had the means to take advantage of it.

Nonetheless, a sizable list of local names appeared in the *Tribune* in August 1887, as investors in the new hotel company. The articles of incorporation called the company the Southern Hotel Company. It would be capitalized for $100,000 with stock selling at $100 per share. Stock subscriptions amounted to $72,300. Large investors included the Pacific Coast Steamship Company, $10,000; Edwin Goodall, $12,000; West Coast Land Company, $10,000; C. R. Callender, $5,000; Goldtree Brothers, $10,000; R. E. Jack, $2,000; E. W. Steele, $2,000; Barrett and Russell Realtors, $2,000; C. J. Russell, $1,000; B. F. Petit, $2,000; J. H. Hollister, $2,000; William Sandercock,

$1,000; S. P. Stow, $1,000; P. W. Murphy, $2,000; William Graves, $5,000. A number of local people purchased one to five shares of stock.

The name of the company, Southern Hotel Company, provided the implication that the Southern Pacific Railroad Company was the owner, and a number of historians make the mistake of assuming this was the case.

Arrangements were formalized on Monday afternoon, August 15, 1887, when stockholders gathered at the Cosmopolitan Hotel. Chauncey Phillips of the West Coast Land Company was elected chairman and R. E. Jack was elected secretary of the group. Phillips called upon Edwin Goodall of the Pacific Coast Steamship Company and Pacific Coast Railway Company to explain the object of the meeting.

Some of the men present were still partially committed to the subscriptions they had made a year earlier for a new Andrews Hotel. Goodall was aware of this, and immediately made them feel at ease. He was here, he said, to organize a hotel company. He didn't want earlier subscribers to feel they would be held to the commitment to Capt. Johnson nor did he want subscribers to the earlier Andrews Hotel organization to feel he was trying to kill their deal. He volunteered to help this group if they wanted to proceed with their plans.

Chairman Phillips, whose past successes were held in high regard, added his thoughts. He said the two hotels would both be needed within twelve months and that San Luis Obispo would have a population of twenty-five thousand people within five years.

Now, as Goodall rolled out the plans for the hotel so that all could see them, the men gathered around. The building was a "Queen Anne" style, Goodall explained, with a frontage of 224 feet. It would be three stories high with two wings. The plan called for 300 rooms, but only 134 bedrooms because there would be many two- and three-room suites.

At dinner time, Phillips adjourned the meeting, but called for another session that evening. Tired but exhilarated, the group gathered again. They quickly reviewed the subscription list which people had signed in the afternoon. The plan had been to incorporate with a capital

THE GOODALL SYNDICATE LANDS,
CITY OF SAN LUIS OBISPO.

Early in '87, Mr. Goodall and associates purchased the most eligible of the unimproved lands in the city of San Luis Obispo. These are all located in the eastern part of the town, the best located, the finest and by far the most valuable and desirable part of the City. The western part of town is somewhat low and open to the coast winds, while the eastern is sheltered, besides having the proper grade and elevation—to give perfect drainage and a perfect view. The lands purchased by Mr. Goodall, viz: the **Buena Vista Addition, the Central Addition,** and the subdivision of **Phillips' Addition** have been all surveyed and platted, and are now offered for sale in subdivisions at exceedingly low prices and on very reasonable terms. Streets have been laid out and graded, sewers laid and many valuable improvements inaugurated, more especially in the Central Addition, in the centre of which the magnificent Hotel Ramona is being built.

In order to make purchases still more accessible and valuable, Mr. Goodall has obtained a franchise for a street railroad, and built same from the depot up-town to and past The Ramona, and right through the centre of the Central Addition, running a line also along Osos Street to the Buena Vista Addition.

The street railroad is now in operation, and is stocked with new and elegant cars.

These various improvements and others which are being made, have added materially to the prosperity of the city.

The parties interested in the Goodall Syndicate Lands in San Luis Obispo have had unusual and unrestricted opportunities of familiarizing themselves with the comparative advantages and prospective prosperity of the different coast counties and cities. After thorough investigation and consideration, San Luis Obispo was their choice.—They knew that while San Diego and Los Angeles were pleasant places to live in, San Luis Obispo furnished the denizens of these Southern Counties the staples of life.—Their wheat, barley, hay, beans, feed, butter, fruit, cheese and live stock, as well as the asphaltum and bituminous rock to pave their streets.

There is no boom in San Luis Obispo now, but there will be when people learn, as they will later, that it offers better land at a lower cost, on which crops can be raised without irrigation, better and more equable climate, surer and larger crops, abundant rainfall, richer soil, finer fruit, more beautiful scenery, a more diversified and interesting country than any county in California, south of San Francisco.

Settlers or speculators cannot make a mistake by purchasing in San Luis Obispo, either city or county, at the present time and prices.

THE BUENA VISTA ADDITION.

Lots in this elegant and centrally located property can now be secured on very liberal terms.

THE STREET RAILROAD

Is completed directly to the property, which is distant but a couple of blocks from the Pacific Coast Railway Co's taack and about 1000 yards from the Court House, and the center of the city. The surveyed line of the

SOUTHERN PACIFIC COMPANY

Is near by, and the new Hotel, Ramona, one of the finest in California, is but a few blocks distant. This property is beautifully located for residence purposes. Strangers will recognize it by

THE TERRACED HILL

In the southern part of the city. The lots now offered for sale lie at the foot of the hill which affords a sufficient elevation to give a magnificent view and perfect drainage. Water is guaranteed to parties buying property on this tract, as the reservoirs are now under construction and pipes being laid to carry water to the top of the hill.

The improvements already made and others projected on and in the vicinity of this property, make these lots unusually

SAFE AS AN INVESTMENT

And exceedingly attractive as a speculation, for the advance in values within the next few months will unquestionably surprise the oldest inhabitant.

stock of $80,000, providing they had over $70,000 in subscriptions. They had $72,000.

There was a long discussion about what to name the company. It had been referred to as the Southern Hotel Company, but now they decided to call it California Southern Hotel Company. They did not decide on a name for the hotel itself at this meeting.

Then they elected temporary directors: J. M. Fillmore, local manager of the Pacific Coast Railway; R. E. Jack, banker and rancher; Ernest Graves, lawyer; Morris Goldtree, an owner of the Goldtree Brothers store and a large landholder; E. W. Steele, large landholder; C. H. Phillips, West Coast Land Company; and Edwin Goodall, principal executive in the Pacific Coast Steamship and Railway Company.

On Tuesday afternoon, September 27, 1887, another meeting of the shareholders was held at the Cosmopolitan Hotel. Finished plans were available for all to see. Chairman Edwin Goodall called the meeting to order. R. E. Jack continued as secretary. That evening the directors met again and executive officers were elected as follows: Edwin Goodall, president; J. M. Fillmore, vice president; R. E. Jack, secretary; and R. E. Jack and Isaac Goldtree, co-treasurers.

They opened six bids and selected Knight and Littlefield of San Francisco as contractors.

C. J. Russell and C. H. Phillips both moved to name the hotel the Goodall. President Goodall expressed appreciation, but urged that some Spanish name be selected. He had enjoyed many successes in his life, and while this hotel was a big undertaking to the local men, it was but one of many promotional undertakings for him. Again, no decision was made about the name that evening.[5]

St. Siena in San Luis Obispo, Cal.

Turn-of-the-century Monterey Street, San Luis Obispo. Unpaved streets, wooden buildings, horses and carriages characterized the view of the main business street.

GRAND AUCTION SALE

AT

Santa Margarita

WILL BE HELD ON

Saturday, April 20th, 1889.

Special ⁜ Railroad ⁜ Excursion

AT GREATLY REDUCED RATES,

With tickets good for 5 days, allowing holders to visit other portions of the beautiful
County of San Luis Obispo.

A GRAND BARBECUE

Will be held on the ground at 1:00 P. M., on the day of sale, under the auspices of
GEN'L P. W. MURPHY, assisted by his Vaqueros.

TERMS OF SALE:

ONE QUARTER CASH, with the balance due in three equal payments, in six,
twelve and eighteen months, with interest at 10 per cent per annum.

For Maps, Catalogues, Etc., address

OR,

F. S. DOUTY,

BRIGGS, FERGUSSON & CO.
314 CALIFORNIA ST., SAN FRANCISCO,
AUCTIONEERS.

Fourth and Townsend Sts.,
San Francisco.

CHAPTER IX

Action On The Santa Margarita

In Los Angeles during early June 1887, a reporter talked to Governor Leland Stanford and one of the managers of the Southern Pacific Company about plans for the coastal line. They told the reporter they expected to continue construction from Los Angeles north to Santa Barbara.

"We expect to reach Santa Barbara in about three months," the manager reported. "There is some heavy grading to be done along the beach, and it is a difficult road to build."

"Will Santa Barbara be made a terminal point?" the reporter asked.

"Only for a few months," Stanford said. "Until the road can be pushed on through to Templeton."

At the end of that month, when a group of engineers of Southern Pacific met in San Luis Obispo, a *Tribune* reporter interviewed them. These men told him that the company would start work to close the gap between Templeton and Los Angeles sometime in the coming October.

At this point, perhaps it will not be redundant to remind the reader that a San Francisco to Los Angeles line already existed inland. A spur track from this valley line was under construction from Saugus to Santa Barbara.

Because of so many disappointments, reports that should have been encouraging were received in the community with mixed emotions. But at least a date had been provided, and reports of a land boom in Southern California occasionally reached San Luis Obispo to give credence to possible action by Southern Pacific.

San Diego and Los Angeles were reported to be "excellent places for men of small means to sink their money." One news item said, "There is nothing to prevent the man who buys a $1,000, twenty-five-foot lot at Coronado Beach from selling it on the following day for $2,000."

So, some landowners in San Luis Obispo County remained hopeful about the future in their part of California. A newly arrived real estate man seeking to share the profits helped stir local pride when he said, "The San Luis Country is remarkably picturesque. There are pretty bits of scenery, fine trout streams and lovely waterfalls to be found everywhere. The men are handsome, the women beautiful, the horses magnificent and the country is grand beyond description."[1]

The big news about the first Southern Pacific train reaching Santa Barbara from the south appeared in the *San Luis Obispo Tribune* on August 26, 1887. It was a re-run of a story printed a few days earlier in the *Santa Barbara Press.*

The train unloaded at State Street a short distance from the beach, and some three hun-

Santa Barbara's first train arrived August 19, 1887. It had rolled in from Saugus through Fillmore, Santa Paula and Ventura. The crowds had waited for hours for its arrival. A special excursion train arrived the next day with visitors from many surrounding communities who came to join the civic celebration.

dred happy passengers disembarked while the Carpinteria brass band played a thrilling march tune. Horse-drawn buses and all three of the city's streetcars were on hand to transport guests to the heart of town. Local people were both elated and weary as they witnessed the arrival of the train. They had been waiting since about 2:30 P.M. The train arrived at 4:00 P.M.

Landmen between Santa Barbara and San Luis Obispo had long anticipated this event. As already mentioned, numerous developments along the expected route north of Santa Barbara were already in progress.

But the rail gap between Santa Barbara and Templeton was still 125 miles. Templeton continued to develop slowly, and there was talk about a "syndicate" headed by a "General Dimond" who was planning a hotel resort at Santa Ysabel, a short distance from the Templeton settlement.

In December 1887, Phillips provided county residents a report of the progress of the West Coast Land Company. The company had sold, he reported, as of November 1, 1887, over 21,000 acres of land representing $600,000 in sales during the previous fourteen months. The land had been sold to 260 settlers coming from as far away as New York State and Canada. Still, the largest number of buyers were from California, including many from San Luis Obispo County.

At the beginning of 1888, surveyors began subdividing the Santa Ysabel Springs purchase. It was part of the Asuncion Rancho, only a short distance from Templeton.

"It is probable," the *Tribune* speculated, that purchasers "will erect a $30,000 hotel on the ground now occupied by the old ranch house. It is the design to run the water of the springs to the hotel, furnishing the guests of the house with water for drinking or bathing purposes."

"We are informed," the newspaper reported, "that the owners intend making a second Del Monte [hotel] on the grounds."

Such statements typified the dreams, rumors and speculation surrounding each new land development along the expected railroad route. Just as so many other dreams never became realities, neither did this hotel.

❧

THERE WERE THREE historically significant Mexican land grants just north of Cuesta grade and south of the El Paso de Robles through which a railroad line would likely pass if it should go through the Cuesta and into San Luis Obispo. These ranchos were the Santa Margarita, the Asuncion, and the Atascadero.

Santa Margarita Rancho is still identifiable as a working stock ranch, and it is surely one of the most colorful in San Luis Obispo County, providing vistas of rolling grazing land and grain fields. The Mission San Luis Obispo Assistencia, constructed of rock and adobe, is still used as a storage barn on the ranch.

The Santa Margarita was the northernmost inland rancho established by Mission San Luis Obispo. The Indians herded mission cattle and sheep across the great open space. They also

Potter Hotel was built above the beach in Santa Barbara in 1901.

This is State Street in Santa Barbara at about De La Guerra Street in 1880. The street was unpaved, a horse-drawn streetcar served as public transportation, and most of the buildings were low and constructed of wood.

planted and raised crops while learning the ways of Christendom at the Assistencia. Mission records indicate that the rancho contributed large stores of wheat to the common larder.[3]

Joaquin Estrada was granted the Santa Margarita Rancho by Mexican Governor Pro Tem Manuel Jimeno on September 27, 1841. In his petition for the land, Estrada rightfully pointed out that the mission no longer used the land, and the local administrator of the mission admitted this fact. The grant included 17,735

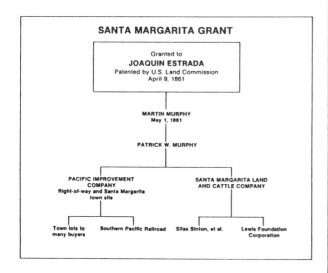

The above illustrates the changes of major ownerships of the Santa Margarita Rancho from original grantee until the time of our story.

acres. Estrada promised in his petition that he would not hinder the mission from using the house on the rancho, but he found the buildings in ruins and unusable anyway. He also promised to respect the acreage used for planting by the mission Indians.

Acting Governor Jimeno had served as a commissioner for the secularization of Mission San Luis Obispo in 1835, so he was somewhat acquainted with the properties under mission jurisdiction, and he undoubtedly knew Estrada.

As was common among grant seekers, Estrada had already occupied the land he sought and built a house on it for his overseer. In his petition he stated that he and his family had cattle and wanted to use the Santa Margarita Rancho to increase their stock. Estrada brought large numbers of cattle to the ranch and began living there in 1843. Inocente Garcia was his overseer and ran the ranch during the early years.

At the time of the conquest of California by the United States, the Santa Margarita's location along the mission trail made it a convenient stopping place. For example, after the United States raised its flag at Monterey in 1846, Mexican Governor Pio Pico and General Jose Castro met at Santa Margarita Rancho to plan strategy to prevent the American take-over. This may have created problems for Estrada. In late November or early December of 1846, Colonel John Fremont ordered Estrada, his majordomo, Inocente Garcia, and his son-in-law, Jose Mariano Bonilla of the Huer Huero Rancho, arrested. However, these men volunteered their services to Fremont as he rode south taking California for the United States, so they were not held.

Tales of high living by Joaquin Estrada are told and retold in San Luis Obispo County. Fellow ranchers and families gathered from miles around to enjoy his genial hospitality, which included week-long rodeos, barbecues, horse racing, and rollicking parties. It is reported that the time came when his worldly goods were largely dissipated—thousands of acres of land, thousands of cattle and horses.[4]

In April 1861, the date the Santa Margarita was patented, title company records show ownership transferring to Mary and Martin Murphy, Jr.[5] The Asuncion and the Atascadero Ranchos soon came under Martin Murphy's ownership also.

RANCHO ASUNCION, AS WERE the other Mexican land grants, was established by the mission priests. Asuncion was north and contiguous with Santa Margarita Rancho. While the Santa Margarita had been under the jurisdiction of

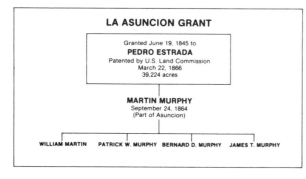

The above illustrates the changes of major ownerships of the Asuncion Ranch from original grantee until the time of our story. Ownership of Asuncion merged with ownership of the Atascadero Rancho after Martin Murphy purchased both of them.

Mission San Luis Obispo, Asuncion had been the southernmost of the Mission San Miguel ranchos.

After Joaquin Estrada was granted the Santa Margarita, Pedro Estrada applied for the Asuncion. It was granted to him June 19, 1845 and

patented in his name by the United States Land Commission on March 22, 1866. It consisted of 39,225 acres. Pedro was an officer in the militia at Monterey. One of his brothers served as majordomo at the ranch. Pedro's brothers, Julian and Jose Ramon, were the grantees of Santa Rosa and San Simeon Ranchos on the coast of San Luis Obispo.[6] One day the San Simeon would become the location of Hearst Castle.

Martin Murphy purchased the rights to most of Asuncion in 1864 and assumed clear ownership after the rancho was officially patented to Pedro Estrada in 1866. The West Coast Land Company also eventually purchased some of the land making up this ranch.[7]

MURPHY'S THIRD HOLDING in that area was the Atascadero Rancho. This one was much smaller than the others, only 4,348 acres.

Trifon Garcia, the son of Inocente (the overseer of the Santa Margarita Rancho) was the original grantee of the Atascadero. His grant was dated May 6, 1842 by Governor Juan Bautista Alvarado. However, his development of the property was constantly harassed by the local Indians, who rustled his cattle and burned the buildings on his land.[8] On March 9, 1846, he

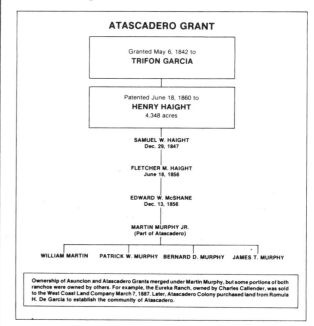

The above illustrates the changes of major ownerships of the Atascadero Rancho from original grantee until the time of our story.

Mexican period casa of Don Jose de la Guerra y Noriega, captain of the Santa Barbara presidio. Now used for several businesses.

sold Atascadero Rancho for only 500 pesos to William Breck. Title records show that the ranch passed from Breck to Samuel W. Haight. Henry H. Haight, a family member, received the United States patent on June 18, 1860. (He was governor of California from December 1867 to December 1871.) There were other owners for a short period before this land was purchased by Martin Murphy.[9]

When Martin and Mary Murphy's son, Patrick, completed a bachelor of science degree at Santa Clara College, he moved to San Luis Obispo County to take charge of the ranch properties of his father, a total of nearly 70,000 acres. Later he became the owner of these properties as well as of the Cojo Rancho of 9,000 acres near Lompoc.

Patrick led a distinguished and successful life in San Luis Obispo County. He served in the State Assembly and was elected a state senator three times. Thousands of head of cattle grazed upon his ranch lands. He was a stockholder and director in the Bank of San Luis Obispo and one of the incorporators of the San Luis Obispo Water Company. His father and brothers were also successful in politics and business in San Jose and San Francisco.

Patrick was a round-faced Irishman with heavy eyebrows, a thick full mustache that curled below the corners of his mouth, and a narrow goatee that started under the lower lip and extended below his oval chin. He enjoyed the old California rancho life. Like the preceding owner, he enjoyed company. He repaired the old ranch house, and entertained hundreds of visitors at barbecues and rodeos.

Patrick's wife, Mary Kate, was the daughter of Dr. P. M. O'Brien, one of the founders of the Hibernia Bank in San Francisco. She had died by the time the railroad activity started in San Luis Obispo County, but was remembered as a lady of many elegant accomplishments.[10]

❦

ALONG WITH ALL OF THE HOPE in the county, there were also occasional expressions of despair. "San Luis has remained so long in an isolated condition," the *Tribune* editor once wrote, "that it is inclined to receive with a feeling of pathetic hopelessness, the suggestion that it is able to do anything. The county communities are widely scattered, and there has grown from this, a separation of interests... Every real estate peddler in the county... thinks

New Arlington Hotel on State Street, Santa Barbara. Built by stock company headed by W. W. Hollister in 1875. Destroyed by fire in 1909, rebuilt, destroyed by earthquake in 1925.

The Southern Pacific station in Santa Barbara does not follow standard railroad architecture. Instead, it is patterned after traditional Spanish styling, with its arches, tile roof, and stucco siding.

it his duty . . . to belittle the attractions of every other part . . . ''

As it began to appear that the Southern Pacific Railroad was no longer taking action to close the coastal gap between Santa Barbara and Templeton, people looked for reasons.[11]

The Santa Margarita Rancho lay to the south of Templeton and the West Coast Land Company development. The *Santa Barbara Press* suggested that one reason the gap could not be closed was that General Patrick Murphy was making exorbitant demands of Southern Pacific in exchange for a right-of-way across his ranch.

The Southern Pacific demanded a free right-of-way through the ranch as well as 640 additional acres of land for a town site. The general was apparently willing to give the land for the right-of-way, but held out against the free land for a town site. He wanted an arrangement in which he would share in the profits arising from the development of a town on his land.[12]

In January 1888, it was reported that Collis P. Huntington, vice president of the Southern Pacific Railroad Company, planned to come to San Luis Obispo County to consider ways of forwarding construction of the line from Templeton through San Luis Obispo to Santa Barbara. Later a tentative date of March 20, 1888 was offered by the newspaper.

In the March 9, 1888 issue of the *Tribune*, an editorial titled "Waiting for the Train" summed up the feelings of San Luis Obispo people. Before the extension of the Southern Pacific line from Soledad, the editor wrote, "we were fairly contented; there was no train due, nothing to expect and no disappointment to suffer." Now, he said, "business is dribbling away into new channels . . . our city is doubtful of its own whereabouts, even, and can only stand and wait and grow exasperated. It does not soothe us to be told that the delay of the Southern Pacific is unavoidable; that there are other roads more important to its interests . . . that progress is financially impracticable . . . [that] the money market is cramped and the company, in fact, hard up."[13]

Then, just when the collective morale of the town seemed lowest, there were some encouraging words.

This old photograph shows a young priest looking out on the gardens of Mission Santa Barbara. The mission was an important attraction for visitors.

In April 1888, the people of San Luis Obispo heard about a report in the *Alta Californian*. Collis Huntington, president of Southern Pacific, arrived from the East, and a reporter talked to him.

"Yes," he said to a question about the Southern Pacific coastal line, "we propose to go on with the construction of the coast line between Templeton . . . and Santa Barbara, but the exact route . . . has not been decided. It will take some time to complete the road as there is a great deal of heavy work to be done this side of Santa Barbara. We desire, however, to complete that road as soon as possible."

This was followed by some interesting local news. Pat Murphy had reached an agreement with the Southern Pacific for a right-of-way through his ranchlands, and the company had agreed to include him in the financial rewards from the town site.

Brooks provided an interpretation for his readers about what to expect. He referred back to the Southern Pacific construction of a line to the last new town, Templeton, and the immediate stopping of construction at that point.

"With the careful consideration of its own interests, which marks the operations of the Southern Pacific, and which unfortunately prevents it from noticing how the interests of others are affected by its action, the railroad crept on to a dead stop at Templeton, paralyzing the business connection of this city with the eastern and northern part of the county.

"Now, apparently, a new Templeton is projected on the Santa Margarita, to be followed by an indefinite postponement of all further work.

"The situation is marked by painful distinctness. San Luis will either degenerate into a small village . . . or she will bend her energies to seek a connection with eastern railroads through the San Joaquin Valley . . . 'Who would be free, himself must strike the blow.'"

Benjamin Brooks was very bitter during this time.[14] Nearly every issue of the *San Luis Obispo Tribune* in 1887 and continuing into 1888 made reference to the need of building a line from the coast of San Luis Obispo County to the San Joaquin Valley, to make a connection with an eastern railroad line. This was among the many proposals that never became realities,

in spite of a number of meetings of men from Kern and San Luis Obispo counties.

The people in Paso Robles and Templeton were not at all happy with San Luis Obispo citizens. They did not like the antagonistic references being made about Southern Pacific. They considered the talks and meetings in San Luis Obispo concerning the construction of an east-west line an affront which could have dire consequences concerning the future plans of Southern Pacific.

By May 1, 1888, West Coast Land Company sales reached $806,661, and Templeton was still enjoying growth. In May a brick building for the Bank of Templeton was in progress, including "a massive safe, vault doors and the steel lining."

By the end of May, all references by the *Tribune* to the possible construction of a line into the San Joaquin Valley stopped, and ads from the West Coast Land Company began to reappear in the newspaper.

A reporter for a Los Angeles newspaper interviewed Charles Crocker about the railroad in early June 1888. "When will you close the gap in the coastline between Templeton and Santa Barbara?" he asked.

"We will assume operations there sometime this fall or winter," Crocker said. "There is some very heavy work on the line, you see, between San Luis Obispo and Templeton, and we will go in to complete the tunnels first."

The *Tribune* reprinted the interview without comment. Crocker's comments were no more definite than Huntington's or those of others before him.

Several months passed, then at long last R. E. Jack, Isaac Goldtree and J. P. Andrews were contacted directly by Southern Pacific officials and asked to procure a right-of-way through the city of San Luis Obispo along with grounds for a depot and machine shops. All of these men were bankers and large landmen in the county, and could be extremely influential. They had already enjoyed financial success by the presence of Southern Pacific in the county. They prepared a joint letter and published it in the *Tribune*:

"To the Citizens of San Luis Obispo:

"The Southern Pacific Railroad Company

By 1893, there were two luxury hotels ready to serve visitors arriving by train or by Pacific Coast steamships. The Arlington Hotel had accommodations for 300 first class guests. It was located at the upper end of State Street with views of both the mountains and the ocean.

have communicated to us the fact that they are about to commence the construction of the railroad, beginning at Templeton, and they desire the right-of-way through the city and sufficient grounds for depots and machine shops.

"The company has authorized us to procure such right-of-way and grounds for them, taking the position that if the citizens of San Luis Obispo desire the road through their city and the location of depots in their immediate vicinity, then they should be willing to furnish the necessary grounds."[15]

In October 1888 the railroad gathered about a hundred and seventy-five workers at Templeton. Sure enough, they were preparing side tracks for construction work in the direction of the planned new railroad town of Santa Margarita on Murphy's ranch. Word was out that the railroad was contracting for great amounts of food to feed its crews—hogs, cattle and all other foods.

During early October the *Messenger*, a small publication in San Miguel, said, "This has been a week of tramp railroad trains. We have heard bells, screaming whistles and brakes at all

hours . . . all bound for the front, bent on the extension of the road from Templeton."

The *Tribune* sent a message to its representative in Templeton asking him to investigate carefully work underway. He wrote back, saying: "This is what I saw and heard while rambling the streets and byways of the flourishing little city of Templeton.

"The first was a part of the Southern Pacific Railroad Company's gigantic railroad building force at work extending their road . . .

"I made it a point to ascertain the facts in regard to the amount of men to be employed. There were on Thursday morning 150 Chinamen, 100 white laborers and 50 bridge carpenters, and 500 more to arrive on Friday or Saturday.

"There is a large store car of Sisson Crocker which furnishes the provisions for the workers—sleeping cars for the workmen and tools of every description to carry on the work of grading and bridge building.

"One mile for grading, almost ready for the ties and rails, has been completed, and large supplies of bridge timber, ties and rails are . . . arriving.

"Chief Engineer Hood was in Templeton on Tuesday, and remained until Thursday morning."

The same reporter noted that land sales had picked up for the West Coast Land Company, and he was extremely optimistic about how quickly all of this would be finished and trains would be rolling between San Francisco and Los Angeles.[16]

On November 9, 1888, the *Tribune* reported that "pile drivers and bridgebuilders have been at work on trestles and bridges over the Paso Robles, Groves and Atascadero creeks." This work was occurring about six miles south of Templeton.

The location for the new town of Santa Margarita remained undecided. First, Southern Pacific wanted to determine the most convenient method of running the line, then they would specify the location of the town. No effort was yet made to prepare a town plot map.

Only one block from the Arlington, the beautiful San Marcos Hotel with spacious lawns and palm trees, accommodated 100 guests.

"On the 10th of last month," [November 1888] the *Tribune* reported, "our citizens were electrified by the news that the first gang of 200 men were actually at work on the railroad (south of Templeton). Now, six weeks later, over 1,000 men are at work."

The camp site of the construction foremen was shifted several times. Now it was located on the Santa Margarita Rancho somewhere near the expected site of the new town. At this point, a great deal of preliminary work had been done between Templeton and the expected new town, but no rails had been laid.

"The town of Santa Margarita will be laid out upon a beautiful elevated plateau a short distance south of the old ranch house," the *Tribune* announced on November 30, 1888. "The rush will come for its choice business and resident sites, and we have the assurances of the owners of the Santa Margarita ranch that a large part of that magnificent domain will be placed upon the market."[17]

Benjamin Brooks made a trip up the Cuesta and joined members of the railroad team. The surveyors lived in pitched tents along the planned railroad route. Mr. Charles H. Lee, assistant engineer, was in charge of the surveyors. Although he was not disturbed by the job ahead, Lee told Brooks that he was encountering problems greater than he had experienced on the Oregon and California line.

Brooks enjoyed lunch with Mr. Lee on the side of the mountain, but he did not eat without some concern. A report he had received a few days earlier said that a number of railroad workers had suffered severe illness as the result of food poisoning. A large quantity of food was disposed of and a Chinese cook had lost his job.

However, Brooks found his lunch to be fine that day, and the foreman was a cooperative interviewee. From his visit, Brooks observed that:

Epifanio Boronda found it profitable to open a general store on his property at the top of the Cuesta to accommodate the railroad workers;

A short distance from the site of the planned town, the railroad line was surveyed and visible by that time;

"Long lines of Chinamen are stretched along the ravine, their shovels flying in the air with monotonous regularity;"

"Carts are filing down the grade loaded with rocks which are brought to a chute just about Boronda's and are plunged down into the gulch";

The Chinese laborers were digging a small canal to divert a stream that would be in the way of planned tunnel work;

"Where Boronda's barn stood, the railroad is to enter the mountain. A black surveyors line marked the line of the first tunnel."[18]

As word about surveys for tunnels through

the Cuesta continued, Brooks found it positively confusing. It was impossible to get authentic information directly from the Southern Pacific office in San Francisco. He obtained a large map of the county, and as he strolled the streets of San Luis Obispo and entertained visitors at the *Tribune* office, he gathered information from all who offered it. He once reported:

"Volunteer reporters who were confident that they were on intimate terms with Hood's [chief construction engineer for Southern Pacific] plans have located so many routes on our map that the original lithograph has nearly vanished."

This latter-day rodeo on the Santa Margarita Rancho helped keep the traditions of its former owners, Joaquin Estrada and then Patrick Murphy.

His map created much local interest, and Brooks tried to encourage it. He had another map made to "give free scope to the crayons of gifted and posted enlighteners."

In late February Brooks received word from one of his many volunteer reporters that the railroad was hauling timbers for a tunnel from the site of Santa Margarita south toward the Cuesta grade. He also reported that work was beginning on a hotel and depot at the new town of Santa Margarita.[20]

∽❦∾

ON FRIDAY, THE NINETEENTH of February, 1889, the *Tribune* announced: "Tomorrow is the birthday of the new town of Santa Margarita." The town had been laid out and mapped, and it was assumed that many people from all over the county would want to see what was happening. Every man in town who had a team

of horses and a wagon that could make it over the Cuesta was called upon to volunteer to haul friends to Santa Margarita. Whether people intended to buy land or not, the occasion would be the largest social function in San Luis Obispo County for many a day.

A new Santa Margarita transportation company announced its intention of running two stages daily between San Luis Obispo and Santa Margarita. The stages would leave San Luis Obispo at 6:30 A.M. and 1:00 P.M. to make connection with the trains.

Brooks received a two-column by twenty-one inch advertisement from the Pacific Improvement Company which he published Saturday, April 20, 1889, announcing a "Grand Auction Sale" at Santa Margarita. The ad announced that Santa Margarita was the new terminus for the Coast Division of the Southern Pacific Railroad. A special excursion train was scheduled to leave San Francisco on Friday, April 19, picking up passengers at San Jose, Gilroy, Pajaro, Castroville, Salinas, King City, and Paso Robles. The San Francisco auctioneering firm of Briggs, Fergusson, and Company would conduct the land sales.

In the same ad, General Pat Murphy announced a "Grand Barbecue" which he and his vaqueros would personally prepare!

The day arrived, and Brooks reported the event as the "biggest camp meeting" ever held

After the Estrada family had sold its ranching interests, they maintained a local country recreation area called Estrada Gardens where major groups held barbecues, picnics and other outings. This is a roadside photo outside the gardens during the annual Swiss celebration, taken about the turn of the century. The Gardens were located outside San Luis Obispo at the foot of the Cuesta.

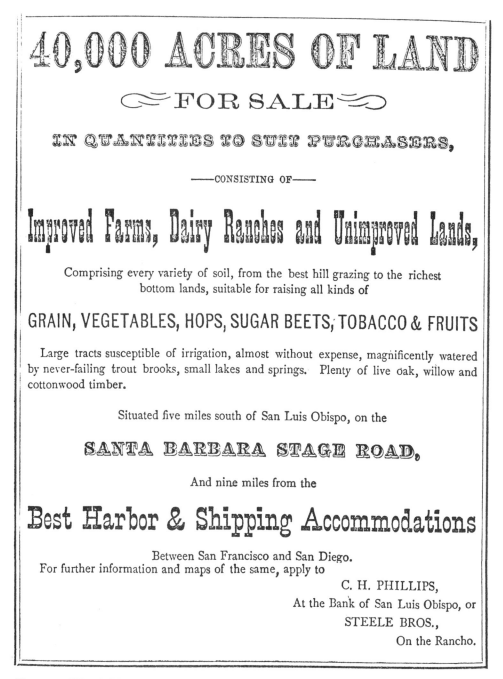

40,000 ACRES OF LAND
~FOR SALE~
IN QUANTITIES TO SUIT PURCHASERS,

----CONSISTING OF----

Improved Farms, Dairy Ranches and Unimproved Lands,

Comprising every variety of soil, from the best hill grazing to the richest bottom lands, suitable for raising all kinds of

GRAIN, VEGETABLES, HOPS, SUGAR BEETS, TOBACCO & FRUITS

Large tracts susceptible of irrigation, almost without expense, magnificently watered by never-failing trout brooks, small lakes and springs. Plenty of live oak, willow and cottonwood timber.

Situated five miles south of San Luis Obispo, on the

SANTA BARBARA STAGE ROAD,

And nine miles from the

Best Harbor & Shipping Accommodations

Between San Francisco and San Diego.
For further information and maps of the same, apply to

C. H. PHILLIPS,
At the Bank of San Luis Obispo, or
STEELE BROS.,
On the Rancho.

Chauncey Hatch Phillips reputation for promoting land sales from the 1870's through the 1890's brought both sellers and buyers to his bank and later to the offices of the West Coast Land Company.

in the county. The crowd was estimated at about two thousand people, most of them coming from the county. Brooks said there were about one hundred and sixty people who arrived by train from the north.

Visitors found the Santa Margarita Valley as "crisp and lovely as old Dame Nature could dress it." The magnificent oak trees were "clothed in their richest foliage, the grasses in richest green, and the flowers of varied hue and choicest color."

The road over the Cuesta from San Luis Obispo was covered by a continual line of carriages, carts and wagons during that early Saturday morning. The Friday train from San Francisco stayed overnight in Paso Robles in order that passengers might enjoy the comforts of the Paso Robles Inn. At 9:00 A.M., it arrived in Santa Margarita with seven coaches full of prospective land buyers and pleasure seekers.

Visitors gathered in the shade of the oak trees or strolled about the town site.

Mr. Fergusson of the auctioneering firm was in charge of conducting the sales. He announced that Pat Murphy soon planned to market ten thousand acres of choice farmlands. This was expected to attract additional population and make Santa Margarita a farming center. He promised that the Pacific Improvement Company intended a large advertising campaign to aid the growth and prosperity of the new town.

"The fun then started," Brooks wrote. Everyone selected his favorite lot. The bidding opened for lot 32, block 84, at the corner opposite the hotel and facing the depot. It started at $100. People bid in $25 increments. Phillip Ready of San Luis Obispo was the first proud owner of a piece of property in the new town. He paid $525 for the lot. That seemed to be the highest bid of the day for town property. Other lots sold for between $160 and $275.

Around noon, the sumptuous smell of barbecued meat drifted with the April breezes from the pits to the auctioneer's stand. This was a decided distraction to sales, so Fergusson adjourned the sale until after lunch.

"If there is one thing more than another that General Murphy knows all about, it is managing an old-fashioned barbecue to a tee-y-te," Brooks reported. "There was beef and bread and salsa for everybody. Beef raw, beef roasted, beef on a stick, beef in hand, beef on a chip, rib tenderloin, round, chuck, briskit, roast stuffed with climate, jerky with scenery salad."

In addition, every local woman in the crowd had a basket containing a delicacy which she had prepared. People gathered in small groups and shared the excitement and their food.

The big sale continued into the afternoon until about 4:45. Fergusson told Brooks that he had sold 102 lots. In spite of the many vehicles on the road that day, no accidents occurred.

Now, after the auction, whatever land sales might be made in the new town would be private transactions. Some people bought land at the auction hoping for a quick profit on their investments. However, within months many people found it best to let their land go at a loss or simply let the land company have their lot without further payments.

So, that was the beginning of the town of Santa Margarita. It had taken the Southern Pacific Railroad nearly two-and-one-half years to extend the line the few miles from Templeton. Santa Margarita did succeed in becoming a community. Ranch hands from the Eagle and Santa Margarita ranches came to town to socialize and a few businesses made a living. It was a small, mostly wooden town of small businesses—a small hotel, saloons, a general store, a blacksmith shop and a few others.[21]

And in San Luis Obispo, the years were passing, and people still waited for the train.

The S. S. Santa Rosa was only one of several in the Pacific Coast Steamship Company Line that docked at Santa Barbara and Port San Luis.

CHAPTER X

New Towns To The South

Myron Angel was still the editor of the *San Luis Obispo Tribune* in 1885. But Angel was much more than the editor of a weekly newspaper in a remotely located small town. He was a visionary and a dreamer, and sometimes he left work behind and went alone on an outing.

One morning in early August 1885 he walked over to Crawford Livery Stable in San Luis Obispo, rented a team of fine trotting horses and a buggy, and set out to observe life in and around Pismo Beach in south San Luis Obispo County.

Although it had been a little too warm in San Luis Obispo, he soon found the day to be one of "unsurpassed loveliness." As he neared the water, a small breeze played about his face as it often does along the coast in San Luis Obispo County.

The scenery was delightful. He drove the team down onto the beach at water's edge near Pismo. Even the horses seemed to enjoy the silence of their hoofs as they trotted in the sand.

Angel played all of that day—bathing in the surf, fishing from the wharf, walking and driv-

BIRDSEYE VIEW OF THE FAMOUS EL PIZMO BEACH TAKEN FROM CAPTIVE BALLOON

Well Located Lots
Selling To-day $150 to $500, on Easy Terms, offers a Handsome Profit.

THE PEERLESS BEACH OF THE PACIFIC
El Pizmo Beach Resort
EL PIZMO, CALIFORNIA

LAND DEPARTMENT

San Francisco Office, 789 Market Street,
OR
Thos. S. Wadsworth   319-320 Douglas Building
Los Angeles, Cal.

Special Excursions
To El Pizmo. We'll Pay Your Way Entire Trip Expense.

In 1885 Tribune editor Myron Angel described Pismo Beach as follows: "For twenty miles the broad beach extends as level as the sea and as smooth as a floor washed by the ever coming and receding waves . . . the sand hardened by the beating of the water so the tracks of horses and wagons scarcely leave an imprint." Taken from a balloon, this photo shows "tent city" just above the beach with real estate promotional copy.

ing the buggy for miles in the sand. "The Pismo beach is becoming famous," he wrote later, "and well it should, for it has not its superior in the world."

The day on the coast lifted Angel's spirits immensely, and he made eloquent notes for the news story he wanted to write. "For twenty miles the broad beach extends as level as the sea and as smooth as a floor, washed by the ever coming and receding waves, the sands hardened by the beating of the water so the tracks of horses and wagons scarcely leave an imprint.

The late Grant and Hazel Hansen with their friend Hugh Cameron at the edge of Tent City in Pismo Beach. The Hansens operated a small general store in Avila when this photo was taken in 1909.

"Eastward and southward are the gently rolling hills of the Ranchos El Pismo, Bolsa de Chamisal and Guadaloupe, with the broad and fertile valleys of the Arroyo Grande, Santa Maria and Laguna Largo opening between."

For miles and miles, Angel witnessed tourists in their carriages silently rolling along the sand, scarcely "conscious of the movement so enraptured with the spell of the experience."

He introduced himself to Mr. M. Meherin, the manager of the recently opened Pismo Hotel, and had a fine lunch for fifty cents. He saw other people from around the county at the hotel, and spoke to people who had come all the way from San Francisco and from San Joaquin Valley towns. He interviewed some of these visitors and found them overjoyed with their chosen holiday spot.

While walking among the numerous campers on the beach and in the grove of trees nearby, he noted that visitors certainly knew how to

make themselves comfortable. They had arranged cooking and dining facilities, nice sized tents for sleeping, rocking chairs and, in some cases, sewing machines. Covered wagons and carriages with sleek horses and strong mules were a part of every camp site.

That day in August 1885, Angel made a prediction: "The Pismo and our grand bay will become the favorite resort of the Pacific Coast."

But Angel was also a businessman. He sold an advertisement in the *Tribune* to Mr. Meherin before he left the Pismo Hotel.[1]

⌘

ONE AND A HALF YEARS LATER, when Angel retired, Benjamin Brooks became the editor and proprietor of the *Tribune*. One day in March 1887, a Mr. P. C. Dolliver, new manager of the Pismo Hotel, came by the newspaper office and asked to see Brooks. He told Brooks that he represented a syndicate of Eastern capitalists, and he expected to remain in the area permanently. His organization, he said, was also associated with Messrs. A. E. Pomeroy and Charles W. Stinson, well known as the "managers and manipulators of the celebrated Long Beach property near Wilmington."

Mr. Dolliver said that he planned a complete "renovation and reconstruction" at the beach and had already hired a work crew. He expected that when the Southern Pacific Railroad came through, it would come very close to his property. Meantime, he planned to sell villa properties to persons desiring homes nearby, and he had already sold lots to a few local citizens.[2]

Crowds gathered at Pismo Beach after church. Typically, all were dressed in their Sunday best.

A summer scene at Pismo Beach. Dress ranges from very modest bathing suits to fully clothed ladies carrying parasols to protect themselves from the sun.

Mr. Dolliver wasn't the only man excited about land development close to the coast. That summer, Bartlett and Russell Real Estate Company of San Luis Obispo announced plans to sell 300 city-size lots in a new town they called Ynocenta.

The town was to be laid out above San Luis Obispo Creek on the San Miguelito Rancho near the warm springs enroute to Avila. The original San Miguelito Rancho consisted of 22,136 acres of land granted to Don Miguel Avila by the Mexican government. Avila served as alcalde in San Luis Obispo for a time during the Mexican period. He and his wife, Ynocenta, had a large family. Port Harford and the town of Avila were both located along a portion of beach front on the rancho, which was now in the hands of Juan Avila, the son of Miguel and Ynocenta.

The new development was inland. The developers proposed holding between thirty and fifty lots for business purposes. They offered residential lots at one hundred dollars each with payments of twenty-five dollars every six months, promoting the location as being only one mile from Avila Beach.

Hoping to reach outsiders in Board of Trade issues of the *Tribune*, Bartlett and Russell used lavish copy. "There are grand mountains from whose breasts flow living fountains, and where is found untold mineral wealth," they wrote. "Beautiful hills covered with verdure rise from rich valleys weighted with grain and fruit and

waterfalls. Trout streams and myriads of generous living springs gleam in the sunlight.... Ynocenta, festooned with vines, sentineled by towering trees, kept green by springs and mountain streams, and made musical by the white waves which break on Avila Beach."

Ynocenta, so named in honor of Juan Avila's mother, comprised 275 acres. South of it, near the creek, the Pacific Coast narrow-gauge line ran to Port Harford. A company called Adams, Nichols & Company had recently announced finding natural gas and hot sulphur water on property adjoining Ynocenta.

As part of their promotional efforts, Bartlett and Russell called attention to an ice cold soda water spring on the property. It had been the favorite beverage of old Don Miguel, they said, and added that "it is said the fair senoritas from many miles away would visit the spring to wash their hair, the soft water giving their luxuriant tresses a lustrous appearance and silky texture. The spring was also the resort of many lavaderas, and there the family linen from many ranchos was washed."

Bartlett and Russell stated that they intended to restore the famous spring as one of the attractions of Ynocenta. They promised wide streets, and a variety of lot shapes. The principal streets would lead directly to the springs and a railroad depot. The promoters promised to plant olive, fir, cypress, orange and eucalyptus trees to beautify the new town.

Unfortunately, Ynocenta was only a dream.

Tent City Pizmo, Cal.

A well-dressed couple at Pismo Beach poses for this postcard photo against backdrop of "tent city." After traveling from the San Joaquin Valley and other distant places, tourists stayed for long periods in these tents set up on platforms.

It never came into existence, even in a small way. However, Miles Station existed on this property as a loading place for farmers shipping goods by the Pacific Coast Railway.[3]

～❦～

THE TOWN OF NIPOMO WAS more successful. During the month of July 1887, the same month the Ynocenta subdivision was announced, land sales were beginning on the Nipomo grant.[4]

The Nipomo subdivision was located upon the Nipomo Rancho, a Mexican land grant confirmed to William Goodwin Dana by Governor Juan B. Alvarado on April 6, 1837. The grant included 37,888 acres.[5] From the town site the rancho extended as far as the eye could see in all directions. The Pacific Coast Railway ran through the ranch, and the route of the train helped establish the location of the town.

Born in Boston in 1797, Dana had sailed on one of his uncle's ships to China and India. He was a cousin of Richard Henry Dana, Jr., author of *Two Years Before the Mast*. He arrived in Santa Barbara in 1825 as the master of the brig *Waverly*. Dana married Josepha, daughter of Don Carlos Antonio Carrillo, who became provisional governor of California in 1835. They had twenty-one children, but only thirteen lived to adulthood. The children inherited the rancho from their mother, divided it among themselves, and sold parcels of the land to others. As late as the 1970s, the Dana family still owned portions of the land in and around the town.[6]

By the middle of 1887, Nipomo had two hotels, a general store, a wagon and blacksmith shop, a schoolhouse, an agricultural implement and hardware store, a livery and feed stable, four real estate offices, three saloons, and a newspaper called the *Nipomo News* that put out its first issue in July 1887.

The Pacific Coast Railway had a depot with a forty- by fifty-foot storage area. The train made one trip each day from Port Harford to San Luis Obispo, Arroyo Grande, Nipomo, Santa Maria, Graciosa, and Los Alamos.

A member of the original Nipomo grant

Pismo Inn was situated high above the beach with a view of the water below. In 1980, a large motel is located on this site north of the wharf.

THE PISMO INN

family, E. G. Dana, was the new town postmaster, and there was a telegraph and Wells Fargo office.

But Nipomo promoters expected to see the Southern Pacific Railroad running through the rancho before long. "There is a fortune in every purchase of land in this county... For cheap homes, come to San Luis Obispo county," the new *Nipomo News* said.[7]

☙❧

IN AUGUST OF THAT YEAR, still another "city" was promoted into existence. Two men named Grover and Gates subdivided the stretch of land between Arroyo Grande and the ocean and called it Grover City. They had an arrangement with Southern Pacific for people in San Francisco who desired to obtain excursion tickets as far as Templeton. The journey would continue by stage to San Luis Obispo and by Pacific Coast Railway to Arroyo Grande. From there, passengers would be transported by wagons, carriages and other miscellaneous horse-drawn vehicles to the new Grover City.

Arroyo Grande people took the occasion to serve as hosts and hostesses in every possible way. The town was all hustle and bustle. Flags were flying, and businessmen exhibited large displays of local fruits and vegetables. Guests expressed amazement at seeing radishes the size of beets, two-pound stalks of rhubarb, forty-pound heads of cabbage, unbelievably large, ripe strawberries and large apples, beautifully polished.

There were "beautiful flowers, prosperous farmers, pretty girls and smiling matrons everywhere," Benjamin Brooks reported. He estimated that a crowd of a thousand people came to see the Grover City development and reported that it was more like a Fourth of July celebration than a land sale. The San Luis band provided good music, and everyone enjoyed the barbecued beef.

At 12:30 P.M. Colonel C. C. Thayer, the auctioneer, appeared upon the platform. He looked over the crowd and gave a little speech about the opportunities in California and the future he saw for this new town. He complimented the crowd for their wisdom in choosing to come to the land sale.

Then he opened the auctioning and the crowd pressed to place their bids, which became very spirited, sales occurring in quick succession. Four clerks were on hand to receive deposits and prepare sales papers.

Later Brooks received word that Grover and Gates had sold 133 lots worth $15,000. At a later second auction, they sold another seventy-five lots for about $7,500. Grover City, it appeared, was off to a highly successful start.[8]

☙❧

In late 1887, a new addition to the town of Arroyo Grande was announced. Four local men had formed a "syndicate" to sell about five hundred lots above and around the main street of town. This property was promoted as Arroyo Grande's "Knob Hill." H. Cox, J. F. Beckett, C. R. Callender, and J. W. Smith were the developers.[9]

Arroyo Grande was an old settlement only a few miles inland from the beach and thirteen miles south of the town of San Luis Obispo. The immediate area around Arroyo Grande was originally utilized for gardens by Mission San Luis Obispo. The fertile land provided potatoes, corn, beans, and a wide variety of vegetables for the mission and the Indians who tilled the soil.[10]

In 1878 Arroyo Grande was described as "a thriving place of from twelve to fifteen houses... [with] two stores, two hotels, a saloon, a stable and a blacksmith shop."[11]

☙❧

AT A LATER DATE, THE MEN handling the Grover City development extended an invitation to a group of San Luis Obispo County businessmen to travel by train to view another development which they were planning in Santa Barbara County. Grover, Gates, and Rosener had acquired the John S. Bell ranch located at the outskirts to the west of Los Alamos, and they hoped they could turn this land into a profitable development. At the same time, the Pacific Coast Railway was extending its line to a new town subdivision called Los Olivos.

Benjamin Brooks was among those boarding the Pacific Coast train a few minutes before 8:15 A.M. that day in early September 1887. He

Early in the twentieth century, this scene was familiar to visitors at Pismo Beach. Old touring cars are parked along the street leading to the dance pavilion which served as a center of recreational activity. The pavilion was removed many years ago.

wanted to see both the Los Alamos and the Los Olivos developments. When the train reached Los Alamos, the tour group was greeted by the developers, who had carriages waiting to take them to the new tract.

Brooks was impressed with the open country. Like most of the great ranches in San Luis Obispo and Santa Barbara counties, the Bell Ranch scarcely showed traces of human habitation. Brooks took note of an occasional grain field, a few widely scattered tenant houses and cattle on distant hills. He saw one lone sheepherder in the distance, and later a hermit tending beehives.

As the teams pulled the carriages through great valleys and rolling prairies in the direction of the ocean, Brooks was aware of his own sense of vast space, empty and unused.

They passed the Bell home on the ranch, an elegant mansion surrounded by lawns and parterres which were skillfully laid out and well kept. The visitors were quietly told that Mr. Bell would receive $350,000 for the ranch.

After seeing Los Alamos, the businessmen were taken to a shady grove of trees at the edge of town where barbecued beef was being prepared. A member of the famous De la Guerra family of Santa Barbara whom Brooks didn't recognize was in charge of preparing the feast. This family, Brooks remarked, was surely responsible for keeping the tradition of the barbecue alive in this part of California.

While they ate, there was much oratory.

Captain Haley, publisher of the *Templeton Times,* had some words for the group. So did Dr. Lucas of Los Alamos and finally, Chauncey Phillips of the West Coast Land Company.

The men retired early at the Los Alamos hotel. In the gray dawn of the next morning, they boarded a construction train that jogged uncertainly toward the proposed Los Olivos town site. The train carried a big water tank. Surface water was scarce along the train route at the end of the summer.

The road bed was a series of cuts and fills through the rolling hills. Brooks counted workers along the tracks and estimated some five hundred men between Los Alamos and Los Olivos.

The town site at Los Olivos was laid out in several broad streets. White corner stakes dotted the flatlands and the gentle hills to the east. The Alamo Pintado Creek flowed through the valley, and Zaca Lake, about twelve miles away, was elevated above the valley and promised to be a source of water for farmers settling the area.

Surely here would be built the "homes of a great population," Brooks later wrote. As he strolled about the town site, he felt almost poetic. Why, he asked, "should men be herded together in struggling, starving masses with hardly room to breathe, with scanty hope of ever sustaining a miserable existence, while here, lonely and unvisited almost, were millions of acres of the fairest, richest lands on earth, ready to reward with profuse bounty . . ."

In buggies and wagons, the visitors rode over much of Rancho Canada de los Pinos. This ranch and a tract of land on the Bell ranch had been acquired by the Steele-Willey syndicate and were being surveyed into many small farms for colonization.

The caravan of horse-drawn vehicles passed through Santa Ynez. Brooks noted that the mission had suffered severely from neglect, but it was better, he thought, than the total obliteration often resulting from poor attempts at restoration.

Later they headed into Gaviota Pass. The men enjoyed a bountiful lunch provided by their sponsors and then headed toward what was announced as the highlight of their journey—Nojoqui Falls. There the rippling water splashing over the boulders in a narrow, darkly-shaded gorge left them "in silent, delighted admiration before the loveliest extravagance of nature that California can boast." The sheer precipice of rock rose 165 feet, its crown canopied with deep green foliage touched only in spots by the midday sun.

It was a beautiful day, and Brooks took copious notes so that he could tell his readers about it.[12]

BY THE ELEVENTH OF NOVEMBER, 1887, the Pacific Coast Railway had completed its narrow-gauge tracks into the planned development of Los Olivos. C. H. Phillips, who was in charge of the sale of the land there, an-

Senorita Blandina Esquer at her wedding to Charles W. Dana, a descendant of William Goodwin Dana and Josepha Carrillo de Dana.

nounced a "grand excursion" and land auction for Wednesday, November 30. In advertisements placed in newspapers throughout California, he promoted attendance at the Los Olivos auction and informed readers at each location of the most convenient way to reach the auction.

For example, people in San Diego could board the northbound steamer *Santa Rosa* on November 28 at 4:00 P.M. Los Angeles residents could board this same ship at 9:40 A.M. the next day, and Santa Barbara people could board it that evening at 9:00 P.M. San Francisco people could board the southbound *Queen Pacific* at the Broadway Wharf at 2:00 P.M., November 29. These ships would both reach Port Harford at Avila in time for passengers to board the Pacific Coast Railway excursion train to Los Olivos on November 30.

At the same time, E. W. Steele placed a large

William Goodwin Dana casa located on the Nipomo Rancho. 37,000 acres was granted to Dana by the Mexican government in 1837. The adobe structure is now owned by the San Luis Obispo County Historical Society.

NIPOMO LAND GRANT

WILLIAM GOODWIN DANA
Received grant from Mexican Governor
Juan Alvarado
April 6, 1837.
Patented by U.S. Land Commission
December 14, 1868
37,888 acres

JOSEPHA DANA
Dec. 26, 1853

JOAQUIN CARRILLO	H. C. DANA		FRANK DANA	FRANCISCO A. THOMPSON
S. A. POLLARD April 4, 1855	BENJAMIN F. PETTIT Nov. 29, 1869		DAVID A. DANA	FRANCISCA THOMPSON
				JOHN F. and HENRY C. DANA Sept. 22, 1874

ELISEO DANA Dec. 12, 1882	JOSEPH VEAR March 16, 1881	PATRICK MOORE June 9, 1882	J. M. STOWE	SAMUEL DANA	ADELINA DANA
		DAVID McKEEN Dec. 23, 1886	DAVID McKEEN June 9, 1882	MICHAEL FOX Oct. 24, 1885	DAVID McKEEN Aug. 1, 1893

In 1886, the Pollard property was partitioned and there were many new land-owners on the Nipomo grant.

When Captain William Goodwin Dana died, the estate came into the possession of his widow, Josepha. Children, in-laws, and others acquired the land from her.

advertisement in area newspapers and also produced a pamphlet announcing the opening of 6,000 acres of choice agricultural lands outside Santa Ynez, on the Canada de los Pinos or College grant. The land was being offered by the Santa Ynez Land and Improvement Company. People were urged to take the Pacific Coast Railway on the same day that the Los Olivos excursion was to occur.

Ben Brooks decided the Los Olivos event was one he should not miss, but he must have had some second thoughts when he awakened that Wednesday morning to find it raining.

He dressed for a wet day, and left for the station on lower Higuera Street in San Luis Obispo. The first stop was Avila. To his amazement, the steamers had reached Port Harford from both north and south, loaded with passengers planning to take the narrow gauge to the Los Olivos development. They "paced the wet decks, balanced themselves against the bouncing billows, looked at the discouraging mist and rain." Some prospects, Brooks reported, gave up the whole notion of going ashore.

But many weathered the storm. Two engines pulled every available Pacific Coast passenger car. The cars were humid with wet people, crowded and uncomfortable. Many had to stand in the aisles. Some of the men squatted in place. Nearly all were growling unhappily. The railway had intended to attach some open cars, but the weather precluded this action.

To his credit, Chauncey Phillips had a temporary covered platform erected at the point where the crowd debarked at Los Olivos. But, Brooks noted, "the soil at Los Olivos is deep and rich, and the plentiful moisture had readily penetrated it, so that the pedestrian could pick up a twenty-five foot lot on each foot in the course of a short walk."

Phillips had hired the San Luis band to provide music, and although the fire smoked and sparked uncertainly in the rain, the delicious odor of barbecued meat tempted the crowd.

"There was a plentiful supply of bread and 'sack'—particularly 'sack,'" Brooks noted, and soon the disposition of the crowd changed under the influence of "sack" to one of very high spirits. People laughed and talked gaily and disregarded the rain, at least partially.

Mr. Phillips took the stage and "palavered the congregation," helping them to see millions in the future city that was about to grow around them. H. W. Weller, an auctioneer from San Francisco, now began his speech in advance of the first offering. Colonel Seely, working for the West Coast Land Company, stood as spotter so as not to miss a bid. W. S. Hinkle set up a table to receive deposits and consummate land deals.

The first lots offered were those close to the depot. They were fifty by one hundred and forty feet in size and the bid went as high as $300 in a few instances.

Then a few lots down the proposed street near the site of the planned hotel were offered and sold. The foundation for the hotel had already been laid with some forty thousand bricks. A windmill was in place and water had been reached at forty-seven feet. T. W. Williams, who had established a lumber yard to serve prospective settlers, announced that he had thirty carloads of lumber ready for immediate sale.

J. W. Smith and P. B. Perfumo from San Luis Obispo bid extremely low on a number of properties, and much to everyone's amazement and their delight, won the bids. They were willing to continue bidding for every piece of land offered. C. H. Phillips and the other investors didn't like the way things were going. They held off for a while, but it became clear that the whole Los Olivos development was going to turn into a financial disaster unless they did something.

Finally, Phillips gave the signal, and all selling stopped. They had sold twenty-nine lots for about $6,300 that day.

The crowd moved to the tables for more food and "sack." The mud grew deeper, the rain fell harder, and food and drink disappeared. At about four o'clock in the afternoon, there was a rush for the train and people settled down, wet and sullen, for the long ride back to San Luis Obispo and Port Harford.[13]

Apparently J. W. Smith was not above making a good land investment wherever it happened to fall, but his real interest was not in buying bargain lots in other men's develop-ments, as he had done at Los Olivos. On December 16, 1887, a short time after the rainy day in Los Olivos, a half-page ad appearing in the *Tribune* announced the subdivision of 9,250 acres in the new Los Berros tract on the Nipomo land grant. C. R. Callender and this same J. W. Smith, San Luis Obispo realtors, had placed the ad. Buyers could purchase land in amounts ranging from five to five hundred acres.

"The Southern Pacific Railroad will pass directly through the tract and the Pacific Coast Railway traverses these lands for three miles and has two stations..." the developers announced. Of course, the developers could not know the plans for the Southern Pacific Railroad, and when the day came to lay railroad bed, the Southern Pacific line ran several miles closer to the coast.[14]

The anticipation of a Southern Pacific line continued to encourage land development all along the coast between Paso Robles and Santa Barbara.

Main Street, Arroyo Grande, in 1908. Taken from a postcard, on which the correspondent wrote: "This is the main street here. Can you imagine what the other streets are like?" But Arroyo Grande had come a long way from its ancestral beginnings as a Chumash Indian village. In 1887, a syndicate of real estate men opened a new subdivision in town which local people still refer to as "Knob Hill."

Steam Engine takes on water and wood fuel.

CHAPTER XI

Two Great New Hotels

Construction of the new hotel in San Luis Obispo, which the Board of Directors had decided to call the Ramona, started late in 1887.[1] By March 1888, the framing had nearly been completed.[2] Work proceeded in spite of many ups and downs about Southern Pacific Company's plans. The hotel's investors were undoubtedly encouraged by the movement of the line to Santa Margarita, even though it was only a few miles.

One Sunday morning in May 1888 the townspeople experienced a big scare. Someone saw smoke in the construction area near the hotel. Volunteer firemen rushed to the scene with the fire wagon and connected their hose to the nearby fire hydrant. The fire was in a large pile of wood shavings and sawdust near the building. One of the men, Madison Graves, succeeded in extinguishing the blaze even before the hoses were connected, but the little episode made street conversation all day. Memories of the Andrews Hotel fire were still fresh in everyone's mind.

People followed construction progress every step of the way, and with thirty-five men working on the job, the progress was rapid.[3] As an edifice, it outdid the Andrews. For one thing, it was reported that the hotel would include a system of electric bells connected between the hotel office and all 144 rooms, as a safeguard against both fire and burglary—another modern innovation.

People were amused by one of the men doing the lathing in the hotel. He could nail 2,500 laths in one day. Reports came out that he kept a mouth full of nails and a cigarette going all at the same time.[4]

Another building was also under construction. For a long time, people had wanted to have a place where the products of the county could be displayed. A main objective of the Agricultural Association, which had grown out of the Board of Trade, was the construction of an Agricultural Hall. Now it, too, was in progress. It was undoubtedly one of the ugliest wooden buildings in California, but its archi-

People of San Luis Obispo County celebrated the opening of the Ramona Hotel on Wednesday evening, October 3, 1888 with music and a supper-dance.

tecture was of little concern because it was needed and wanted by so many.[5]

In spite of this show of progress in San Luis Obispo, most things remained largely the same in 1888. On Monterey Street in front of the courthouse, pedestrians, horsemen and wagon drivers nearly always had to "shoo" their way through a herd of cows.

There was continuing illicit activity on Palm Street. In 1888 one of the girls doing business became so demoralized that she tried to take poison and end it all, but a good local doctor successfully pumped out her stomach and saved her.

The Chinese were running fan-tan games on Palm Street, too. One day in May of that year, several of them were arrested, and two of them were charged heavy fines. The others were discharged because officers couldn't identify them as game operators.

Among the identifiable marks of progress, the new Crocker Brothers store building was completed that year.

One day in July, Brooks was invited to join a group of investors on an inspection tour of the Ramona Hotel. He was surprised to see the amount of progress that had been made inside the building. The interior finish work had started. From the top floor windows of the rooms facing west, he enjoyed the view of the whole town, including the mission with San Luis Obispo Mountain as its backdrop and the Irish hills beyond the Los Osos Valley. Looking east, he saw the beginning of Cuesta Pass and the backdrop of the Santa Lucia Mountains.

"We may not have a railroad," Brooks wrote, "but if people once find their devious way to the Ramona, we have no shadow of doubt that they will remain until compelled to depart."

A man by the name of S. B. Rathbun had been hired to manage the hotel, and he was busy recruiting local people for the staff.

Mr. Fillmore, manager of the Pacific Coast Railway, said the furniture had been selected and would arrive by steamer from San Francisco as soon as it could be placed in the hotel.[6]

At last, the time for a grand opening arrived. The celebration occurred Wednesday evening, October 3, 1888. Hotel manager Rathbun had been working day and night for weeks to be

This building was constructed as an Agricultural Hall at Monterey and Toro Streets in 1888 and was used for fairs and agricultural exhibitions. Later, the building was referred to as the pavilion. At the time this photo was taken, it was used as the Women's Civic Club. Many road shows were staged in this building in the new century.

ready for this long anticipated occasion. At last, the furnishings of the hotel were in place, the kitchen was in order, and he was ready to serve. He had many bosses to please among local stockholders.

Residents from all over the county arrived in town for the celebration. People from over the Cuesta and from the southern part of the county took rooms for the night and settled in for the swankiest celebration the county had experienced since the grand opening of the ill-fated Andrews in 1885.

Mr. Rathbun was a calm person with a pleasant smile. He flattered the patrons as they arrived, and kept a watchful eye for the smallest disorder. He was "a prince of hosts," Brooks wrote.

The hotel was ablaze with lights from its entrance to the turret. The drawing rooms and ballroom were adorned with heavy drapes and decorated with masses of flowers.

Local people began to arrive about nine o'clock. Drivers waited patiently along the carriage-way for their turn to guide their horses to the steps of the great veranda where the music of the San Luis Obispo band made each person's arrival exciting.

At 9:45 that evening, the music for the grand march began. Mr. Rathbun could draw a deep breath. The big event was underway.

The ladies of San Luis Obispo had never looked more beautiful. Mrs. J. H. Hollister, there with her husband from Chorro Ranch, was wearing black lace over apple green silk and a diamond necklace that Brooks felt compelled to try to describe. Mrs. Edwin Goodall, whose husband had promoted the hotel, wore "blue moire, white lace draperies."

Chauncey Phillips, down from Templeton, proudly watched his daughters on the dance floor. Miss Lyda wore a cream-colored silk dress and Miss Jennie wore nile green and lace. R. E. Jack danced with Mrs. Jack, who wore a beautiful pink moire with a gauze overdress. She, too, wore diamond jewelry.

Mrs. J. M. Fillmore, whose husband managed the local Pacific Coast Railway, caught everyone's eye in her lavender silk gown with lace overdress. Judge Beebee's wife wore a cream silk and black velvet drapery with hand-painted flowers and birds. Her jewelry included both pearls and diamonds.

Mrs. C. W. Dana was stunning in her black velvet and red silk gown. Mrs. H. W. Fiske wore cream Nuns' veiling and flowers, and Mrs. Venable, the judge's wife, wore a black silk entrain with jet trim. Mrs. H. M. Warden pleased the crowd in garnet silk and velvet.

Brooks called on his wife to help him record all that he was seeing. Mrs. Brooks wore an attractive claret gown with a golden train and a diamond necklace and brooch.

Many of the men, especially the young bachelors, wore swallow-tailed coats and diamond studs to please the unmarried daughters of San Luis Obispo's elite families.

When dancers wanted a break, they adjourned to the hotel's breakfast room and selected from a bountiful table of good things to eat. They also strolled on the wide veranda across the front and alongside the hotel.

Brooks observed activities from the sidelines, the dance floor, the veranda, and the buffet table. He talked to everyone, and listened to the waltzes. The evening was filled with talk about money, politics and a variety of intrigue. All seemed well with the world.

At the end of the evening, with a packet of notes, Brooks hurried back to the newspaper office and hand-set the type for a story.[7]

AT ABOUT THE SAME TIME THAT San Luis Obispo people celebrated their new hotel, a grand opening for the great new Del Monte Hotel in Monterey was also being planned.

There was also a great deal of activity in Paso Robles. Until the arrival of the railroad, Paso Robles had been little more than a private village. But soon afterward, F. P. McCray of Hollister was hired to lay out a town site around the hotel. G. F. Spurrier and Van R. Elliott later completed the survey begun by McCray. Lots were sold in a series of auctions with much promotion and a brass band.

Blackburn and James set aside two full city blocks for a public park in the heart of the new town. This park exists today. After the park was laid out, a planting day was held and each citizen brought his donation. For a long time afterward, trees and bushes in the park were referred to by the names of their donors—"Dr. Call's tree," "Mr. Shackleford's pines," etc. A bandstand was built with funds raised through a series of stage shows featuring local talent.

At a later date, its now historic Carnegie Library was built in the park. However, the town was not without a library before that time. The first town library had opened in a room of the Blackburn home with one hundred donated books. Miss Lillian Wright was the librarian.

At the time the city was laid out, Drury James was clearly the dominant person in the hotel and land development partnership. Daniel Blackburn was seventy years old, and James Blackburn was dead. Cecelia, Daniel's wife, was trustee for James Blackburn's estate.

Paso Robles was incorporated in an election held on February 25, 1889. Drury James was the first president of the new city's Board of Trustees. Dr. J. H. Glass, who became resident physician at the resort, was also a trustee. Other trustees were W. E. Grant, John M. Van Warmer, and R. E. Jack, who was treasurer. W. R. Stokes was appointed city attorney.

During the same year the city was incorporated, plans for a completely new Hotel El Paso de Robles were unveiled, the biggest event in the history of the resort. The structure would take at least two years to build, and it was to be the grandest hotel ever built in San Luis Obispo County.

Without fanfare, the new Hotel El Paso de Robles opened for business October 12, 1891. Spurred by the arrival of the Southern Pacific Railroad, the town incorporated. Featuring its hot springs, the hotel continued the tradition of the earlier hotel as a health spa and resort.

People of the new town and the county watched with anticipation and excitement. The newspapers followed the event closely. In September of that first year, the *Tribune*'s stringer-reporter wrote: "The new hotel looms up grandly now that the kitchen and dining room walls are done and work has been so pushed that the main front is halfway up the window sides. The carpenters will soon begin finishing the roof on the rear."

At the same time, grain teams moved in and out of the town burdened with the fruits of bountiful crops. Two new warehouses had been recently built to meet storage needs, one by the Southern Pacific Milling Company and the other by the Grangers' organization.

However, construction of the hotel did not go smoothly. Apparently the owners met with financial difficulties which completely stopped work for many months. It was a sad sight to see. Located in the very heart of Paso Robles, this incomplete building, larger than anything in the town, simply waited while financial help was sought.

During June 1890, the *Leader* announced that work would again begin on the hotel. It also announced that Drury James did not go to San Luis Obispo to pledge stock of the hotel company in order to raise money to complete the structure.

In addition to financial difficulties, there was also some faulty construction. Architect Len-

zen ordered the brick work over the east and south entrances to the hotel torn down and relaid because it had settled in misshaped fashion. The lack of work at the hotel had some bad effects on both the economy and the optimism of the town, but people were quickly encouraged when the sounds of hammers and saws were heard again.

Meantime, the old Paso de Robles Hotel continued operations. In the heart of the summer in 1890, the *Tribune*'s stringer wrote: "The Hotel Paso de Robles has between 150 and 175 guests and more coming on every train. Cripples of every description, invalid chairs, crutches and canes are too numerous to mention."

At the same time, the town was getting an "electric light works." The franchise had been granted to the Southern Pacific Milling Company, and by November 1890, they announced that a dynamo was ready for use. Stores, offices and residences were being "fitted up" with incandescent lights. Light poles were first erected on Eleventh, Twelfth, Spring, Oak, and Pine streets.

Land sales in and around the town seemed to be active again and the trustees wrestled with the decision of establishing a street railway line.

When the year of 1890 came to a close the new hotel had been painted on the outside and plastered on the inside, but there was still much to do.

It was not until June 5, 1891 that a most

historical change in the ownership of the hotel occurred. A new round of excitement passed through the town, for it was generally known that new owners and fresh capital would hasten the hotel's completion.

The *Tribune* was quite blunt about the reasons for the change. "It had appeared," the newspaper announced, "that there was a certain lack of harmony in the old management which seriously interfered with the energetic prosecution of the plans for the development of this celebrated property. Times have changed and the easy-going management which for a generation past met all the necessities of travel will no longer answer."

Early day swimmers and attendants pose for this postcard photo of the Paso Robles Hot Springs Plunge.

For years the hotel's bathhouse was nearly a mile from the hotel, but eventually this one was built on the hotel grounds.

So, then, the Blackburn name was no longer associated with the property which Daniel Blackburn had built in that wilderness spot so many years earlier. Drury James was now controlling stockholder.

The new corporation was called El Paso de Robles Springs Company. It had issued 1,000 shares of stock at $500 a share. While James and his wife, Louisa, were majority stockholders, two other men were now large shareholders. They were Hiram Shackelford and W. M. Coward. E. F. Burns, the hotel's manager, owned four shares and B. D. Murphy held two shares.

On October 12, 1891, the new Hotel El Paso de Robles opened its doors for business. It was

With its reputation for hot springs, the city of Paso Robles built a municipal bathhouse near the park in the town center.

not an event. The manager and the owners
simply declared this day as the beginning of
operations. The day before, a Sunday, the dining room had begun serving meals.

It was fully expected that the hotel would be
the beginning of extraordinary growth for the
new town. "There is not a vacant store room in
Paso Robles today and more are in the course of
construction and are rented in advance," the
Paso Robles Leader reported. "Our mechanics
and artisans are all busy, and everything ahead
looks as though a season of prosperity has come
to our city."

*An early photo of guests relaxing on the veranda of
the El Paso de Robles Hotel.*

*This old photo displays the in-
terior architecture of the Solarium at the El Paso de Robles at
the turn of the century while
guests relax in cane-seated rock-
ers and wicker chairs in an
atmosphere of indoor plants.*

The hotel was three stories high with 285 feet
of frontage. Circular towers extended over the
north and south wings, and a solarium had
been built into a large square tower rising over
the center of the building. It provided both
sunshine and a magnificent view of the countryside. The veranda was sixteen feet wide and
ran around three sides of the hotel. It served as a
spacious, covered open-air promenade. The
main entrance to the hotel led into a large
lobby.

"The large rooms in front on the ground
floor consisted of parlors, billiard rooms, reading rooms, club meeting rooms, a saloon and a
barber shop," the *Leader* said.

The dining room would "comfortably" accommodate three hundred guests.

The building was constructed of solid ma-

sonry with handsome sandstone arches, and the
Tribune said that it was "absolutely fireproof."
It had cost $160,000 to build.

"The Hotel El Paso de Robles," the *Tribune*
said, "is furnished throughout in elegant style,
the parlors being equal to those in the first
hotels of San Francisco.[8]

Large hotels now existed in both of San Luis
Obispo County's largest communities, but
Paso Robles had a clear edge for growth because
railroad line from San Francisco went through
it. San Luis Obispo still waited.

CHAPTER XII

Land Subscriptions

Interest continued among businessmen and landowners in developing an east-west railroad running from Fresno and Bakersfield to the coast. At the beginning of 1888, a group of San Luis Obispo businessmen succeeded in stirring interest in the prospect of a railroad line from Port Harford to the San Joaquin Valley, and before its demise later that year, the San Luis Obispo Board of Trade had held a number of meetings on the subject.

It was difficult to estimate the motivation of some of the men discussing this movement, but

erally understood to be the peculiar and sacred function of some bloated monopoly. But the bloated monopoly in its inception has been usually the confederation under some high-sounding name of a gang of lean and impecunious gentry with no knowledge of railroad construction, but with a healthy and assorted lot of unscrupulous and predatory instincts.

"The open secret of this success is to stock the road for four times its cost, bond it for enough to build with, and then charge four freights to pay the interest and dividends.

When local speculators discussed construction of a railroad from the San Joaquin Valley to Port Harford, they envisioned the development of this port at Avila where the Pacific Coast Railway carried goods and passengers to meet Pacific Coast Steamship Company vessels. In this old photo, the little narrow-gauge engine pulls two passenger cars along the wharf where passengers boarded the waiting ship enroute to either Los Angeles or San Francisco.

most of them were disgusted with the seeming lack of action by Southern Pacific, and some might have hoped that such a railroad line would be their path to riches.

Certainly Benjamin Brooks had become unhappy with Southern Pacific and was going out of his way to encourage a line from inland California to the coast. Southern Pacific construction had stopped, as Brooks had predicted, after arrival of the line at Santa Margarita.

"Railroad building," Brooks wrote, "is gen-

"Incidentally, there are unconsiderable trifles to be picked up in town sites, ranches to subdivide and sell on shares, warehouse privileges and 'trusts' which eke out the boodle."

So, Brooks strongly advocated that local investors get behind the development of a railroad from the coast to the inland valley, and not worry about Southern Pacific and its continuous demands.

The various developers kept advertising, however, hoping to convince people of the

Luigi Marre with a partner built the Marre Hotel at the edge of the wharf in 1885. It served visitors into the new century as they arrived by ship or railway. Until a few years ago many local people recalled the social activities at the old hotel.

money-making opportunities of buying land before the railroad arrived.[1]

❧

WHEN CHRISTMAS ARRIVED in 1888, people throughout San Luis Obispo County took pause to count their blessings, admittedly mixed. There was tragedy for some.

People who frequented the Ramona Hotel for various social occasions made up an informal group which the *Tribune* liked to refer to as the "Ramona Club." This group sponsored a hop on Christmas Eve which included good music, dancing, and a late supper. The Cosmopolitan Hotel offered a big Christmas Eve dinner which also attracted people, and all of the local saloons in town provided a special egg nog drink for celebrants.

There was a Christmas party for employees at Crocker's General Store, and they surprised Crocker with a gift of a very elegant and costly cane. At both Maenorchor and Sauer Halls, there were celebrations that included beautiful Christmas trees loaded with presents, singing and dancing.

But for the citizens of the town of San Miguel, celebration turned into chaos and tragedy.

The evening started happily. Most of the people in the small town gathered in San Miguel Hall. The orchestra started playing and people began to dance. The place was crowded, and since this was a family occasion, there were many children present. Some of the entertainment had been planned especially for them.

Frank Marshall's three-piece "orchestra" entertained on Saturday nights at the Marre Hotel. In an early issue of La Vista, the late Hazel Hansen recalled the many times that she and Grant walked from their general store in Avila with the baby in arms to dance until the wee hours before walking back home.

Publisher Burns of the *San Miguel Messenger* didn't arrive at the party as early as the others, but after he closed the print shop he hurried along the muddy street toward the hall, enjoying the music on his way.

That's when he caught a glimpse of the red flickering in the dark on Mission Street. There was no doubt about what he was seeing. He started running toward the hall to tell everyone.

The sounds of merriment stopped immediately with Burns' cry of fire. It was about 8:30 P.M. People rushed to the door to see where Burns was pointing, toward the roof of the little Central Hotel on Mission Street. In the dark December night, flames already lighted second floor windows and flickered above the roof.

Every able man and woman rushed to help. Women filled water buckets, bucket brigades formed at the nearest well, and people appeared with blankets to fight embers flying across the dry wooden buildings of the town. In moments, the hotel was a cauldron of flames, and it was too late to remove contents.

Firefighting equipment was nonexistent in San Miguel, and the fire threatened to destroy the town unless its path was somehow hurriedly blocked. Some citizens concentrated on removing and saving merchandise from the general store and from the shoe store, but if these buildings were foreordained to burn, the fire would also spread to others. A crew began the fast destruction of Methener's building. They literally dragged the building from its lot, and succeeded within a short time in making a fifty-foot space in the path of the raging fire. Eugene Gorham worked so hard and so long that he fell in a faint with exhaustion. While wetting down the roof of Neal's Drug Store, Ralph Reed fell and was badly shaken. Fortunately, he wasn't injured. Charley Davis lost one of his shin protectors when he got caught up on a nail in dismantling Methener's building.

people were late to church, but there was a special thanks because all were alive, none seriously hurt, and most of the town's buildings had been saved.[2]

❧

ON THE FIRST DAY of the new year, 1889, John Geiger, the county agent, accidentally took a big dunking at Port Harford. The steamship *Queen of the Pacific* was leaving Port Harford while Mr. Geiger was still on board. As the *Queen* moved gingerly away from the wharf, Mr. Geiger concluded his business and stepped from the ship's deck.

At that moment, a big wave rolled the vessel, and Geiger found himself falling between the ship and the wharf into the water. He struggled to regain the surface just as another wave rolled him against the piles of the wharf and within reach of a dangling rope.

Geiger seldom removed his hat outdoors, but the cold water over his balding head told him that he had lost it during his fall. He looked desperately about him, saw his hat and grabbed

In this rare photo at Port Harford, a Pacific Coast Railway engine as well as the warehouse and a steamship are visible. This photo was probably taken from a window of the Marre Hotel.

But at last, the fire was confined to the hotel and the buildings next to it. The bucket brigade continued throughout the night until those buildings were smouldering ashes.

In the morning, with the battle won, exhausted and dirty citizens walked slowly home, talking and wondering how the fire had started. Did it start with a careless match? A defective flue? Mr. Burns reasoned that the fire started in the hotel entrance hall from an upset lamp.

That Christmas Day in San Miguel, a few

it, quickly clapping it back on his head. Some of the dock workers soon pulled him out of the water and up to the wharf.

A little later someone asked him about the temperature of the water. "Two or three degrees above zero," he remarked dourly.[3]

❧

IN APRIL OF THAT YEAR, word came down the Cuesta to San Luis Obispo that the Southern Pacific Railroad depot at Santa Margarita was completed. It had five rooms upstairs and handled passengers and freight on the ground floor.

The Southern Pacific Milling Company established a warehouse near the tracks in the new town to accommodate farmers in the vicinity. Mr. Sheerin, the company's agent, had disappeared temporarily, and the word around town was that he would soon reappear with a wife from San Jose.

With railroad construction ended at Santa Margarita, people reported that things were very quiet. "The new paint glares in the sunshine, the flies buzz, the cattle graze in the distance," a *Tribune* stringer reported.

❦

During an interview with reporters in San Francisco, Southern Pacific Company's president, Collis Huntington, said that he might travel to the end of the coastal line and look around. True to his promise, Huntington and a party of executives and consultants arrived in San Luis Obispo about 2:00 P.M. on April 9, 1889. They had come by train as far as Santa Margarita, then by stage through the Cuesta to the Ramona Hotel.

Huntington was accompanied by the vice president, Charles Crocker; the superintendent of the Coast Division, A. C. Bassett; the chief engineer, William Hood; and the president's secretary, G. E. Miles.

Although Huntington sent little advance notice, the word spread quickly, and he agreed to speak in the new agricultural pavilion that evening. An estimated fifteen hundred people packed the pavilion.

Judge Adams opened the meeting and called for a president of the evening. E. W. Steele of Arroyo Grande was immediately nominated and elected. Several prominent citizens were then named as vice-presidents of the evening, and they were asked to sit on the stage. Myron Angel was elected secretary. Charles H. Johnson, L. M. Warden, H. E. McBride, R. E. Jack, and several others were called upon for an expression of sentiment.

The big man of the Southern Pacific Railroad Company was in the town of San Luis Obispo sitting on the stage of the new pavilion on Monterey Street. What an occasion! It was time for the leaders of the town to shine, and each provided his best oratory.

Then Collis Huntington was introduced to tumultuous ovation. He was tired and said so, speaking very frankly: "Now, we are sixteen miles from here, and if you were to give us the right-of-way, and it was all straight and the title was perfect and the ground that we would want for the shops and depot purposes was provided, I expect we might commence work at the building of the road.

"As far as I am personally concerned I would just as soon you would be ten years about it as not—in fact, rather.

"I have been working steadily for fifty-three years," he said tiredly, "and I feel I should like to quit, but still, I think that we will have to work along."

Both Huntington and then Crocker intimated that the expense and difficulty of building tunnels through the Cuesta was discouraging. Crocker, too, said that Southern Pacific would wait for clear right-of-way and other concessions before commencing construction through the Cuesta.

L. M. Warden heard the words of Huntington and Crocker as a commitment that if right-of-way land were provided over the grade and into San Luis Obispo, Southern Pacific would build a line into the town. He moved that another meeting be held the next evening in the pavilion.

Huntington and his party excused themselves at the earliest possible moment and returned to the Ramona Hotel.[4]

The next morning the visitors boarded a special train of the Pacific Coast narrow gauge. It took them to Los Olivos with stops enroute. At Santa Maria a delegation of citizens boarded the cars with special offerings of local flowers, fruits and gifts. Huntington was so pleased that he had the gifts loaded on top of the stage that took him back to Santa Margarita that night.

A much smaller group was present the next night at the pavilion in San Luis Obispo. A committee of twenty-one men was appointed to develop a plan. The twenty-one were L. M. Kaiser, R. E. Jack, L. M. Warden, E. W. Steele, J. P. Andrews, H. E. McBride, P. H. Dallidet,

Jr., J. M. Felts, H. M. Warden, Morris Goldtree, B. Sinsheimer, Ernest Graves, C. H. Johnson, L. Rackliffe, E. P. Unangst, W. Sandercock, Benjamin Brooks, W. W. Hays, V. A. Gregg, J. N. Turner, and George T. Gragg.

With the word from Huntington establishing the fact that the railroad wasn't in a hurry to continue construction to San Luis Obispo and that, in any case, they did not intend to wrangle or get caught up in lawsuits or hold-ups by landowners about rights-of-way, the committee of twenty-one was beginning its work from zero.

Some people felt that landowners along the proposed route of the Southern Pacific were duty bound to give up land for the cause and for the good of all. For large landowners, it was generally conceded, giving land to Southern Pacific was a sound business deal. The line through their land increased values and offered bright new money-making opportunities.

However, there were also many small landowners. What about them? A railroad line through small holdings would ruin homes and orchards, and split small acreage into useless divisions. What was their duty to the cause? All kinds of advice were offered.

"All this criticism of our efforts and methods," Brooks wrote, "this vigorous prodding of this city, this wise advice of how to do and how not to do, these assurances that the eyes of our neighbors are upon us, strike us as exhibiting a profound degree of magnificent and cold-blooded gall."

Brooks made it clear that the railroad might not be initially good for everybody and criticism of those who had nothing to gain and much to lose was nothing more than "insolent interference."

"If it is agreed that it would be profitable and advisable to grant the right-of-way," Brooks said, "it remains to be ascertained by whom. When it lies through a great ranch like the Paso Robles or the Santa Margarita or through a city like San Luis Obispo, other interests may be so remote that they cannot be expected to contribute.

"But with respect to lands...[like those] lying between the summit of the Cuesta grade and the boundaries of this city... the tracts are small through which the road would pass, but... [for the owners] are very valuable. No one will say that they will be benefited by the building of the road through them.

"... [These] owners must be fairly compensated—But who should pay it? Certainly not the city of San Luis Obispo. This city will be sufficiently burdened if it provides the right-of-way through its own limits. In our opinion the [money] should come from all the landowners to be benefited. From the Wardens and all the property owners of the Los Osos; from Messrs. McCoppin, Grant, Steele, Orcutt, Goldtree, Hollister, Venable, Hersman, Murphy, the West Coast Land Company and the land owners clear to San Jose. From the beneficiaries should come the cost..."

Brooks wasn't making friends among the affluent with this kind of editorial, but he surely made the problem clear to everyone.[5]

The committee of twenty-one began calling upon property owners known to have land along the proposed railroad route. They sought contracts of sale from owners which they intended to use as a basis for a subscription drive within the city and county. E. P. Unangst was secretary to the committee. William Hood of the Southern Pacific said that maps showing the proposed route through the Cuesta pass and through the town of San Luis Obispo had been completed and would be sent to the committee.

By May 3, 1889, committee members had succeeded in acquiring contracts of sales for fifty-five lots, forty-two of them at an average price of about $185 each.

At a meeting held at the Cosmopolitan Hotel, the committee determined to raise money from taxpayers through contributions to buy the property. Different rates were applied for landowners within the city, those owning property within a radius of five miles of the city, and those whose land was even more distant.

Brooks explained the details of assessment to his readers: "Saturday morning [May 11, 1889] our citizens may expect the visit of committeemen to secure their promise to pay 3% of the value of their property, according to the county assessment roll of 1888 to purchase the right-of-way for the railroad. We trust there is no taxpayer in this city who will refuse."

The monied men of the town, Brooks said, were fairly well committed and were setting the example. The town had been divided into fourteen districts, and a subscription agent had been appointed in each district. Committee members lived in the districts for which they were responsible. Brooks listed the following: R. D. Loomis, P. H. Dallidet, Ernest Graves, J. M. Felts, W. W. Hays, B. Sinsheimer, Morris Goldtree, J. C. Castro, E. W. Steele, Ben Brooks, H. M. Warden, George Gragg, C. J. Russell, and William Sandercock.

The executive committee sometimes met all day organizing and planning the details of their undertaking. Brooks published a list of property owners to be contacted and followed up with a list of those who agreed to an assessment of three percent, exemplifying the spirit of the undertaking. He headlined one news story, "Preparing for Today's Canvass; The Subscription Agents Ready to Go on the War Path."

"From present appearances," he wrote, "the community is practically a unit in the determination to meet the propositions of the railroad, and with that spirit general success is certain."

As Collis Huntington prepared to leave San Francisco to return to the East Coast, a *San Francisco Call* reporter asked him about plans in San Luis Obispo County. Huntington left the West Coast saying, "The matter is in the hands of the people there. As soon as they have obtained the right-of-way for us, as they have promised, and made arrangements to give us depot grounds, we will go ahead. Until then, our terminus will be at Santa Margarita."

At a meeting of the committee, the secretary, E. P. Unangst, read a letter he had received from Colonel C. F. Crocker of the Southern Pacific Company: "Referring to my letter of the 26th [April], I send you by express today, maps made in two sections showing on a large scale the right-of-way and depot grounds shaded in pink. In order to facilitate your work, we have concluded to accept either one of two sites for the depot, and I therefore send you tracings of both: one near Osos streets and one near Hathway Avenue . . . "

He promised to send another map showing which streets it would be desirable to close after San Luis Obispo citizens determined where they wanted the depot located.[6]

So, the town buzzed with activity during the month of May 1889, but things did not go perfectly, by any means.

Brooks wrote an editorial calling attention to the problems. "We have heard it intimated, and we have heard it with shame and regret, that there are those amongst us who by position and fortune ought to be considered as our leaders who announce that they will do nothing. Nothing! Imagine it!"

He scolded these local landmen: "Now," he said, "they refuse to share even to the trifling extent proposed because in their cold-blooded shrewdness, they conclude that they will be able to evade their just share of the public burden; that their fellow citizens will make up for their meanness and penuriousness and will pay their share for them."

Brooks called the situation a crisis. He predicted that if the citizens of the county failed in this effort to clear railroad right-of-way land, the town would be abandoned by half of its businesses. It would lose its place as county seat to Paso Robles, and much of its land would become practically worthless.

"We race out at great speed for a short distance and then we stop," he said. "We must go ahead, and instantly."

Certain monied individuals were holding out against contributing to the cause and although Brooks never mentioned these men by name, everyone in the community probably knew who they were. Strong community pressure was brought to bear, and Brooks, in his editorials, scolded and coerced them, always leaving the door open for them to change their minds. "They will soon see the light," he suggested. "They will not let the community down."[7]

Clever contributors provided Brooks with satirical material to help get certain people in line. For example, here is a piece of verse which was published and signed Greenleaf.

A Railroad Soliloquy

A stage coach or a railroad? That is the question!
Whether 'tis better for the town to suffer
The Antinomians to control her destiny,
Or to whip out the laggards.

And by opposing, end them. To die, to sleep,
And by a sleep, to say we end
The close-fisted silurians and misers
The town is cursed with! 'Tis a consummation
Devoutly to be wished. To die, to kill
   trade,
   business.
To paralyze business: Ay, there's the rub;
For in that paralysis what other towns may grow
When this one shuffles off the railroad?

The Shakespearian verse was aimed directly at those who declined to contribute three percent of the assessed value of their property to buy land for the railroad. The "third book" of Chronicles was also brought to bear on the subject of the railroad in a long list of verses using local names. Some of them read:

1. Now in the first year of the reign of Benjamin the Hoosierite, and in the second of Waterman, the local governor, behold there came unto the town called San Luis, one Collis, whose surname was Huntington, and one Charles, whose surname was Crocker;

2. And these men were mighty in the building of tunnels and of roads, even railroads.

3. And the people of the town went out to meet these men, saying we have heard of the great multitudes going from east unto the west, even unto California; but lo, they come not here; neither do we see the color of their shekels.

4. We pray thee, therefore, to grant us a means of transportation, that we may dispose of our herds and our olives and the blood of the grape and the orange and the pomegranate.

6. Then Collis, who was also called a king, made answer and said, O people of San Luis, I am greatly troubled and sore vexed at suits at law, wherein some of the subjects of Andrew, whose surname was Jackson, are determined to take much silver and gold and treasure out of my coffers.

7. Therefore, to the end that peace may reign in the land, we beseech thee to procure for us the land upon which to lay the rails of our road.

8. Then Collis leaned heavily on his staff and looked at the people, and saith further, I am weary and full of years and care not any more for honor or flattery.

9. So make not resolutions, but give up thy loins and go out and seek the owners of these lands and get upon parchment the roll of the people and of the peoples' shekels, and come and give to me the deeds; and on that day shalt the building of the road be begun.

10. Then, the people raised a great shout and went and took Edgar, whose surname was Steele, and put him in a high place before them, and demanded of him that he appoint messengers, even one and twenty messengers, who should go out among the people, at their houses, and wrestle with them and exhort them unto righteousness and progress.

The author tells of E. W. Steele, chairman of the committee of twenty-one, appointing men of the community to seek subscriptions. He tells of some of their successes, but . . .

14. But there lived in the midst of the community one man who was mighty by reason of having much gold and silver and precious stones.

15. And this man was a changer of money and did dwell in a house built with iron and stone.

This man was apparently difficult to approach, and he gave those contacting him about contributing a very bad time. People also listened to him when he suggested the whole undertaking was a bad business venture. So, some people began to have serious doubts about the undertaking. The writer then predicted the end in his "Chronicles."

23. So there fell down slain of San Luis four thousand men and women and children.

24. Thus the mighty man, with his gold and his silver and precious stones, lived in the land alone and his treasure soon became a burden because the people had been gathered to their fathers.

Finally, the "Chronicles" predicted, even the rich villain died.[8]

A letter to the editor in the May 17, 1889 *Tribune* said, "Disguise the fact as you may, flatter yourselves if you will, nevertheless, today our prospects for complying with the requirements of the railroad company are very poor.

"The committee [members] are trying to 'whistle through the graveyard,' but they must acknowledge the fact that, at this time, they have but very little hope of success.

"...Now if the banks, hotels, owners of large tracts of land, the water, gas, telephone and other companies, who will receive the greatest benefit, do not immediately come to the rescue, the cause is lost."

The writer made a final point: if the individuals and businesses most able to solve the problem were not interested, the committee should not attempt to continue.

L. M. Warden, whose ranch holdings were in the Los Osos Valley, considered failure of the committee disastrous for both farmers and businessmen. "If we don't make it," he said, "we can only expect destruction, bankruptcy and coyotes." He willingly pledged his three percent subscription.

J. P. Andrews, San Luis Obispo's most successful banker, believed in the community, and all of his financial interests were within the county. He was the major stockholder in the bank and many other local enterprises. He felt that the railroad had no choice but to build through the town, but was less committal than some others about donating three percent of the assessed value of his business to the cause. "I am called a kicker," he said. "Perhaps I am, but I believe in San Luis...I will be my own judge of my actions, but you may depend upon it, although I do not always show my hand, I am friendly to public enterprises..."

It was generally known that Andrews favored routing the railroad along Stenner Creek. William Hood of Southern Pacific disagreed and wrote Andrews accordingly.

Opinion ran rampant, but too many of the men who should have been participating remained noncommittal.[9]

Greenleaf provided more parables comparing San Luis Obispo's plight to the flood and Noah's Ark, and Brooks kept the honor list of contributors on the front page of every issue of the *Tribune*. At the same time, it was hard to write enthusiastically about the prospects of the railroad.

"These are rather gloomy days for the county town," Brooks said. "Its friends are few. Its sister towns regard it with rather unfriendly eyes. The San Francisco papers...lose no opportunity of maligning us." But he had to admit that some landowners were holding their property at exorbitant prices determined to make a killing from its sale.

There had been continuous objection by the men who made up the syndicate that owned the Ramona Hotel about Southern Pacific's plan to build track at the very back door of the new hotel. R. E. Jack, chairman of the citizens' committee raising subscriptions, asked Edwin Goodall, president of the company that owned the hotel, to explain his position. Goodall expressed his view in a letter to Jack:

"...I very much regret that the protection of the property in which the syndicate is directly interested makes it necessary for me to appear as an obstructionist.

"There is an old and generally accepted maxim that self protection is the first law of nature. I think it is unreasonable for one property holder to expect another to voluntarily make sacrifices; in other words to ruin his own property for the benefit of his neighbor or the public....I am not sufficiently patriotic or philanthropic to ruin my own property for the benefit of others.

"The building of the railroad along Johnson Street [in back of the hotel] would in my opinion practically ruin the Ramona Hotel... I was informed...by the railroad...that the road could be thrown back another block without...additional expense...What I would very much prefer, even to this, would be to see the road run down around the other end of the town, say, along Stenner Creek.

"I am...willing, on behalf of the syndicate, to pay my proportion, [providing] the line is changed as suggested, but I certainly will not contribute anything, nor will I grant any right-of-way [under the present plan].

"If the line of the road is thrown back another block...I am willing to contribute the right-of-way through the Central addition and through the Ingleside lots [both city subdivisions developed by the company]."

In this letter, which was read to the committee by R. E. Jack and reported in the *Tribune*, Goodall clarified the position of the company which owned the hotel.[10]

The subscription committee met with many property-owner demands along the proposed route. Lots considered to be worth about one hundred dollars suddenly became valued at three or four hundred dollars for railroad beds. Suburban land selling for fifty dollars an acre went up to seventy-five. Chaparral lands worth seventy-five cents to five dollars an acre had new prices as high as two hundred and fifty dollars an acre.

The proposed change of route by Goodall from the east to the west side of San Luis Obispo now left the committee helpless. It was decided to submit a new road plan to Southern Pacific for acceptance before wasting additional energy seeking land that would not be used.

With a new road plan in hand, a committee of stalwart citizens was appointed by R. E. Jack to go to San Francisco and talk to Southern Pacific officials. But everything had to be delayed for the celebration of the Fourth of July.[11]

༒

A "GRAND FREE BASKET PICNIC" was planned for Independence Day at Hot Sulphur Wells near Avila with music provided by the San Luis Military Band. Judge Adams was going to provide oration and appropriate exercises to

Pacific Coast Railway warehouse, Lower Higuera and old French road, now Madonna Road. Original location of roundhouse and railroad repair shops.

This Pacific Coast Railway trestle across San Luis Obispo Creek at Avila was a standing remnant until the middle 1980's when it collapsed on the beach during a heavy storm.

suit the occasion. Dancing and entertainment were also planned.

The *Paso Robles Leader* produced a three-sheet poster promoting the holiday events in Paso Robles—a picnic, barbecue and ball with patriotic oration by Captain W. D. Haley.

Los Alamos announced a "Monster Fourth of July Celebration" on large posters printed in red, white and blue. Among the attractions was the "celebrated puzzle" called "Pigs in clover" played with live porkers.

Both Cambria and Cayucos planned music, picnics and entertainment for the day.[12]

Throughout that summer of 1889, towns and organizations in the county collected donations and held money-making events to assist victims of the tragic Johnstown flood. The *Tribune* office served as headquarters for the receipt of funds and forwarded them to a headquarters office in Johnstown.

That same summer a utility plant placed poles and wires for providing electricity in San Luis Obispo. Incandescent lights were soon available. The charges for service at a given location were $1.25 a month for lights burning until 9:00 P.M., $1.75 for lights burning until midnight, and $3.25 for lights burning all night.[13]

When San Luis Obispo's Board of Trustees asked for suggestions from citizens about needed conveniences, one citizen suggested that one street be designated as the "wood market." He suggested Garden Street between Higuera and Marsh be used for this purpose. The objective was to reduce congestion downtown by getting wood peddlers' wagons off the business streets. This same citizen recommended building a watering trough at some central location other than on the main business streets. This idea was also offered as a partial solution to solving the heavy horse and carriage traffic on downtown streets.[14]

San Luis Obispo's delegation to San Francisco was most hospitably received by William Hood at Southern Pacific Railroad offices located at Fourth and Townsend streets.

The members of the delegation first discussed their desire to change the railroad routing in San Luis Obispo from the east to the west side of town along Stenner Creek. Then, most politely, they were ushered into a large executive office to be greeted by none other than the former president of the railroad, Leland Stanford; the vice president, Charles Crocker; and A. N. Towne, general manager of the San Francisco office.

Once again they explained their desire for a change in road routing. Hood gave his bosses assurance that the plan was workable. Finally, Crocker said that he would submit the plan to the company's Board of Directors, and it would

Front view of the Victorian-styled lighthouse above Port San Luis. In 1990, a celebration hailed its centennial year. In 1992, the U.S. Coast Guard transferred its ownership to the San Luis Obispo Harbor Commission. In 1993, the Nature Conservancy opened the Pecho Trail for docent-led hikes to the lighthouse.

be given the same attention as if it had originated with the company's own engineers.

The committee left the offices of Southern Pacific Company feeling successful.[15]

ONE DAY IN LATE JULY 1889, Benjamin Brooks hurried from the newspaper office, jumped aboard a horse-drawn streetcar on Higuera Street and arrived at the depot on lower Higuera just in time to board the narrow gauge to Port Harford.

The Pacific Coast Railway manager had extended an invitation to a number of local businessmen to inspect progress being made by

scow. The scow delivered and dumped the boulders along the line of the breakwater. During the previous winter, one scow had been driven ashore and wrecked upon the rocks. Its remains were still visible.

"Looking along the shore toward the Pacific Coast Railway wharf and thence to Avila," Brooks wrote, "one [can] see where, in the future, [there will be] a succession of piers where hundreds of vessels [may] find ample accommodation."

Whenever railroad activity bogged down, it was encouraging to review again the schedule of cargo and passenger steamships docking regularly at Port San Luis.[16]

The town of Avila in 1912. The Pacific Coast narrow-gauge line continued its regular runs to Avila at the time.

a government construction crew on a breakwater at Port San Luis. Upon arrival at the wharf, the party boarded small boats and were rowed to the little island just off the point at the harbor. Brooks inspected a rock breakwater that had been laid between the island and the mainland, a distance of about one hundred yards. It would soon be extended beyond the island into deeper water.

He found a shed on the high point of the island where a blacksmith and his helper were constantly at work welding chains broken in connection with the harbor work.

On shore, where the rocks were being quarried, the editor watched boulders being girdled with chain. A small steam hoisting engine lifted the boulders and swung them on board a

With the passage of time and no word from Southern Pacific about the committee's proposal for a change of route, R. E. Jack wrote a note to Col. Crocker. After proper reminders of the San Francisco meeting, Jack wrote:

"We are willing and anxious... to do the best we can in any direction as soon as the definite word is spoken... We respectfully request that, thereafter, we may consider it forever settled.

"... In procuring right-of-way thus far, we have taken many bonds running 90 days from their date and expiring now in about 40 days..."

we have received subscriptions amounting to $32,000 for . . . buying right-of-way and depot grounds.

"Is it agreeable on your part to give us such assurance, which this committee deems absolutely necessary for a further prosecution of its labors? Otherwise, the Van Winkle influence permeating this burgh will have fully mastered us, and you will hardly hear from us again for a thousand years."

No word came from Crocker, so Jack tried again in July 1889. At last, Crocker answered: "There is nothing new to be said . . . regarding the extension of the line from Santa Margarita; no change in the line as located has been made, and it is not probable that one will be made.

"With regard to a guaranty or pledge from the railroad company in the matter of construction, I am unable to add anything to what has already been said on this subject."

Time passed again and the committee received no word from Southern Pacific about altering their proposed route within the city of San Luis Obispo. The group was beginning to feel that the Southern Pacific executives were simply ignoring them. Some of the 120 contracts of sale initiated with landowners along the proposed railroad route were running out.

In late August 1889, R. E. Jack agreed to take a steamer to San Francisco to see if he could get some kind of a report. When he first arrived at Fourth and Townsend streets, no one was available to talk to him. After several fruitless visits, he succeeded in getting an appointment with Crocker. He told Crocker that the people of San Luis Obispo hoped for some specific assurances that if rights-of-way were secured for the railroad, work would actually begin within a reasonable time.

Crocker said he was not prepared to make any promises. The right-of-way must be given to Southern Pacific without any conditions. He pointed out to Jack that this line would cost the railroad nearly one and a half million dollars. The $30,000 or so which the people of San Luis Obispo might spend to acquire the land was not significant to the company.

Crocker spoke quite bluntly to Jack. He said the citizens' group in San Luis Obispo had been at work for nearly four months and had accomplished nothing. If they could not procure the right-of-way, they could let the matter rest, and when the railroad was ready to begin work, they would do so—condemning the property they needed.

Crocker said that the railroad was thoroughly familiar with San Luis country. He doubted that the oldest settler could tell them anything that they didn't already know. The railroad had adopted the route which they considered most feasible, and they could see no reason for changing it to suit a few local citizens or the syndicate that owned the Ramona Hotel. For all of the consoling efforts of Crocker and Stanford during the committee's previous visit, it appeared that communications with Huntington in the East had not convinced him that he should accept the proposal for the changed route.

Before leaving on the trip, Jack had talked once more to Goodall about the feelings of the Ramona Hotel syndicate. Goodall had remained firm about not wanting railroad track through the hotel property, especially at the back door of the hotel.

When Jack returned from San Francisco, committee members Steele, Rackliffe, L. M. and H. M. Warden, Sandercock, Kaiser, Castro, Unangst, Maddux, Brooks, and a few other interested citizens gathered at the Cosmopolitan Hotel to hear his report. Most people present were ready to drop the project, but E. W. Steele urged a more determined attitude. The town was defunct without a railroad, he said, and he urged the group to continue gathering agreements from landowners—to keep pushing. He felt strongly that there was nothing to lose, and everything to gain, by trying.

Chauncey Phillips of the West Coast Land Company was present in the group after a long absence. The committee urged that he join them in their efforts. At this point, Phillips stood and wagered J. P. Andrews a champagne supper that work on the railroad would commence within six months. People could not garner enthusiasm to match his challenge.[17]

During that same month, J. A. Fillmore, general superintendent for the Southern Pacific, was encountered one day at the Los Angeles depot by a reporter from the *Los Angeles Tribune*. Fillmore had arrived on the Sacramento, a

This imaginative painting depicts early San Luis Obispo Hot Sulphur Springs health spa. In 1993, it serves as a spa named Sycamore Springs.

special car of the railroad from San Francisco through the valley. He was with J. H. Wallace, superintendent of track laying and maintenance, and H. J. Small, superintendent of motive power. "When will you begin closing up the gap in the Ventura division between Elwood and Templeton?" the reporter asked.

"Not for ten years if I have my way," Fillmore remarked. "We have built to the mountains on either side and opened up a vast new country for development. To cross the mountains will entail a heavy expense and result only in a virtual paralleling of our own line to San Francisco.

"Of course," he said, "we will go into the town of San Luis Osispo, but it will be several years before there is an actual need of a through line there. We are ahead of the country now."

"What is the meaning of the accumulation of ties at San Pedro?" the reporter asked.

"They are for repairs. We will need about one million ties for repairs on the line this year."[18]

❦

GEORGE A. FAYLOR, THE EDITOR of the *Moon* at Paso Robles, didn't make it to the office to do any work that month of August, because of an accident.

He was driving a buckboard at the time. The floor of the vehicle was constructed of loose slats. He was carrying a double-barreled shotgun, the butt of the weapon resting on the slats. As he guided his horse along the winding, dusty trail in the direction of Templeton, he saw the gun slip through the slats. He reached and grabbed it at the top of the muzzle, but the butt

struck the ground and the gun discharged. He felt a sharp pain in his hand and fingers.

Alone on the trail, hand bleeding and blackened, Faylor sat shocked for a short time. Then, by sheer will, he resisted the pain and aimed the horse for Templeton as fast as he could travel. There he found assistance. The top of his thumb and index finger and all of the other fingers were shattered beyond recognition. With his permission, a doctor loaded Faylor with strong whiskey and amputated his fingers.

❦

Brooks received Southern Pacific Superintendent J. B. Fillmore's remarks about not extending track quite objectively. He found the statement consistent with Southern Pacific philosophy and the comments of other officials of the company during the year.

"Probably their immediate gains would not be largely increased by the completion of the through connection . . . meantime, they avoid the large outlay consequent upon crossing the formidable mountain barriers at the Cuesta and Gaviota passes," he wrote. " . . . While we are satisfied that the railroad people have a friendly regard for this city . . . we cannot . . . expect that they will put their kindly feelings to the painful test of consulting our interests," he told his readers.

The *San Francisco Bulletin* provided its readers a report about San Luis Obispo and the Southern Pacific Railroad. Among other reasons it gave for a holdup of the railroad was the fact that the right-of-way desired by Southern Pacific cut through the grounds of the Ramona

Hotel, an enterprise controlled by the Oregon Improvement Company, owners of the Pacific Coast Steamship Company and the Pacific Coast Railway.

"These companies," the *Bulletin* reported, "operating both the steamers . . . and the Pacific Coast Railway running southward from San Luis Obispo to Los Olivos, naturally have no desire for competition, and when it comes to granting right-of-way for such competition, strong objections are urged."

In San Luis Obispo, the committee of twenty-one seemed to have disbanded. There were no more meetings and no new plans. "Some of our readers may remember that there was formerly an institution known as the Committee of Twenty-One," Brooks wrote. The effort to change the right-of-way to follow Stenner Creek, a controversy about the location of the depot, and the complaints from the Ramona Hotel faction "rather sickened the gentlemen of the Committee," he said.

But the committee did meet to decide whether or not they should quit. Somehow, they could not really decide. Quitting, it seemed, would spell certain doom for San Luis Obispo.

Then, in September 1889, C. F. Crocker confirmed San Luis Obispo's worst expectations. He told a reporter with the *San Francisco Call*

that "when there [was] sufficient development to warrant it the Southern Pacific would build to San Luis Obispo and Santa Barbara . . . and not until then . . ." He said that there was "neither sufficient population nor development to justify further construction . . ."

Since activity related to the possible extension of the railroad through San Luis Obispo dominated the year 1889, Brooks felt compelled to refer to it in his editorial summation of the old year. He noted that the San Francisco press had made continuously slanderous remarks about San Luis Obispo and its citizens, and misrepresented the people in San Luis Obispo County.

He also felt that the people of San Luis Obispo had been betrayed by Southern Pacific. "Our citizens," he said, "were permitted to go on with their efforts to secure the right-of-way . . . for the road until we reached the point where condemnation was essential." At this point, assistance from the railroad was needed, "and it became manifest that the railroad company did not want anything done."

"We start the new year [1890] without any glittering mirage . . ."[19]

Five years had passed since the railroad first arrived in the county. The gap from Santa Margarita to Santa Barbara remained.

Engineer and fireman pose proudly on old Pacific Coast Railway engine 101 that pulled President Teddy Roosevelt's car when he visited San Luis Obispo County. American flags and Roosevelt's photograph decorate the nose of the engine.

CHAPTER XIII

Gathering New Hope

Startling news reached San Luis Obispo on January 25, 1890: the almost new wooden hotel in the new town of Los Olivos had burned to the ground. W. C. Davis, manager of the hotel, sent details to the *Tribune*. "As usual, at about eleven o'clock last evening," Davis recounted, "every fire was carefully extinguished. I made the rounds myself and satisfied myself of the fact."

There were a number of guests staying at the hotel, and all had retired at the time Davis made his check. He then retired himself to the sound of rain and heavy winds. At about 4:00 A.M., he suddenly awakened to the smell of smoke. Then he realized the whole building was in flames. He sprang from bed and ran down the stairs in his underwear, shouting, "Fire, fire!" Guests came scurrying behind him.

George Cullems, a hotel employee, helped Davis attach hoses. They found they had a powerful stream of water, but even as they worked, they felt the hopelessness of the task. Flames seemed to be all around them.

Employees and guests stood helplessly in a torrent of rain, leaning against the wind, watching the conflagration. A half-dozen men pulled the big piano from the sitting room into the rain. Suddenly, with one great terrifying explosion, the roof caved in.

The Los Olivos Hotel had been constructed by the same syndicate of men associated with the Pacific Coast Railway and the Ramona Hotel. They included John L. Howard, J. M. Fillmore and R. E. Jack. William Evans had served as architect and superintendent of the job. The building had cost about $20,000, and had opened in May 1888.[1]

The heavy rain in Los Olivos during the

Established by the same syndicate of interests that built the Ramona Hotel, San Luis Obispo's horse-drawn streetcars traversed the length of town between the Pacific Coast Railway depot and the Ramona. Here one of the cars is shown with the Castle Saloon and the Crawford Stable in the background.

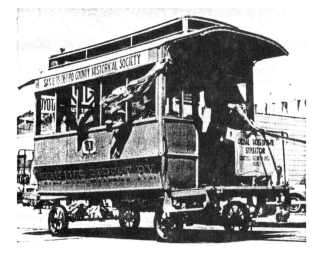

Preserved by the San Luis Obispo County Historical Society, horse-drawn streetcar No. 1 is under the tight control of this book's author in his role as conductor during La Fiesta parade in 1967.

hotel fire was the beginning of a terrible storm which hit San Luis Obsipo, too, and all along the coast. Brooks found the lines to the local telegraph office down and the Associated Press dispatches for the newspaper didn't reach town. Later dispatches informed him that the storm was general all along the coast of California and that it was coming in from the north.

Superintendent Lewis at the county hospital measured rainfall of 2.78 inches in twelve hours. This brought the season total to over thirty inches.

"The placid and usually bad smelling San Luis Creek [is] a raging, muddy torrent," Brooks reported.

At the Pacific Coast narrow-gauge depot on lower Higuera Street, the creek overflowed and threatened the railroad bridge. The railroad yard and track were under a foot of water in several places. One day the train from Port Harford was stalled three miles from town. William Evans, the town's leading architect, was a passenger on the stalled train, but he was determined not to be detained. He left the train and waded in water waist-deep until he reached the waiting horse-drawn streetcar at the depot.

The steamers scheduled to deliver freight at Port Harford didn't attempt to reach the wharf. Instead, they waited out the storm at sea.

Business was slow in January, but at the end of the month C. H. Phillips placed a large ad in the *Tribune* for the West Coast Land Company, and some people read this as a good sign.

The streetcar line had been having difficulty getting through town during bad weather, so the company finally laid a rock bed along the center of the streets to support the tracks.

"If we can get the city to keep the streets as well as it requires the horse-drawn street railway to maintain its tracks," Brooks wrote, "we'll be in good shape." Petitions addressed to city officials requesting bituminous rock paving on both Monterey and Higuera streets were distributed around town, but nothing happened.

The weather was hard on the roads all over the county. A stringer for the *Tribune* from Creston commented upon the condition of their county wagon roads that rainy January in 1890. "They are impassable for wagon traffic," he reported. The mail carrier between Templeton and Creston had given up delivery by stage

Museum Curator Louisiana Clayton Dart was given special recognition during La Fiesta in 1967. Here, in special costume, she steps from the historic streetcar amidst the cheers of onlookers.

wagon. He strapped his mail bags across his horse and reverted to pony express delivery.

The Creston stringer pointed out that the really important things in life were not dependent upon the weather, and the folks in that part of the county were enjoying the usual number of love affairs, marriages and births.

Still, the roads were a serious problem. "The roads we make are not roads," Brooks wrote. "The simple plowing up of a piece of soft earth into the shape of a road does not make one.

In the late 1880's, Robert E. Jack, a San Luis Obispo developer, along with John Wise of San Francisco sought landowners signatures to this form in an effort to obtain railroad right-of-way land between the Bay of San Luis Obispo and the inland counties of Kern, Tulare and Fresno. They were unsuccessful.

What we have amounts only to a stretch of land to which teams [are] confined instead of wandering broadly over the country . . . these narrow enclosures . . . become troughs of dust, then the rains come and . . . teaming is ended."[2]

At the first meeting of the City Trustees of San Luis Obispo in 1890, Mr. Remick, representing the San Luis Bituminous Company, asked the city to support the merchants on Monterey and Higuera streets in their efforts to get paved streets. His company proposed to do the job for ten cents a square foot. The cost of the undertaking was to be shared by the merchants, the horse-drawn street railway company and the city. The trustees agreed that although times were hard, the city should do its share if the businessmen were in agreement.[3]

IT WAS NO SMALL THING when Chauncey Phillips announced that the West Coast Land Company was negotiating to purchase the Ramona Hotel and the attached town subdivision lands referred to as the Goodall syndicate interests. He also said the company planned to buy all of the town subdivision making up Los Olivos. Since there was an overlap among owners of the West Coast Land Company, the Pacific Coast Railway and Steamship Company and the Los Olivos development, this change was one of convenience and responsibility rather than ownership.

"I desire to state," Phillips said, "that I expect to see in the near future one hundred thousand people within the present limits of this county, [and] San Luis Obispo a city of thirty thousand and, ultimately, the largest and most important city between San Francisco and Los Angeles." He urged the City Trustees to "sewer the town and pave streets and cause sidewalks to be constructed . . ."

Now it remained to be seen whether Phillips could get another boom started. Was he acting on inside information? Was the railroad going to start work toward closing the coastal gap between San Francisco and Los Angeles?[4]

About this time, R. E. Jack was urged by various leaders in town to run for City Trustee. As a stockholder in the West Coast Land Company, he would make an excellent liaison between the city and this company which could have so much influence on the future.

The Los Olivos Stage, loaded with passengers, begins trip to Santa Barbara, pulled by six-horse team. Passengers from the north could travel by Pacific Coast Railway from San Luis Obispo, but had to transfer to the stage to continue their trip.

During April 1890 word spread that Chauncey Phillips and R. E. Jack had suddenly left town for San Francisco. It was at a time when the Southern Pacific Company was holding an annual conference of its principal executives on the coast. No explanation was ever provided, and their trip may have been for naught.

Brooks called attention to the various articles and references made about the San Luis Obispo area in Southern Pacific Company's magazine, *California.* This publication was distributed in the eastern states. "It is hardly possible that this fact should be wholly without motive," Brooks wrote. "Obviously, it is intended to induce heavy immigration in this vicinity, but the

Wagon train hauling grain to Southern Pacific warehouse in Paso Robles.

completion of the railroad is essential to the success of such plans . . ."

So, a new line of speculation was developing.

IN LATE APRIL WORD REACHED town that the lighthouse above Port Harford and Avila would be finished and turned over to the government on May 10. On that day a federal employee, the lighthouse keeper, would arrive to take charge of the new beacon and the adjoining structures. All but the fog whistle would be ready for operation. Some thirty local men had found employment during construction of the lighthouse, and they hoped for early resumption of work on the breakwater to provide continued employment.[5]

Any activity by Southern Pacific Railroad was cause for talk and some of it spurred local activity in 1890.

First, Collis P. Huntington had recently succeeded Leland Stanford as president of Southern Pacific Railroad. This change had occurred after some rough exchanges at a company board meeting where members discussed Stanford's use of railroad funds for political campaign purposes. The incident received such an unusual amount of publicity that Huntington finally released a letter which he had sent to Stanford in which he apologized for his own words.

Meanwhile, in San Luis Obispo, C. H. Phillips, P. W. Murphy and various other powerful men in the county still hoped to achieve a full right-of-way for Southern Pacific into the town of San Luis Obispo. They talked at various times about their common cause and the individual sacrifices necessary to get the railroad through the Cuesta and into town. A positive step was their success in electing R. E. Jack to the San Luis Obispo City Trustees that year. He was then unanimously elected president of the trustees, a strategic position for uniting city government and the West Coast Land Company in a common effort.

Phillips and the others also talked quietly to landmen who had held out along the proposed route. Charles H. Johnson, an influential man in the area since the fifties, had been among those who held out against signing over a right-of-way to a large parcel of his land. To do so, he felt, meant destruction of some excellent land worth at least twenty-five thousand dollars. But now he relented and took the big step which only a few had dared hope for. He authorized the committee pursuing land concessions along the right-of-way to announce that he would "donate without charge" to the Southern Pacific a right-of-way through his property.

"It is an action that merits public recognition and is worthy of all praise," Brooks wrote.

General P. W. Murphy sent a public letter to the *Tribune* from the Santa Margarita Rancho upon receiving word about Johnson's generous move: "I can assure Mr. Johnson that [the people] appreciate the enlightened generosity which prompted [him] to act, as all can understand the great advantages which a transcontinental line will give to this section of the country."

Simultaneously, C. H. Phillips said that the Southern Pacific Railroad Company was at liberty to cross West Coast Land Company land as necessary even if their line went through the Ramona Hotel, over which that company now exercised control. Phillips wrote a letter to the *Tribune*, too, in which he congratulated Johnson on his public stand and reiterated the West Coast Land Company's offer of land under its control.[6]

It had been over a year since Collis Hunting-ton had publicly announced that Southern Pacific would consider building through the Cuesta only when land right-of-way was clearly established and deeded to the railroad. Now Huntington was president of the company, and right-of-way had been promised, but it remained to be seen whether these new conditions could result in a railroad all the way through San Luis Obispo County.

On Sunday, May 31, 1890, Huntington, C. F. Crocker and an entourage of railroad officials visited Santa Barbara. Santa Barbara City and County officials hoped the visit would offer them a clarification of when the Southern Pacific line would be extended.

Huntington was frank and answered their questions freely. He said the finances of the railroad would not permit the start of work along the coastal gap between Ellwood and Santa Margarita in 1890. He also said that he would never build another railroad where he had to fight for the right-of-way. He felt that landowners had more to gain financially by providing land than the railroad had.

He would make no pledges, he said, but it was probable that work along the gap would begin in 1891, and the road could be finished within a year of starting work.

While Huntington talked to one group of Santa Barbara leaders, Crocker spoke to another group. One man asked, "Would it be any encouragement to the company to begin work providing the right-of-way were given?"

"Yes, it would be some encouragement," Crocker answered, "but as it will cost about three million dollars to complete the road, the right-of-way, providing we had to pay for it, would be a comparatively small matter." He said that the Gaviota Pass had been practically abandoned as a route. A coast route would be used because of the more favorable grades.

The *Santa Barbara Press* noted that the five counties of Santa Clara, Monterey, San Luis Obispo, Santa Barbara and Ventura were equally interested in a connection with the transcontinental railroad. The *Press* urged a conference of delegates from these counties to pool their efforts.[7]

This horse-drawn street car was first used in the City of San Luis Obispo in the early part of the twentieth century. It can be seen under the roof of the Ramona Hotel depot located on the Dallidet property, San Luis Obispo.

CHAPTER XIV

The Search For Outside Support

In June 1890 a group of concerned citizens of Santa Barbara appointed Ellwood Cooper to write a letter to representative citizens in those counties they thought were likely to be the most concerned about the gap in the coastal rail route. Cooper addressed a letter to R. E. Jack in San Luis Obispo, among others. C. H. Phillips also received a letter at his Templeton office.

Jack discussed the letter informally with several San Luis Obispo leaders and called a meeting of the old executive group of the committee of twenty-one. The meeting took place in the San Luis Obispo office of C. H. Phillips, and its purpose was to deliberate the usefulness of meeting with committees from the counties between Santa Barbara County and Santa Clara County. Among those present were Benjamin Brooks, L. M. Warden, Benjamin Sinsheimer, and Dr. W. W. Hays. Chauncey Phillips read the letter he and Jack had received.

The letter called for the selection of a five-man delegation to represent San Luis Obispo County in negotiations with other counties. There was a little hassle about which men could most successfully represent San Luis Obispo, but in the final analysis, five of the strongest among the San Luis Obispo landmen were appointed. They were: C. H. Phillips, the most prominent land promoter and developer on the coast; D. W. James, owner of most of El Paso de Robles Rancho and the developer of the town of Paso Robles; L. M. Warden, largest landowner in the Los Osos Valley; L. Rackliffe, chairman of the committee of twenty-one; and John F. Dana, who represented Nipomo Rancho and southern county interests.

Word soon reached the appointed delegation that a conference would be held in San Jose to discuss the common interests of all the related counties along the proposed coast route of the railroad.

As he had done at other times, Ben Brooks took the occasion to look frankly at the Southern Pacific Railroad's viewpoint. He summed up and paraphrased various ideas the Southern Pacific had expressed, writing in first person as if the words came directly from the officers of the railroad:

"We cannot see that it would be for our interest at the present time to give you the through rail connection that you require. We have built a railroad from San Francisco to Templeton. We have also built from Los Angeles to Ellwood. We receive satisfactory rates on all the products of the country raised along the lines of the road built.

"Between Ellwood and Templeton good freight rates are also obtained by the Pacific Coast Railway and Pacific Coast Steamship Company. Why, as a business proposition, should we proceed?"

Brooks didn't answer his own question, but he was obviously preparing the way for the delegation in San Jose. He felt that all counties must be ready to make generous concessions to Southern Pacific if they expected to succeed. He painted a picture of a very dismal future along the coast if a through railroad line were not established.[1]

Brooks wound up going to San Jose as one of the county's delegates on June 24, 1890. He and the other delegates took the train from Santa Margarita to San Jose and hired a cabbie who took them from the San Jose depot to the Vendome Hotel, where the meeting was to take place.

Santa Barbara, Santa Clara, Ventura, and Los

Railroad promotional delegations from Santa Barbara, Santa Clara, Ventura, Los Angeles and San Luis Obispo Counties gathered at the Hotel Vendome in San Jose, mapping strategy to persuade Southern Pacific to complete the coastal line between San Francisco and Los Angeles.

Angeles county delegates were already present. Monterey, Santa Cruz, and San Francisco delegates were due the next day. That evening Ellwood Cooper of Santa Barbara was elected chairman. Benjamin Brooks was elected secretary, and C. H. Phillips was appointed to the committee on permanent organization, rules and order of business.

Above all, delegates agreed, their purpose was to work with Southern Pacific and to determine what they could do to induce action. They did not want to agitate or aggravate the railroad's management. They resolved to work together to obtain right-of-way land between Santa Margarita and Ellwood, including land for depots. They also resolved to subscribe $500,000 in Southern Pacific Railroad bonds at five percent interest if the railroad would take action to close the gap within three months.

By the end of the first day of meetings, the convention had telegraphed C. F. Crocker of Southern Pacific asking him to attend their meeting, and he accepted the invitation.

"We are bound to say," Brooks exclaimed later, "that in the opinion of every member of the convention, he [Crocker] could not have been more frank, candid and friendly."

A *San Francisco Examiner* reporter had an opportunity to talk to Crocker during the convention, and he faithfully wrote down the railroad executive's remarks: "We were indisposed to pay fancy prices for rights-of-way, especially when the road gave but little promise of paying interest on the bonded debt that would be required to construct it...

"The offer [by the convention] to procure us a free right-of-way, therefore, is one that cannot but be considered by us in the same spirit that prompted it...

"It is an important factor in hastening our deliberations as to commencing work on the Santa Margarita-Ellwood gap."

The convention had wound up offering three percent interest for three years ($105,000 a year) on a mortgage bond debt of $3,500,000, the estimated cost for completing the line. Crocker doubted that Eastern capitalists would be interested in low interest bonds for constructing a line with such a doubtful future, and he didn't feel that Southern Pacific dared make the financial sacrifice involved in selling bonds below par to compensate for a low-interest yield. He was still recalling that $100 par value bonds for the Oregon-California line had sold on the Eastern market for only $90.

Nonetheless, he assured everyone by saying that "Huntington will be consulted immediately on the San Jose convention proposition, so that the company's action in the matter can be ascertained shortly."

The *San Jose Mercury* reported that the convention had a real "friend in court" in C. F. Crocker. "it is but natural for the railroad people to look at the proposition from a conservative and businesslike standpoint . . . the position taken by Col. Crocker was commended because they [convention attendees] knew they could expect more rather than less than intimated . . . ''

The convention left Brooks feeling elated. "We have no time to lose," he wrote. "We want to check the dry rot and get new life into our business conditions, and if there is, indeed, a new and grand era before us upon which we can enter if we will, it would be insanity to delay. Our task is to do our share of that which has been promised by the convention.[2]

C. H. Johnson and the new Hotel Ramona owners remained steadfast in their offer to donate right-of-way through their lands to Southern Pacific Company, a genuine encouragement to others along the proposed line.

SAN LUIS OBISPO MAY HAVE HAD the biggest and best Independence Day celebration in its history that year. The weather was brilliant, the sky cloudless.

Brooks estimated crowds amounting to eight thousand people. A Pacific Coast Railway excursion train from the south was loaded. The roads from all directions were lined with teams headed for town.

When the first rays of the sun reached courthouse hill, "the boys were ready." The cannoneer let go a magnificent burst announcing that Independence Day had arrived. This was the signal for everyone in town to raise the flag. "For the next few hours, the city was alive with horsemen dressed in parade regalia, bands playing, visitors arriving and all the flutter and bustle of such an occasion," Brooks reported.

Arriving in San Jose from isolated San Luis Obispo was undoubtedly a stimulating contrast, because the entire county of Santa Clara was already a busy, relatively fast-moving area. This illustration from an 1892 copy of the San Jose Mercury depicts the County Courthouse along with the hustle and bustle of cabbies, streetcars, and buggies. San Jose had enjoyed railroad connections with San Francisco and surrounding communities for years—and with these connections, ample markets for its agricultural products.

Even while the delegation met in San Jose, the former president of the Southern Pacific Company, former governor of California and United States Senator Leland Stanford and his wife noted happily the near completion of nearby Leland Stanford, Jr. University. It was only one of several developing colleges and universities in that county. Taken from the October 2, 1891 San Jose Daily Mercury, this illustration accompanied the news story announcing the opening of the university on October 1, 1891.

General Pat Murphy was president of the day. A. R. Estrada was standard bearer. A triumphal carriage presented San Luis Obispo's own Goddess of Liberty with forty-two young ladies in the procession representing all forty-two states of the Union.

There was a deeply moving program at the pavilion. Gen. Murphy limited his remarks to only a few words. Miss Muscio captured everyone's heart with her recitation, "Independence Bell." The school children sang "America," the Reverend Mr. Mather provided a moving address about the birth of America, and everyone was thrilled by the reminders that he or she was an American.

Our flag is the symbol of our freedom, the Rev. Mather told his audience. It has meant protection, liberty, equality, and the peaceable pursuit of happiness for refugees from Europe for a hundred or more years, he said.

The balloon ascension was the major event of the day. For nearly an hour the crowd milled around the baseball diamond watching Professor Baldwin's every move in preparation for the ascent. Finally, word circulated that the balloon was being inflated. It gradually grew and swelled and swayed in the light afternoon breeze. Suddenly it shot skyward, trailing a long, narrow bundle of canvas behind it, then a long rope, and on the end of it dangled the daring Professor Baldwin.

The crowd stood astonished and breathless. Hundreds of feet in the air, the "aeronaut" climbed hand-over-hand up the rope. With a great stretch, he reached the ring of his parachute. The balloon rose to over two thousand feet in altitude.

Suddenly, Baldwin dropped fast, perhaps three hundred feet, and his canvas parachute opened. The crowd broke into a roar of applause as he floated toward the ground. The sun, low in the sky to one side of San Luis Obispo Mountain, gilded the parachute, and it looked like a gigantic flower in space.

Professor Baldwin landed as lightly as a bird within two hundred feet of the place where he had started. His abandoned balloon reached ground soon afterward. The ascension of a man to two thousand feet in the air had been a rare and wondrous sight.

The electric light company contributed to the celebration by stretching a line of red, white and blue incandescent lights across Monterey Street. Quintana Brothers, Prefumo and Vollmers,

"For Mrs. Stanford and myself this cermony marks an epoch in our lives..." said Leland Stanford at ceremonies celebrating the commencement of Stanford University on October 1, 1891.

Goldtree Brothers, the First National Bank, the Ramona Hotel, the courthouse, and several other businesses decorated their buildings with red, white and blue streamers.

It was a great day in San Luis Obispo.[3]

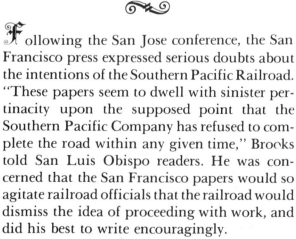

F̵ollowing the San Jose conference, the San Francisco press expressed serious doubts about the intentions of the Southern Pacific Railroad. "These papers seem to dwell with sinister pertinacity upon the supposed point that the Southern Pacific Company has refused to complete the road within any given time," Brooks told San Luis Obispo readers. He was concerned that the San Francisco papers would so agitate railroad officials that the railroad would dismiss the idea of proceeding with work, and did his best to write encouragingly.

But the letter from Charles F. Crocker dated July 29, 1890 that reached Ellwood Cooper, the president of the committee that had met in San Jose, seemed to confirm the doubts of the San Francisco press. Crocker had sent the committee's proposition to the members of the Southern Pacific board in New York City. They replied: "We have favorably considered your

proposition and will make an agreement with an authorized committee covering the construction of the line of railroad between Santa Margarita and Ellwood, asking, however, that the Standing Committee appointed by the convention shall strike out the limitation of time mentioned in the resolution for completing the road."

A telegram was addressed to R. E. Jack from Cooper in Santa Barbara, providing news of the railroad's general acceptance of the proposition. The word spread quickly through town and everyone was elated. The time factor somehow did not discourage anyone. People talked about getting out the band, firing a salute, and other ideas for celebrating, but, in the end, they confined themselves to excited talk.[4]

A second state committee of delegates met in San Jose August 9, 1890. Among those present were Chauncey Phillips of San Luis Obispo, and Ellwood Cooper from Santa Barbara. Colo-

After Senator Stanford's death, the university suffered some financial setbacks. To help meet the university's needs, Mrs. Stanford sold her precious jewels. The school was named for their only son, Leland Stanford, Jr., who had died a few years earlier. In recent years, Stanford University was recipient of the Santa Margarita Rancho in San Luis Obispo County.

nel Charles Crocker represented the railroad. There were also delegates from Los Angeles, San Jose, and San Francisco. The news Crocker presented this time was discouraging. He said that Southern Pacific did not wish to try to complete the rail line in less than four years.

Mr. Calkins of Santa Barbara said that delegates felt as if a long icicle had been inserted down the back of their necks. With Crocker's announcement, there was a good five minutes of very depressed silence. Before the meeting adjourned, C. H. Phillips and Gen. H. I. Willey were appointed to consider new avenues of approach to the problem.[5]

❦

THE WEATHER IN JULY AND August of 1890 was exceptionally nice. Pismo Beach enjoyed a tourist boom. The beach was lined with tents, covered wagons and camping equipment. People were arriving by the wagonload along the rough mountain roads from Merced, Fresno, Tulare, and Kern. Crowds gathered for campfires each evening and entertained each other with music, singing, speech contests, and other spontaneous activities. It was a hard trip from the interior, and when they arrived, people stayed to enjoy the sea breezes for as long as a month.

❦

On Monday, August 11, 1890, the Standing Committee of the coast county delegates again conferred with Col. Crocker. Finally, the railroad agreed to begin construction to close the gap within thirty days after being provided a right-of-way. San Luis Obispo's committee of twenty-one received a report about the meeting from R. E. Jack and C. H. Phillips.

So, once again stirred by hope, a county subscription committee was appointed to begin the task of obtaining right-of-way lands and raising money to buy land from some small owners.

Committeemen set aside regular work and began the task of calling on their neighbors for subscriptions. At best, their efforts were very discouraging. Very few landowners along the right-of-way refused to help, but neither did they subscribe generously.

The West Coast Land Company placed an occasional full page ad in the *Tribune* reminding locals of their existence and encouraging people to feel optimistic about the future. Nonetheless, two "grand obstacles" to success loomed, according to Brooks. Those persons subscribing money hadn't subscribed enough, and landowners along the right-of-way were asking too much for their land.

San Luis Obispo people wanted help from the people of Paso Robles, San Miguel, Templeton, Arroyo Grande, and Nipomo, but subscriptions were even smaller from these towns. Before the railroad line had been laid to Santa Margarita, land in that northern section of the county could be bought on long-term loan for as little as ten dollars an acre.

Brooks claimed that land along that route was now worth three times that much. The difference in land values amounted to millions of dollars, he estimated, and he bawled out neighboring towns for not recognizing their great opportunity by contributing to the purchase of right-of-way land.

As members of the committee continued the struggle to gain right-of-way agreements, they still didn't feel assured that Huntington really agreed with Crocker about starting construction to close the gap. R. E. Jack and C. H. Phillips, representing San Luis Obispo County, went to San Francisco to negotiate a firm agreement with Southern Pacific Company.[6]

On October 23, 1890, Benjamin Brooks received this wire from Phillips: "Contract signed by Huntington, Stanford, and Crocker for the railroad company, and by Jack, myself, Eddy, and Calkins for San Luis Obispo and Santa Barbara Counties. Work to go on as originally agreed upon. All satisfactory to us."

When Phillips and Jack returned to town they were heroes. A crowd of businessmen and landmen received them at the Ramona Hotel. E. W. Steele was chairman for the occasion. Drinks were available in ample supply. Steele congratulated Phillips and the members of the committee who represented the coastal counties in San Francisco.

As Phillips and the others who had returned from San Francisco talked that evening, it became evident that some earlier commitments which they thought they had had from Crocker had not been at all acceptable to the other Southern Pacific Company executives. At this latest meeting with the railroad executives, they found themselves starting all over again, but now they felt they had at long last negotiated a definite plan. They were cheered and toasted over and over again.

Brooks' story about the reception turned on the pressure to get the job done. He frankly sought to embarrass large landowners and businessmen who had declined to contribute generously to the right-of-way campaign. "... Our own people, who are to be enriched [by the agreement] are still doubtful, we regret to say, but we have the satisfaction of knowing that there is a further resort, a jury of ... peers and countrymen ... who have the right to judge ... between the impulses of greed and the needs of the people."

After so many years of effort to obtain a railroad line between San Francisco and Los Angeles along the coast, the people of San Luis Obispo were finally seeing results to those efforts. A written agreement signed by the railroad now existed. It remained to be seen whether these local committees could actually obtain right-of-way land to uphold their end of the agreement.[7]

In late December 1890, the committee acquiring San Luis Obispo town lots along the railroad right-of-way tried to wind up its contacts with property owners. In the case of each property, they had determined the maximum amount they would offer an owner. If an owner refused to accept the established maximum offered, the committee intended to begin condemnation suits. The *Tribune* reported that cooperation among landowners was good, and only a few suits would be necessary.

In Santa Barbara, property owners came to a a central location, and if satisfied with the amount offered, they signed a deed. Contacting absentee owners was the most difficult problem.

There was a great deal of vying for favorable consideration among small towns along the route. All wanted the line to pass through their town. Santa Ynez people wanted the line to run through Gaviota Pass and into their newly established town. Lompoc people were hoping

the railroad would be routed along San Julian Pass and through their town.

W. D. Gillette, a road engineer for Southern Pacific, came through San Luis Obispo in November to observe the work of a company surveying party. The cost of construction, he told Brooks, would largely determine the route.

In San Jose, a San Luis Obispo committee was warmly received. C. H. Phillips, speaking at the San Jose Board of Trade meeting, told the group that San Luis Obispo needed twenty thousand dollars more than it could raise locally in order to complete purchase of railroad right-of-way land. The members of the board expressed keen interest in helping, and the committee left feeling assured that the San Jose board would conduct a money-raising campaign to close the coastal railroad gap.

A San Luis Obispo lawyer, William Graves, made a trip to San Francisco to talk to Southern Pacific officials and others about documents and proceedings for beginning county condemnation suits along the right-of-way.

By early December nearly all of the property along the right-of-way between Boronda's property at the top of the Cuesta and the Santa Maria River had been acquired. But an interesting thing was happening. The deeds obtained for property south of San Luis Obispo remained unrecorded. The committee informed residents that the deeds hadn't been recorded because there was no money to pay for them, but that $20,000 from the San Jose Board of Trade was expected soon.

In San Jose, a local Railroad Committee had been appointed by the Board of Trade and Chamber of Commerce. It included the Honorable B. D. Murphy, D. B. Moody, Lawrence Archer, W. A. Parkhurst, W. G. Hawley, J. H. Flickinger, Captain W. T. Adel, and C. M. Shortridge. To these men, it was said, $20,000 was a pittance in terms of the possible return for a through route to Los Angeles. San Jose had spent $30,000 for a road to Alum Rock, a recreation park, only seven miles from town. A road up Mt. Hamilton had cost $65,000, with most of the cost borne by the city.[8]

❧

West Hall.   East Hall.   Conservatory of Music. Central Hall. South Hall.   Observatory

Santa Clara County was justly proud of its many developing colleges and universities. University of Pacific, now located in Stockton, California, was founded in Santa Clara County in 1851. This illustration depicts it as it existed in 1892 in Santa Clara County. U.O.P. serves as headquarters office for the Conference of California Historical Societies. At this time, San Jose University was developing as a normal school in San Jose, and Santa Clara University was a growing institution in that city.

AT THE END OF THAT YEAR, 1890, the *San Francisco Examiner* published an elaborate holiday edition featuring a line illustration and a biographical sketch of the richest taxpayer in each California county. In San Luis Obispo County, that person was R. E. Jack. The article noted that Jack, who owned the great Cholame Rancho, was a millionaire.

Jack was asked what advice he would give to a young man just starting his career. He quickly recommended buying forty acres and planting fruit trees. In the handling of his business, Jack advised that a young man should engrave on each of the corner posts of his land this legend: "Be bold. Be bold. Be bold." But, on the fourth corner post, he should remind himself: "Be not too bold."

For a while, at least, San Luis Obispo County people continued to live on a diet of rumors about the railroad. The *San Francisco Chronicle* announced at the beginning of 1891 that Santa Barbara County had successfully acquired all needed land for railroad right-of-way through its county. San Luis Obispo people had been under the impression at the time that Santa Barbara was still hung up by the uncertainty of the route the railroad would follow in that county, so there were doubts about the *Chronicle* reports.

L. M. Warden had returned to San Luis Obispo on Christmas evening 1890, after a weary trip to San Francisco and a stop at San Jose. Among those he talked to that day in San Jose, he found little enthusiasm about the railroad, especially about the earlier promises of San Jose's committee to raise $20,000 to buy right-of-way land in San Luis Obispo.

On February 6, 1891, C. H. Phillips published a report of the activities of the San Luis Obispo Railroad Committee, of which he was secretary. "Nearly all of the right-of-way through the town of San Luis Obispo has been secured," he reported, "and this is the case from Santa Margarita into this town and from this town to the Santa Maria River; in other words, I think we have more than five-sixths of the work done. We have prepared papers through our attorneys for condemnation in several cases, and we are corresponding with other parties where we are liable to reach satisfactory settlements."

He said that a committee composed of Judge George Steele, R. E. Jack, and R. M. Shackelford planned a trip to San Jose and San Francisco to urge those groups to fulfill their commitments. Other men were planning trips within the county, hoping to get support in Paso Robles, San Miguel, and Arroyo Grande. The committee still needed $20,000 in subscriptions to buy the land along the right-of-way. The appointed committees made their trips out of town and were back by Monday, February 9, to make their reports.

Jack, Steele, and Shackelford had made their presence known in San Jose through an interview with a reporter from the *San Jose Mercury.* Jack was spokesman. "We are not here on a begging tour," he told the reporter. "We [are] representatives of the people of San Luis Obispo County [here] to consult with the people of Santa Clara County on a matter of vital importance to us all." He told the *Mercury* reporter that residents of San Luis Obispo had raised $30,000. He hoped other counties along the route would consent to raising another $20,000.

Jack himself had contributed right-of-way land in the city of San Luis Obispo and had contributed $2,000 in cash to buy property from small landowners along the right-of-way.

The San Jose Board of Trade Railroad Committee gathered at the Commercial and Savings Bank to meet with the men from San Luis Obispo. D. B. Moody was chairman, C. M. Shortridge acted as secretary, and J. H. Flickinger and W. A. Parkhurst were also present.

The committee decided to make an all-out drive through San Jose. They would issue 20,000 certificates at one dollar each and distribute them. The certificates would read:

The Connecting Link

This certifies that the bearer has given one dollar for the purpose of securing the right-of-way for the completion of the Southern Pacific Railroad from Santa Margarita in San Luis Obispo County to Ellwood in Santa Barbara County.

D. B. Moody, Chairman
Charles M. Shortridge, Sec.[9]

◌◌◌

AS A NEW YEAR'S RESOLUTION, the San Luis Obispo City Trustees had determined to lay a gravel sidewalk along one side of Santa Rosa Street between Monterey and Peach streets, a bituminous (paved) rock walk along Broad Street between Higuera and Buchon, a gravel walk along Broad between Bushon and Islay, a bituminous walk along Nipomo from the bridge near Monterey Street to Buchon, and a bituminous rock walk along Monterey Street between Nipomo and Essex streets.

In February 1891 the City of San Luis Obispo held a bond election to raise money for city improvements. It took a two-thirds vote in favor of the bonds to win. Citizens voted themselves an indebtedness of $14,628.50 for new bridges across San Luis Obispo Creek at Broad, Chorro, Court, Osos, and Higuera streets. $16,939.73 was voted to construct retaining walls along the creek on Higuera Street between Court and Santa Rosa streets. Another $2,500 was voted to condemn and acquire land for widening Chorro Street between Monterey Street and the creek. Money was also voted for grading and opening Pacific Street. At last, too, the city planned for sewers along Higuera Street between Santa Rosa and Nipomo streets, along Monterey from Osos to Nipomo streets, on Nipomo between Monterey and Marsh, and along Marsh from Nipomo to the junction of Higuera. It sounded good. Now, all they had to do was sell the bonds.

One week in February 1891, I. K. Fisher, a member of the right-of-way committee in Santa Barbara County, visited San Luis Obispo. He reported that nearly all needed land in Santa Barbara had been acquired, but that their committee was being slowed by landowners near Guadalupe who were holding out for higher prices.

That same month, condemnation suits were started against some San Luis Obispo landowners who wanted higher prices than the committee offered. Among those whose land was involved were Epifamio and Beatrice Boronda, who owned land along the Cuesta. A few years earlier Boronda had sold about ten acres of land to Southern Pacific Company for $1,600. Then the company learned that the land was a homestead claim, and they had to negotiate all over again. Boronda kept the money, and Southern Pacific finally gave up the fight.

Now the Railroad Committee took Boronda to court. Expert witnesses testified that the land had little value. Very little of it was suited for agricultural use. The court awarded Boronda an additional $310 for the land and closed the case. So, Boronda realized a total of $1,910 for his land, a generous pay-off, everyone agreed.

◌◌◌

WORD REACHED TOWN FROM Washington, D.C. in early March that one of the county's largest landowners, Senator George Hearst, had died in the capital on February 28. His large holdings were left to his wife, Phoebe Apperson Hearst, and to his son, William Randolph.[10]

❦

Although difficulties in obtaining railroad right-of-way from some landowners persisted, it was far more difficult to raise money to buy land where agreements had been reached.

By March 1891, San Luis Obispo citizens were feeling bitter toward San Jose businessmen. Their money-raising plans had not really been started, and they were obviously indifferent about helping San Luis Obispo buy right-of-way land.

The San Luis Obispo Railroad Committee received a letter from the secretary of the Santa Barbara committee in April. He wrote: "We hope to have our right-of-way work completed by or before the tenth of April. Will you be ready by that time?

"We will have but few condemnation suits, mostly estates with minor heirs.

"Mr. Hood [Southern Pacific Railroad construction engineer] has shown a disposition to facilitate our work . . .

"We hear that Mr. Crocker is expected home about the first of April and shall be disappoint-

ed if he does not commence work as soon as we fill our part of the contract."

With San Jose remaining silent about raising money, a delegation of San Luis Obispo businessmen decided to try in San Francisco. Messrs. Mehlman, Brunner, J. C. Castro, C. H. Reed, Nathan Goldtree, and Mark Lasar traveled to the City. Benjamin Brooks received a telegram from this group one evening in April saying that they had succeeded in making some good contacts with San Francisco businessmen. So far, they had raised about $1,800, and they hoped to get $5,000.

Then in May, D. P. Moody, chairman of San Jose's Board of Trustees, wrote the committee to say that subscriptions were now being successfully obtained there. At the end of May a check for $1,077 was received from San Jose. The total contribution from San Jose as of that date was reported to be $3,222. Moody was largely responsible.

In June 1891, Brooks reviewed the railroad situation: (1) R. E. Jack had talked to Charles Crocker in San Francisco, and Crocker had given his usual assurances that action would begin after all right-of-way land was acquired; (2) Southern Pacific's construction engineer, William Hood, reported that railroad lawyers were actively engaged in the preparation of condemnation suit papers; and (3) the Railroad Committee had succeeded in making contracts of sale with three more "problem land owners," thus reducing legal difficulties.

Early postcard depicts 30-horse harvester team on Carrisa Plains. Southern Pacific rail lines opened major economic and agricultural opportunities.

CHAPTER XV

Railroad Work Really Begins

Mr. Staniford of the Pacific Coast Stage Company received word in early December 1891 that Mr. R. H. Pratt, the general superintendent of Southern Pacific Railroad Company, along with an entourage of company executives, was coming to Santa Margarita by special train and that they would want a special stagecoach to transport them through the Cuesta to San Luis Obispo.

Sure enough, Pratt's party arrived in Santa Margarita late at night on Saturday, December 5. They continued sleeping in their private car until early Sunday morning. Staniford was there to meet them before daylight, and carefully delivered his passengers across the grade. By 7:45 A.M. they had arrived at the Ramona Hotel in San Luis Obispo. The hotel manager knew they were coming and had planned an extraordinary breakfast for them, but didn't expect them until around 8:30.

It had been a cold trip over the Cuesta, and Pratt and the others enjoyed gathering around the crackling fire in the big fireplace in the hotel reading room. Then, just as breakfast was nearly ready to be served, the group left the hotel and started walking down Monterey Street toward town.

One of the hotel guests pursued Mr. Pratt to tell him breakfast was ready, but Pratt said that they would return in about a half hour. The men in his party included J. H. Walker, Assistant General Superintendent; Arthur Brown, Assistant Engineer in charge of rights-of-way; Mr. Haydock, Division Superintendent; Mr. Murdock, Roadmaster; and one other company official.

Hurrying toward the hotel along Monterey Street, C. H. Phillips, L. M. Warden and L. Rackliffe "chanced" to meet the party as they walked along near the mission. Phillips expressed regret that Mr. Pratt was investigating San Luis Obispo with such haste, and told him that several businessmen in town hoped to negotiate contracts for construction of the road bed. Pratt told Phillips that it was much too early for such planning. First, he said, they would bore a large tunnel on the Cuesta, then they would contract for road building.

No matter which member of the party was addressed or what questions were asked, all made the same statement: "There is no significance to our visit."

Perhaps annoyed, the railroad officers never returned to the hotel. After about an hour, they went directly to the stage office, called for a coach, and headed back to Santa Margarita.[1]

But within a day or so, a story came out in the San Francisco papers that sounded most convincing. "The Pacific Improvement Company will begin work about January 15 on the tunnels in the first five miles of the Coast Division gap south of Santa Margarita," one paper said. "It has called for bids for the construction of two tunnels, one 3600 feet and the other 1400 feet long."

News about events planned in San Luis Obispo County often reached its people this indirectly and with so little advance notice. Soon after this news arrived, the railroad agent at Santa Margarita wired William Sandercock, the drayage man in San Luis Obispo, to bring teams to Santa Margarita for moving camping equipment to the location along the Cuesta where the first tunnel was to be constructed. Some railroad men at Santa Margarita said that construction trains were already made up in San Francisco and would be coming any day.

Word also reached San Luis Obispo from

Stewart Clemons pauses in front of early Southern Pacific Depot in San Miguel. This structure was dismantled after passenger service ceased.

Santa Margarita that a railroad representative had contacted R. Bean on the Cuesta stage road about leasing land near the mouth of the first proposed tunnel. The railroad, it was said, intended to establish a labor camp at that location.

Then word spread that "a gentleman known to be a contractor for railroad work was taken out to the end of the road..." Another gentleman "in a shiny plug hat attracted attention yesterday." Someone penetrated this man's disguise and said that he was Fred de la Guerra, the "celebrated" tunnel contractor.

On Sunday, December 19, 1891, A. N. Cunningham reported seeing a Southern Pacific Company's engineers' camp near Boronda's place along the Cuesta. With camera in hand, Cunningham photographed the camp and delivered the picture to the *Tribune*.

"If the Tribune had the facilities," Brooks wrote, "the picture is...one which we would like to reproduce...It is an historic scene, and the details of these beginnings will be the most interesting...hereafter. The photograph... shows the long line of tents with the numerous

company of engineers grouped in front of them."

Most San Luis Obispo people didn't travel over the Cuesta often, so they depended on Brooks and occasional travelers through town to confirm railroad activity.

Meanwhile, the local railroad committee was rushing around trying to close all land deals along the right-of-way to assure smooth construction once it started. After raising nearly $45,000 with some outside help, they found themselves short by $2,500 as of Christmas Day 1891. They still did not have clear title to all land needed for the right-of-way.

The *Tribune* promised to print a "roll of honor" soon, showing names of contributors to the cause.[2]

☙❧

WHEN THE PEOPLE WHO GATHERED each day at the stagecoach office to wait for the mail looked up Monterey Street toward the Cuesta one evening in December 1891, they saw unmounted horses racing toward them with dangling harnesses. As the horses galloped along the street, men rushed out to stop them. They were obviously the stagecoach horses.

It had rained intermittently for several days. The stagecoach road on the grade was slippery and dangerous, and the worst was expected.

Two stages had left Santa Margarita together, and it was not until the second one arrived that the story of what had happened could be pieced together. The second stage was crowded with disheveled and anguished people who had survived an accident on the first stage.

Jim Myers, the driver of the first coach, hustled to the ground and assisted the people who had been riding with him. He had started from Santa Margarita with a six-horse team attached to a mud wagon. The December night was black along the Cuesta grade, and the mud along the trail was deep and slippery. As they descended the grade, the horses suddenly acted frightened and began moving too fast. Myers pulled on the wagon brakes and held them for all he was worth, but it didn't seem to deter the team. The horses dragged the stage through the soft mud dangerously fast. Myers struggled to slow them and thought he had gained control

Editor Benjamin Brooks, vigilant and continuously attentive to the needs of the community, poses with the staff of the San Luis Obispo Tribune. Brooks is at left with galley proofs in hand.

again by the time the wagon reached the bridge halfway down the grade. Then the horses again acted alarmed and frightened and began racing down the grade out of control. At a steep turn, the wagon jerked and rolled over, spilling passengers, baggage and freight. Fortunately, the wagon tipped in the direction of the bank.

Mrs. Knight, one of the passengers, fell under the wagon and suffered a cut on the side of her head. Other passengers had small cuts and bruises and were badly skinned.

Frank Smith, driver of the second coach, found the horses desperately tangled in their harness. They had fallen together a short distance beyond the overturned wagon. Three of the horses were on their backs. The other three were dovetailed on top of them. They were a wild mass of kicking, struggling animals. With dexterity and care, Smith cut the harness that bound them, and as quickly as each animal was free, it sprang to its feet and raced down the road.

Now safely arrived in San Luis Obispo, all of the injured passengers were methodically bandaged and patched by Dr. Nichols, and they bedded down in the Ramona Hotel.

There was a general prayer of thanksgiving in town as the year 1891 ended. The rains offered promise of good crops and the beginning of railroad construction suggested prosperity, employment and growth.[3]

Benjamin Brooks served as editor and publisher of the Tribune for forty years. He sold it in 1925 to Rollins Company. His role in bringing the Southern Pacific line to San Luis Obispo cannot be overestimated. He cheered, threatened and cajoled the community year after year.

Chauncey Phillips took a stagecoach ride over the Cuesta on business in early 1892. While there, he checked the activities of the Southern Pacific Railroad. Including engineers, masons and laborers, he found a force of forty men at work. Three carloads of construction materials, including heavy timbers and cement, had arrived at Santa Margarita. There were six teams hauling from the end of the railroad line in Santa Margarita to the planned mouth of the first tunnel. Stakes were driven from Santa Margarita to locations next to two sites where tunnels were planned.

Much of the work that had been done in 1889 between Santa Margarita and the location of the first tunnel was now being repeated. That earlier road bed had disappeared in thickets and high grass. A small dam-like structure was built to control water flow from the hill above the first tunnel. Many preliminaries had to precede actual construction of a rail bed. It made everyone impatient.[4]

Brooks estimated that some thirty or forty contractors had appeared in the area from as far away as Seattle and Denver, all seeking construction contracts with Southern Pacific.

∾

THE TRIBUNE BEGAN A campaign for contributions to build a city library in February 1892. People were urged to contribute to the library fund, and the newspaper published the names of donors as money came in.[5]

∾

During the many months of waiting for Southern Pacific to start action, another San Luis Obispo group continued to pursue the possibility of a narrow-gauge rail line between the San Joaquin Valley and Port Harford in San Luis Obispo County. They called their organization the San Luis and San Joaquin Valley Railway Association. The officers were J. H. Wise, president; R. E. Jack, vice-president; and Myron Angel, secretary.

Actually, Myron Angel was the principal promoter of the idea. He said that the grain of the San Joaquin Valley needed an inexpensive outlet for shipment by water. At this time, the federal government was building a breakwater at Avila and this made the plan seem that much more feasible.

Angel had contacted most landowners across the plains between Bakersfield and San Luis Obispo County. They generally expressed a willingness to take stock in the enterprise to the extent of a dollar an acre for land that might be used by a railroad. Angel figured this would make the company immediately worth five million dollars.[6]

∾

The San Luis Obispo Building and Loan Association was another organization that came into existence during these years. With land prices increasing and speculators looking for money, pioneer businessmen put their heads together in this venture. *Tribune* editor Benjamin Brooks was president of the association. Other officers were: C. O. King, vice-president; M. Lewin, secretary; R. E. Jack, treasurer; and E. P. Unangst, attorney.

∾

C. H. Phillips announced in the *San Jose Mercury* and the *San Luis Obispo Tribune* in April 1892 that he had acquired and was subdividing and selling the Morgan Hill and San Martin Ranches. Among the various land promoters between San Francisco and Los Angeles, none seemed to have his fingers in so many land developments as Phillips.[7]

∾

Brooks broke some "news" about the railroad in the *Tribune* of Tuesday, April 12, 1892. He had met a man named Emil Haltier who had arrived in San Luis Obispo from Durango, Mexico. Haltier announced that he had been working for nearly three years as a tunnel and road builder for the Southern Pacific Company. There, he said, the Southern Pacific was running a line to connect with the Atchison, Topeka and Santa Fe.

Now, he had been dispatched to Santa Margarita, and he had a gang of forty workers with him. They had come by steamer from the Gulf of Mexico to San Diego, he told Brooks. From there, they traveled by ship to Santa Barbara and by stage and the Pacific Coast narrow-gauge railway to San Luis Obispo.

Haltier explained his method of operation to Brooks. He said that he worked his men in three shifts of six hours. When tunneling, they drilled deep holes into the rock, filled them with dynamite, discharged the explosives and then cleared the shattered rock.

Haltier said his gang of workmen were Germans, Russians, and Belgians, and that many of them were fine musicians and made an excellent band. He promised they would make San Luis Obispo's Fourth of July jubilee a memorable event.[8]

William Sandercock received word from Pacific Improvement Company at the beginning of April 1892 that he had been awarded a contract to build some wagon roads to planned tunnel openings. These roads would start from the stage road at Santa Margarita and run to the first two tunnel sites on the Cuesta.

Pacific Improvement Company, which was Southern Pacific's own construction firm, continued to build culverts and generally prepare the way for tunneling and road building.

But for people in San Luis Obispo, nothing really exciting was yet happening. "If there ever was a community that was a massive and monumental instance of that heart sickness that comes from hope deferred, it is the country sunk in the 'gap,'" Brooks reported.[9]

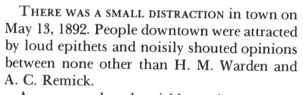

THERE WAS A SMALL DISTRACTION in town on May 13, 1892. People downtown were attracted by loud epithets and noisily shouted opinions between none other than H. M. Warden and A. C. Remick.

A group gathered quickly at the corner of Chorro and Higuera streets where these well-known local men questioned each other's moral standing and veracity. They were startlingly frank. Suddenly one of them took a poke at the other, and all dignity was set aside. The town needed a diversion, and Warden and Remick provided it.

They swung at each other with genuine vehemence, but neither man seemed quite able to make a decisive blow. The whole thing was so much fun that no one tried to break it up. The crowd grew larger while Warden and Remick continued swinging. But the battle finally attracted the attention of police officers Kiernan and Cushing.

The officers escorted both esteemed citizens to Recorder Loomis's office where they were inspected for damage. It was discovered that Remick had split his pants up the back and

This early photo of the San Luis Obispo City Hall was taken in 1906, but it was already twenty-five years old. The building served as both City Hall and the fire department. In this photo, volunteer firemen pose with their teams and fire-fighting equipment. The sign at right promotes "Eiler's Big Rip Van Winkle Show." It probably took place at the agricultural pavilion.

Warden's left ear was temporarily shaped like a horseshoe. Both men were ready to go it again, but the officers insisted that they go separate directions.

For no good reason, it seemed as if fights broke out all over town for the next several days.[10]

The weather in San Luis Obispo County was generally beautiful all through May. One weekend a troupe of professional entertainers set up business at Sycamore Springs near Avila and sent notices throughout the area about their Sunday show. The Pacific Coast narrow gauge made a stop at the resort on its way to Avila, transporting many passengers from San Luis Obispo. Someone counted 204 horse carts, carriages and wagons full of people attending the occasion.

The combination of good entertainment and the health baths made Sycamore Springs very popular during that spring and summer.[11]

There was scarcely standing room in Arroyo Grande during its flower show in 1892, which was sponsored by the Arroyo Grande Floral Society. San Luis Obispo people crowded the narrow gauge to Arroyo Grande for the occasion. In addition to the flower exhibit, visitors enjoyed homemade lemonade, ice cream, and locally picked strawberries.

There was a Maypole dance, a flag drill, a rainbow march, and music by the local orchestra.[12]

From the time San Luis Obispo citizens began to consider the likelihood of a through railroad, a certain consciousness of the town's backwardness came to many of them. They could tolerate conditions themselves, but they felt obliged to tidy up for company.

Throughout San Luis Obispo history, cesspool drainage from property along the creeks had drained into the water. During the summers, the result was a terrible stench in the downtown business district. Along with the ankle deep dust in the streets, droppings from horses, and cattle herded through town, the place was sometimes infested with flies and insects.

Although the town had voted to issue bonds for a sewer, more than a year had passed without action because they couldn't sell the bonds. It was not until May 1892 that money was raised and a contract let to a San Francisco firm for sewer lines.

A line would run along Monterey Street from the corner of Osos to Nipomo. On Higuera Street, one would run from Santa Rosa to Nipomo. Line would also run along Nipomo Street between Monterey and Marsh. The city owned a lot on Marsh Street and planned to erect a large cesspool there.

That same month, the city opened bids for laying bituminous sidewalks on Broad, Monterey, and Higuera streets. Gravel sidewalks were planned on some other streets.[13]

On June 24, 1892, a San Francisco-bound freight train met with an accident. Pulling five cars loaded with cattle, one car of oak wood, and several others containing other freight, the train that left Santa Margarita that day partially derailed near the Pear Tree Ranch, about one mile north of a bridge across the Salinas River.

The car with the oak wood broke an axle and was thrown from the track into a ditch. Its load flew in every direction. The five cattle cars were derailed, but they remained upright.

For several hours the regular northbound passenger train was detained at San Miguel while the tracks were cleared and damaged freight cars were hauled back to San Miguel.

t the end of May 1892, William Sandercock came into town from the Cuesta. He was sunbrowned and vigorous. He said that he and his crew needed another month to complete grading and road building along the site of the Southern Pacific line, and reported that the stone masons constructing water conduits at the site of tunnel number two were nearly finished with their work. He estimated that there were about ninety men working in various ways along the line.

Sandercock had predicted the needed time accurately, for at the end of June 1892, he announced that he had completed his wagonroad contract for the railroad and was disbanding a fine local labor force.[14]

ON THE FIRST DAY OF JULY, 1892, lots were advertised for sale in the new town of Grover located at Huntington Beach. "It is a fact disputed by none," the town's promoters wrote, "that this is the finest beach on the coast, and it is the first point where the Southern Pacific Coast (planned) route . . . touches the beach."

The town of Grover was laid out with lots 100 by 120 feet on a slightly elevated sandy plain sloping toward the beach. With nothing built up between the town site and the water, every lot seemed to offer an open view.[15]

Historian and former *Tribune* editor Myron Angel struggled with various small railway possibilities, and he gathered associates wherever he found them for each new idea. In July

1892, he sought partners and incorporated to establish a short line between San Luis Obispo and Moro, a new subdivision developing in what is now Baywood Park. As it was with most business promoters, capital was always short, and that kept Angel's ideas from developing.[16]

ఌఞఌ

In Santa Barbara, people were becoming weary with the seeming lack of progress of the Southern Pacific. The distance between their city and the Cuesta was such that they felt sure that nothing significant would ever happen. Certainly, it wasn't happening in Santa Barbara County.

At last, William L. Eddy, a local banker and member of the Santa Barbara committee to acquire right-of-way land for the Southern Pacific line, appointed himself a committee of one to travel to San Luis Obispo and go up the pass to see with his own eyes what was happening. L. Rackliffe, a San Luis Obispo friend, met him, and they took a buggy to the scene of operations.

Eddy didn't make any discoveries that people in San Luis Obispo hadn't already heard about, but at least he could see that preliminary work was underway, and that the whole idea wasn't humbug.

Brooks caught a rumor from a New York man who was in town for a few days. It seemed that this man had written to Collis Huntington a few days before beginning his trip to the Pacific Coast, and Huntington had personally sent a return note saying that the California coastal line would be finished in two years. Since this man was a pastor in a large New York church, Brooks felt people could take store in what he said.

ఌఞఌ

WHILE DIGGING TRENCHES for the sewer pipe along Higuera Street opposite the City Hall, a workman struck a box about ten and a half by fourteen inches in size. It contained human bones. Upon investigation, he discerned Chinese characters on the outside of it. It turned out that about eight years earlier these same bones had been found in about the same place while someone was laying gas pipe. That time, workmen had put the loose bones into a wooden tea box and reburied them. Less sentimental workers this time tossed the bones to the winds.

The pavilion was located on the north side of Monterey Street a few blocks east of the county courthouse. It was a two-story wooden structure used for a variety of activities including the local fair in September.

The fair was an event worthy of good news coverage. Nearly everyone participated in it, so Benjamin Brooks took careful notes at each exhibit. Upon arrival at the pavilion that year, he immediately went upstairs to the art exhibit. One painting in particular held his attention. It was an oil painting of "Pueblo de San Luis Obispo de Tolosa," painted in 1868 by L. Troussett as he viewed it from the residence of Frank Rodriques. Brooks had heard that the Rodriques' place stood on the old fortification thrown up by General John Fremont. He noted

Present-day bunkhouse on the Santa Margarita Ranch once served as stagecoach depot.

In the early part of this century, Southern Pacific Railroad operated the largest ferry in the world between San Francisco and Oakland and other ports located in San Francisco Bay. It carried freight cars as needed.

that this painting would give future residents of the city a good idea of how San Luis Obispo looked in 1868. In 1980, this painting hangs in the Mission San Luis Obispo gift shop.

The work of hundreds of individual school children was on exhibit at the fair, and someone from Cholame showed a ninety-pound watermelon.

The University of California agricultural experimental station exhibited a remarkable collection of California grapes. The exhibit suggested what was possible for San Luis Obispo farmers.

Horse racing was included among fair events, with $525 in prize money. People gathered from throughout the county in their carriages to see the races. There was also a cattle parade and a horse parade in which farmers showed the best of their stock.[17]

Through the late eighties and nineties, San Luis Obispo enjoyed a musical organization called Maenorchor. It started as a musical society for men. Its members were largely citizens of German birth or parentage, although this was not crucial criteria for membership in San Luis Obispo. Members met regularly in Krebs Hall to sing, and they often entertained the townspeople.

They were so successful as an organization that in August 1892 they announced purchase of a lot on the north side of Marsh Street, fifty feet west of Garden Street. They planned to build their own building. William Evans was their builder-designer and superintendent of

construction. A reception room and auditorium were planned.[18]

On Saturday night, October 14, 1892, the new Maenorchor Hall was opened. William Evans received endless compliments upon the building's acoustics and pleasing design.

E. P. Unangst was speaker. He was introduced by President E. Fluegler during the evening program. Unangst told the crowd that "Maenorchor" meant "male chorus." The organization's membership had one important commonality. All loved "music, song, and social intercourse," Mr. Unangst said. They had first organized in 1888.[19]

❧

By early autumn of that year, railroad activity along the Cuesta seemed to have stopped and San Luis Obispo and Santa Barbara citizens had become convinced that the railroad had given up or indefinitely delayed plans to build the line across the pass.

R. E. Jack wrote a letter to A. N. Towne, the general manager of Southern Pacific's San Francisco office, and the answer was good medicine for the dampened hopes of those who had worked so hard acquiring right-of-way land for the line. Mr. Towne wrote:

Dear Sir:

Referring again to your letter of the 29th September, enclosing one from Mr. Eddy. Our President, Mr. C. P. Huntington, is now here and intends to go on with the proposed work on the Coast line. If you should happen to be up this way, please drop in to see him as I am satisfied he will satisfy you of his intentions.

Yours truly,
A. N. Towne

W. M. Eddy in Santa Barbara received a note directly from C. P. Huntington which included similar assurances.

Upon receipt of the letter, Jack went to the newspaper to see Ben Brooks, who published it in the Friday, September 30, 1892 issue of the *Tribune*.

In the same issue, A. F. Hubbard offered "Carisa Lands for Sale to Actual Settlers" at prices ranging from seven to ten dollars per acre. He wanted one-third cash and eight percent interest on the unpaid balance.[20]

Not long after R. E. Jack received the letter from Towne suggesting that he might like to talk to Collis Huntington in person about the company's plans, Jack made a trip to San Francisco and was ushered into the plush office of the railroad president. Huntington told Jack that he intended to take action on the coastal line soon, and he promised to send word as soon as he could give Jack some firm information.

Sure enough, Jack received a letter from San Francisco dated October 19, 1892, containing information that the people of San Luis Obispo and Santa Barbara counties had hoped to hear:

My Dear Sir:

The last time I saw you, I told you that we would let you know when we were ready to commence work to close the gap between Santa Margarita and Ellwood. I write now to say that we have closed a contract for the work between Santa Margarita and your city, and that work is to be commenced in a very few days.

Yours very truly,
C. P. Huntington, President[21]

The *San Francisco Chronicle* announced the arrival in San Francisco of J. A. McMurtrie, a civil and mining engineer, and formerly chief engineer of the Denver and Rio Grande Railroad. McMurtrie, the paper announced, had secured the contract for the construction of the tunnels along the coast route.

Shortly after these announcements a construction train arrived in Santa Margarita loaded with tools and men. Work camps were established at both ends of the first tunnel. The contractors led seventy mules to the mouth of the tunnel, along with tons of hay to feed them. The mules would be used to haul dirt from the tunnel.

Mr. McMurtrie and his partner, Mr. Stone, came into San Luis Obispo, and everyone in town tried to talk to them. They told people they hoped to finish their job in about a year. At present, they had a few men building work camps on the Cuesta, and they wanted to start work by the middle of November.

While in town, the contractors purchased provisions for their crews from G. L. Motz and Company, Goldtree, Lazar, and A. Sauer. Now, the money was going to flow in San Luis Obispo, everyone whispered. Someone predicted that the railroad would spend two million dollars in their town within the next year. It was unbelievable!

Soon "gangs of men" were seen leveling ground for a storehouse and clearing undergrowth along the main line out of Santa Margarita to the mouth of the first proposed tunnel. This had been started two other times in previous years, but both times Southern Pacific had stopped the project before it was finished.

Ranchers around the Santa Margarita settlement immediately found a market for whatever they could offer—teams of horses, wagons and food. They also hired out to haul lumber by wagon from freight cars in Santa Margarita to construction sites.

Brooks soon wrote, "A start has been made at both ends of the big tunnel, and the dirt is flying in a very encouraging fashion..." He estimated that there were a hundred and fifty men on the job.

But there was no special celebration in town. If this was truly the beginning of railroad construction through the Cuesta, it was anticlimactic for most people.

Brooks looked back eighteen months. Excitement about the possibility of a Southern Pacific line to San Luis Obispo had reached a "white heat" at that time, but it had been changed by delays. "...Hope deferred made many heartsick, drove many exhausted citizens to other [places] or into bankruptcy. Stocks dwindled . . . merchants diligently burrowed down to find bedrock. . . . Things adjusted to new conditions, merchants got rid of superfluous clerks . . . competition diminished."

Now, things were starting again and the promises looked real.[22]

THE TOWN OF SAN LUIS OBISPO was awakened at 3:30 A.M. on Tuesday, November 8, 1892, by continuous blowing of the steam whistle in the machine shop of the Pacific Coast Railway on lower Higuera Street. The watchman had spotted flames at the south side of the coach shed in a lumber pile.

The regular firemen sounded the alarm calling volunteers to duty. The hook and ladder companies responded immediately.

Earlier in the year, the railroad company had requested that the City Trustees install two fireplugs on lower Higuera, but the council had not taken action. The nearest fireplug was several blocks away at Marsh and Higuera, and the firemen were dependent upon a company tank with only ten feet of water. It was soon exhausted, and the flames consumed both the coach and grain sheds. The loss included 1,800 sacks of beans and grain, five empty flat cars, a section boarding car, two caboose cars, a mail and baggage car, four passenger coaches, and nine flat cars loaded with lumber. Engineers had managed to remove the engines from the roundhouse.

The burned buildings and grain smoked for days. Pacific Coast Railway continued its regular service the best it could, and it placed an order for more coaches and cars, but it was some time before they were in service.[23]

During early November the *San Francisco Chronicle* carried a news item stating that once again Southern Pacific Company planned to stop work at Santa Margarita. The news spread quickly in San Luis Obispo, so Ben Brooks asked County Coroner Nichols to join him in a

trip. He hitched up his buggy and the two of them headed up the Cuesta to find out what was happening.

They found Stone of McMurtrie and Stone, the contractors, who assured them that the story was simply untrue. Stone said he had orders to hurry the work of grading to the face of the first tunnel out of Santa Margarita so that construction trains could run that far. He hoped to meet that objective by the first of February 1893. However, he was faced with blasting and moving an immense amount of rock, and a tremendous amount of fill was needed to take care of low places. A construction train would eventually help the whole job move faster.

Brooks watched a group of men blasting rocks along the mountainside. Some of the rock would be used for facing at the tunnel site. There were men already working underground at the Boronda tunnel. He reported seeing "great piles of heavy timbers" all along the grade and at Boronda's and all along the way into Santa Margarita. He said that he saw "a veritable army of men and horses and scrapers and carts and dump cars . . . busily engaged in earthwork."

On both sides of the wagon road, just before Boronda's tunnel, Brooks saw "numerous new houses" erected for boarding and lodging the workmen. There were also stables, storehouses, a blacksmith shop and repair shops. Railroad workers were living in an assortment of tents and temporary shelters. Surely, the *Chronicle* story was wrong![24]

DURING DECEMBER RAINS FELL heavily along the Central Coast of California. Santa Barbara stages found the mud and slides along the San Marcos wagon trail so bad they could not make their regular runs.

In San Luis Obispo, Brooks urged the city government to hire Sandercock to scrape the mud and accumulated horse manure from the city streets before it dried in an impassable crust.

Regardless of weather, 1892 was ending on a positive note.

CHAPTER XVI

Tunnel Building

Southern Pacific Railroad construction train positioned to remove loose rock at tunnel entrance along the Cuesta. Track laying moved along much more quickly than tunnel digging, so contractors frequently laid off crew workers preparing track beds so that tunnel crews could keep up. Typically, tunnel crews were limited to about forty men since only so many could work at one time. Workers in the tunnels received $2.50 per day, higher wages than crews on the outside because of both the danger and the hardship.

The *San Francisco Chronicle* included a prognostication of the future of San Luis Obispo in its issue of January 6, 1893. In part, it said, "The truth is that for thrice seven years San Luis Obispo has writhed beneath the frowns of fortune. Men have grown gray waiting, waiting, waiting for the railroad that never came. All this is now at an end . . .

"Within eighteen months at most, more probably within the year—the scream of the locomotive issuing from the big tunnel will be a familiar sound. The huge overland Pullmans will be seen skirting the great scenic transcontinental route which will then be open to the public."

The *Chronicle* predicted that 100,000 persons would pass through San Luis Obispo County annually. "In time, San Luis Obispo will rival Los Angeles, perhaps surpass it. What will the 1900 census show? Qui vivra, verra![1]

But for a time, the thoughts of people in San Luis Obispo were distracted by a frightening

During the years of building the Southern Pacific coastal line, the Pacific Coast narrow-gauge railway handled freight and some passengers coming to and from steamships docking at Port San Luis.

threat—the prospect of a smallpox epidemic. Word reached town in early January that this dread disease had broken out in a Southern Pacific camp on the Cuesta.

Unbeknown to most people, one worker, feverish and out of his senses with the disease, had been brought down the grade to the county hospital in a drayage wagon.

At that time, the county hospital housed the aged and the poor who could not pay for treatment. Persons with a communicable disease were usually placed in special isolated quarters away from the regular facility. However, the Southern Pacific laborer was apparently brought to the hospital before diagnosis and consequently, many people were exposed before the man's condition was recognized. As soon as the disease was diagnosed, a yellow flag went up to warn all to stay away, the "pest" house was put in order, one special nurse took charge of the case, and all communication with the sick man ceased. Fumigations and disinfectants were put to immediate use in the rest of the hospital. Unfortunately, another railroad worker who appeared in town sick was placed in the pest house without clear diagnosis.

Word spread in town that free vaccinations were available for all who applied. The school superintendent announced that children who were not vaccinated would not be permitted to attend school.

The Board of Health quickly called for strict measures to prevent tramps from entering town and to compel those present to leave at once. Mission school was closed indefinitely and did not open for weeks.[2]

Since people were so frightened, they readily believed rumors that circulated quickly about town. Perhaps the worst rumor of all was that smallpox was running rampant in the railroad camp on the Cuesta.

When George Stone of McMurtrie and Stone appeared in town, he was almost immediately surrounded by people along Monterey Street. He was most emphatic in declaring that what people were hearing was only dreadful rumor—that only a single case of smallpox had originated in camp. It had occurred five weeks earlier, and the man was now nearly recovered, he said. He denied rumors that some camp tents and tool sheds had been ordered burned.

The crowd that gathered around Mr. Stone expressed relief. However, a day or so later, the first victim in the pest house died. The second one escaped in his night clothes, but he was recaptured and locked up again.

Throughout January hundreds of people lined up at City Hall, where all the physicians in town took turns during long days of vaccinating all comers. By the end of the month, doctors felt they had acted quickly enough to avert epidemic, and no new cases developed.[3]

❧

Land sales had been slow for two years in and around the county, but with the new year, the West Coast Land Company reported several sales in town. All the Terrace Hill property, the Central Addition, and lots in the Phillips Addition were once more for sale, C. H. Phillips said.[4]

In February 1895, A. S. Austin, a reporter for the *Tribune*, undertook an eyewitness investigation of activity at the railroad front. He arrived in Santa Margarita early in the morning on February 11 and proceeded to look around.

In "railroad circles" he found everything "whooping and booming," he said. Three engines were giving off steam and several railroad cars were loaded with steel rails and cross ties. The banks of a hillside north of Santa Margarita had provided needed gravel, and Austin counted forty railroad cars loaded with gravel. He talked to the railroad engineer on board a "90-ton mountain engine" and to Conductor E. Stanwood, the man in charge of the train.

He also talked to John Higgins, "captain" of a forty-man crew responsible for track laying. The men called Higgins "Black Jack." He was "tough and hard as they come," they said, and of all the track laying "captains" in the country, he had the reputation for getting the most track laid in a day. In the last day and a half, Higgins' men had laid five-eighths of a mile of track. They worked in three separate groups— one group handled and laid ties, another placed the rails along the ties, and the third bolted on the fishplates and drove the spikes.

The immediate goal, Black Jack said, was to lay three miles of track. This would provide rail line up to the mouth of tunnel number one on the Cuesta, the main tunnel. All of the materials were on hand in Santa Margarita to get this much of the job completed.

Austin asked many questions about the tunnels, and Higgins took pleasure in explaining things to him. There would be six tunnels dug between Santa Margarita and San Luis Obispo. The main tunnel, number one, would be about thirty-six hundred feet long; number two would be about fourteen hundred feet; and the other four would range between seven and eight hundred feet each.

When Austin saw tunnel number one, about three hundred and eighty feet of digging and timber work had been completed from the north entrance and about three hundred feet from the south entrance, but the timber work inside the tunnel was incomplete.

Work was also underway at tunnel number two. Workmen had dug about a hundred feet into the mountain at each end of this tunnel.

Two gangs of workers were employed on ten-hour shifts, and work continued night and day. Austin reported that diggers used tallow dips for light in the tunnels, but an electric light plant was nearing completion, and very soon Southern Pacific expected to provide electric light in the tunnels for more efficient construction.

Austin heard that a man named Erickson had been given the contract for a large cut and several fills between the second tunnel and San Luis Obispo. He also heard reports that Erickson intended to establish a mountain camp for about two hundred workmen at the south end of tunnel number two.[5]

⚕

REPORTS ABOUT RAIN IN flood proportions came in from all over the county during the middle of February 1893. The San Luis Obispo City main water line was damaged during the storm, and so while people waded about town, there wasn't any drinking water.

A landslide on the Cuesta stage road about parallel with railroad tunnel number one prevented passage on the Cuesta that month. Mail delivery stopped, and people received no news about the outside world for a few days. The Pacific Coast narrow-gauge railway coped with about three feet of water on lower Higuera and gave up its regular run to Arroyo Grande, Nipomo, Los Alamos, and Los Olivos for a few days. Word came that bridges at Arroyo Grande and Santa Maria had been carried away by the water.

A big sycamore tree was uprooted near the Ramona Hotel and washed down to the Marsh Street bridge. People expected the bridge to be destroyed but, somehow, it held until the waters subsided and the tree could be cut up and removed.[6]

⚕

A most extraordinary doctor appeared in town in February. He set up headquarters at the Cosmopolitan Hotel and announced that he could cure "most of the ills of the human flesh" by calling upon the "angel world."

Two *Tribune* reporters visited the Wizard's rooms to test his expressed ability to communicate with the dead. The Wizard tried hard by various questions to identify the dead from a list of names provided by the reporters. When Benjamin Brooks, the newspaper editor, was identified as among the dead, the reporters left the hotel convinced that the good doctor wasn't that good.

Still, the *Tribune* reported that "the lame and halt are flocking to his rooms by the score."[7]

A. S. Austin, the roving reporter, took a trip to the southern part of the county to report on activities there. Among other things, he reminded his readers about the "extensive deposits of bituminous rock" beginning about eight miles south of San Luis Obispo and extending toward Arroyo Grande. Austin, who had previously been unfamiliar with this substance, discovered that it was the black tar stuff used to pave streets in the big cities.

A company called the San Luis Obispo Bituminous Rock Company was mining this rock on about twelve hundred acres of land, he said. The company employed as many as thirty-five workers at times and provided "large boarding houses and ample accommodations for their workmen," and had facilities for processing the raw bitumen for commercial use.

Austin visited a second operation called the Occidental Bituminous Rock Company, about a half mile east of the first one. This company was leasing land from George Steele and had an open pit mining operation. Unfortunately, the land was not near Pacific Coast Railway line, so the product had to be hauled by wagon for some distance to reach port where it could be transported by ship.

Austin also visited the hot springs resort called Newsom Springs, to the south of Arroyo Grande. He reported that Newsom owned about fifteen hundred acres of land adjoining the springs. "The springs," he wrote, "are situated in a natural cliff in the hills that is peculiarly lovely and romantic. The wagon road passes up through a gulch from the south and the depression at the springs of a few acres in extent is protected by high hills in all directions except to the south." He reported a strong smell of sulphur from the spring waters, which poured out at about one hundred degrees Fahrenheit.

Newson was building new bath houses, Austin said, and constructing a "curbing around the spring." He had eight furnished cottages for rent to tourists at rentals ranging from fifteen to thirty dollars per month.[8]

Austin did a good job of traveling around and reviewing conditions in the county. On February 18, he took a ride on the construction train out of Santa Margarita to the mouth of tunnel number one. As they came within one-half mile of the tunnel's mouth, double track had been laid to accommodate extra engines for doubling over the grade, he said.

He saw men at work at both ends of tunnel number two. Beyond this tunnel he found men clearing the banks, burning and grubbing brush. About two miles beyond tunnel number two, a construction camp was being set up by Higbee and Bernard Construction Company. Austin estimated that forty men were putting up tents. He also reported that a camp for another two hundred men was expected to be set up about three miles outside of San Luis Obispo near Chorro Creek.[9]

In the early morning on February 16, 1893, a huge fire broke out in a wooden building used as a paint shop at Los Alamos. It spread quickly out of control, burning Arana's Barbershop, the Alamo Hotel, McLaughlin's Drug Store, and the general merchandise store. One entire business block was destroyed. The whole town pitched in to remove merchandise from the stores as the fire raged, and the effort was successful. People were convinced that the fire had been started by tramps who had a grudge against the paint store owner.

Since the town had no facilities for fighting the fire, its people could only try to save merchandise. They did attempt to pull down small buildings between larger ones, hoping to separate key buildings from direct flames, but they were not successful.[10]

Austin made another trip to the tunnels at the end of February 1893. This time he talked to a Mr. Marsh, the engineer in charge of constructing the tunnels. He reported that workmen had dug three hundred and twenty-five feet into the north end of tunnel number one and two hundred and seventy feet into the planned south entrance. At the second tunnel, they had advanced another fifty feet on the north side and about thirty feet at the south end since his last report. Marsh said he had two hundred men engaged in tunnel work, and he estimated that they were progressing about thirty-five feet each week at each end of every tunnel.

At the same time, grading for the railbed was underway. The finished grading of the bed between Santa Margarita and the main tunnel, a distance of three miles, was nearly completed. Within a few days it would be ready for laying permanent track, the engineer said.

On February 24, 1893, Brooks wrote that "constant processions of men and scrapers, great wagons filled with indescribable paraphernalia... tools and implements... [passing through town] tell their own story of the progress of the army that is at last connecting San Luis Obispo with the world at large.

"We are reaping the tardy results of the movement that three years ago was undertaken with so much misgiving and carried out at so much personal self-sacrifice by the people of this city.

"If ever the history of that movement is written, and we plan it shall be, it will be an interesting monument of pluck and enterprise, a widespread, united effort that was only to be expected of this city . . ."[11]

෬ක෨

AFTER THE FIRE WHICH destroyed the Pacific Coast Railway Depot along with some warehouses and some coaches, the railway company had been forced to rebuild. The result was an important improvement in San Luis Obispo. The earlier warehouses had been really decrepit and sway-backed, but because they served their purpose without requiring the expenditure of capital, they had been continued in use.

By March 1893, a new depot and new warehouse buildings were operational, and an artesian well had been sunk to assure the availability of water in the event of another fire. The railroad also purchased some new coaches and laid asphalt walks and driveways around the depot in place of the wooden planks used in former years.

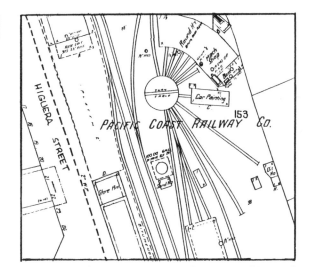

In March, 1893, the center in San Luis Obispo for Pacific Coast Railway activity had been restored following a devastating fire. This is a section from a 1905 map showing the locomotive turntable and roundhouse. Located on lower Higuera street at Madonna Road where a modern shopping center has incorporated architectural features of the original warehouses.

The new warehouse for storing grain was forty-five by three hundred and fifty feet. It was constructed on a brick foundation wall that was five feet high. The rest of the siding and roof were constructed of galvanized metal siding, and the floor was asphalt and gravel. There were large sliding doors on each side of the building facing both the railroad track and the County Road. In 1980, this warehouse is still in use as the quarters for a farm and garden supply business.

The new coach shed was two hundred and twenty-five feet long and had three sets of tracks leading into it. It was built to house between ten and eighteen coaches at one time. The Pacific Coast Railway had ordered four new passenger cars, one combination baggage and passenger car, and one baggage and mail car from Hammond and Company in San Francisco for delivery March 15, 1893.[12]

While Southern Pacific Railroad track was being laid, people living in San Luis Obispo County could still travel slowly by both land and sea, provided they were hearty and patient. Pacific Coast Steamship Company steamers traveled both north and south, making twice-weekly stops at Port Harford. Four ships in service stopped regularly at the port. They were the *Santa Rosa*, the *Los Angeles*, the *Corona*, and the *Eureka*. Roundtrip fare was $11.60 for a cabin, less if one traveled in steerage.

The Pacific Coast Railway had daily roundtrip service between San Luis Obispo and Arroyo Grande, Los Berros, Nipomo, and Santa Maria. It included stops at Miles (a planned development that never developed), Sycamore Sulphur Springs, Avila Beach, and Port Harford. One train each day continued to Los

Alamos and Los Olivos. Roundtrip fare from San Luis Obispo to Los Olivos was $5.80. Six-horse, eighteen passenger Concord stages met the train at Los Olivos to provide passage to Santa Barbara. The roundtrip Sunday excursion fare to Sycamore Sulphur Springs or Port Harford was fifty cents.[13]

❧

In early March, *Tribune* reporter A. S. Austin was back on the construction train between Santa Margarita and the first tunnel. Heavy

A family gathers at the beach to see the wrecked S.S. Santa Rosa. Although people wore working clothes during the week, they dressed well on Sundays, even for an after-church buggy ride to the beach.

On July 7, 1911, the Santa Rosa, one of the ships making regular stops at Port Harford and Santa Barbara on runs between San Francisco and Los Angeles, went aground and split completely in half. The Santa Rosa was one of four ships of the Pacific Coast Steamship Company in service during the 1880s and 1890s.

rains had slowed grading and rail laying. A camp of wooden buildings had been constructed at Chorro Creek for workers and equipment. He heard that Erickson's Construction Company, with a crew of eighty men, planned to start grading operations in that vicinity very soon.

Six miles up the grade, according to Austin, another work force estimated at one hundred and fifty men was at work for the Higbee and Bernard Construction Company, which had the contract for the grading from the south end of tunnel number two to the north end of Erickson's section.

Tunnel number two was still under construction at this time. Workers had advanced from the south end about seventy-five feet, but only about forty feet on the north end. At tunnel number one, work crews had dug more than four hundred feet in from the south and five hundred feet in from the north.

In earlier digging, workers brought out traces of coal in the large tunnel, but no major deposits appeared.[14]

Excitement in town reached a virtual clamor among certain local people on March 15, 1893, when word spread that a group of railroad officials was in town. What were they here for?

It was soon confirmed that H. E. Huntington, the nephew of the great Collis Huntington, had indeed arrived at the Ramona Hotel by stage from Santa Margarita. He was accompanied by the company's engineering superintendent, William Hood; W. Solomon, who was a member of the banking firm of Aug. Spyer and Company, New York; and G. L. King, Mr. Huntington's private secretary.

They had a big meal at the Ramona Hotel, then rented a surrey and a fine four-horse team from McKennon's Stable. Huntington seemed interested in surveying the town. The streets were still muddy from the rain and it was cold, so they returned to the hotel after only an hour.

Townspeople called at the hotel that evening to pay their respects to the distinguished visitors. Huntington and the others talked pleasantly with all comers for several hours. As it turned out, the officials were taking a ten-day tour from San Francisco to Los Angeles to learn what they could about the resources all along the proposed line that might support a railroad freight and passenger business. They had stayed at the Del Monte Lodge on the Monterey Peninsula the night before arriving in San Luis Obispo.

People hoped that Hood would answer some questions about planned railroad construction south of San Luis Obispo, but as usual, he was reticent to talk about future plans, though he was quite willing to discuss work that was already completed.[15]

After the smallpox scare that originated with Southern Pacific workers on the Cuesta, the railroad constructed its own small hospital, a two-room building under supervision of Dr. Nichols at the foot of the Cuesta. This was almost necessary since local people were not happy about the whole town's being exposed to some dread disease that might be brought in by railroad crews. There was also the possibility of hospital facilities' being inadequate during an emergency.[16]

Over the months the Southern Pacific hospital repaired dozens of men who suffered minor accidents and illness, but occasionally, victims were beyond repair. One Friday in April 1893, an unexpected explosion occurred in tunnel number two. Two men were horribly injured and died from their wounds. A number of others escaped with only small injuries.

CHAUNCEY PHILLIPS, R. E. Jack, and others who joined them as partners in one or more land ventures, tried hard to keep well ahead of Southern Pacific track laying. Even before the railroad arrived in San Luis Obispo, they surveyed land farther south and made investments. In April 1893, they heard that a depot was planned on the Cienega Ranch southwest of Arroyo Grande, so they formed a syndicate and negotiated with Coffee Rice, the owner, for purchase of acreage around the land Rice had given Southern Pacific Company for right-of-way and a depot.

Among the partners of Phillips and Jack in this venture were John Adams and a Mr. Stowell of Paso Robles. The partnership announced its intention of developing about sixty blocks of lots for a summer resort. Railroad engineers staked out right-of-way land, and C. O. King and Van R. Elliott were employed by the syndicate to survey and map a new town. The "town" eventually became Oceano, a community supported principally by truck crop agricultural products and a vegetable processing plant.

The tract was laid out in lots one hundred and ten feet deep with twenty-five- and fifty-foot frontages. Around the edges, they laid out "villa" sites ranging from two to ten acres in size. In the center of the town, the developers planned a fountain and announced their intention of constructing a "grand" hotel, but

The Coffee T. Rice three-story mansion at Oceano as it appeared early in the century. It's balconies, turrets and gingerbread trim make up an outstanding example of California Victorian architecture of the 1890's.

typically, most of the grandiose plans never came to be.[17]

After disposing of the ranch, Rice moved to Santa Cruz, but his large Victorian home still stands in 1980 as a landmark in the community of Oceano.

ℐn April 1893, William Hood announced in San Francisco that Southern Pacific was having difficulty finding enough construction laborers and that he expected to find it necessary to employ Chinese labor. At the time, the railroad paid workers one dollar a day and board.

Hood also said that work on the extension was difficult and that he did not expect to build beyond San Luis Obispo during 1893.[18]

That same month, a reporter with the *San Francisco Chronicle* interviewed Colonel C. F. Crocker, who had returned to San Francisco from the East after an absence of three months. He said what people in all of the coastal communities wanted to hear: "The only construction that we consider of great importance at present is to complete the gap in our coast line between Santa Margarita and Ellwood. We are very desirous of finishing that work as soon as possible."

But some of the news wasn't that good. "We do not pretend to be able to complete that stretch of road without placing bonds on the market . . . It will take, I should judge, fully five million dollars to finish the coast line."

"Do you think it probable that the gap will be closed this year?" the reporter asked.

"Oh, no, indeed," Col. Crocker answered. "If we had our bonds all placed and three thousand men at work we could not finish the road this year."

"Will it be finished in 1894?" the reporter asked.

"I certainly think that it will. We are working away at the tunnels between Santa Margarita and San Luis Obispo, but that work is not being pushed ahead nearly so fast as it would be if we were in a position to rush the rest of the line."

Later in April the *San Francisco Bulletin* carried a long interview with Chief Engineer William Hood in which he elaborated on his concern about the labor problems the company had been experiencing along the gap. "There are now from 1,000 to 1,200 men down there at work," Hood was quoted as saying, "but there are changes all the time, and we have to keep sending down new gangs. Not a Chinaman has yet been employed—except as a cook—but the work has to be done, and we may have yet to employ Chinese laborers.

"We have been sending men down to the front from San Francisco, but we have poor luck in getting men who seem willing to stay and do the work. If we want fifty additional men, we have to send down from a hundred to a hundred and fifty, before we can get the number required."

San Francisco, July 9, 1895.

R. E. Jack, Esq.,

County Bank, San Luis Obispo.

Dear Sir,

I am directed to advise you that we will put in the spur track from Oceano to the beach if you and your associates can arrange to do the grading of this spur ready for the track as laid out and cross-sectioned by our Engineers and be graded under their direction. We will put in the culverts necessary for the grading and will lay the track forthwith on completion of the grading.

You will notice this gives the Oceano people a chance to share the expense of the construction of the spur and hence share in the responsibilities as to having it worth while for us to have the spur exist.

If you decide to do this please telegraph me at once that I may procure the necessary track material in time as we are a little short of some items, also that I may have the culverts built.

R. E. Jack and his partners built a pavilion at Oceano Beach as a recreational attraction. They negotiated with Southern Pacific to construct a spur track from the main line to the beach and to run excursions to Oceano. Apparently this speculative venture enjoyed only moderate success.

He said that many of the men were "trampers." After getting the trip south and a good meal, they disappeared without touching a pick or shovel. Of course, the work on the seven tunnels and winding road on the Cuesta was heavy and difficult. Hood compared it to the railroad construction through the Tehachapi and Siskiyou mountains.

The *Bulletin* article also said that the Southern Pacific line would cross the narrow-gauge Pacific Coast road several times, "often enough to worry the managers considerably." [20]

One way people in San Luis Obispo witnessed the excitement of daily railroad construction was in seeing the procession of work teams headed for the camps along the Cuesta. Teams carried food, construction equipment, and supplies of every kind. Fifty head of mules from Santa Maria formed one part of an outfit

that came in from the south along the county road and down Monterey Street and up the Cuesta one day in April.

The town was now feeling proud of itself after experiencing rejection and failure for so long in the pursuit of a Southern Pacific line. San Luis Obispo only had a population of about three thousand people and yet the town had raised $50,000 to buy right-of-way land for the railroad.

Taxpayers had also assumed an indebtedness of $40,000 for local improvements. Among other things, the city had walled in a long stretch of its creek. A system for sewage drainage had been developed, but much work still needed to be done. Macadam sidewalks had been built on Monterey, Higuera, and some side streets between the two. However, the streets were still only covered with gravel. The city also had the

Ramona Hotel, a large wooden structure with excellent accommodations that only needed guests.[21]

A reporter for the *San Luis Obispo Tribune* accompanied Dr. Nichols, the Southern Pacific doctor, to a camp established by the construction company of Higbee and Bernard. This camp was known as Camp No. 4, and was located in back of Nevada House (or Lyman's) on the Cuesta road. The reporter counted about twenty-five tents. Each tent contained eight double bunks for workers.

He learned that Higbee and Bernard's major task at the time was dynamiting away part of a mountain. The dirt resulting from the explosions was pushed over the side to fill a gulch below.[22]

Toward the end of April an article in the *San Francisco Bulletin* helped keep alive a rumor of long standing in San Luis Obispo. With some logic, perhaps, people had the feeling that the Pacific Coast narrow gauge had probably long since been purchased by Southern Pacific. Land promoters around Los Olivos, Santa Ynez, and Ballard had good reason to hope and to promote the idea that the Southern Pacific would pass through those communities enroute to Santa Barbara, and the Pacific Coast Railway had line to Los Olivos.

C. O. Johnson, the manager of the Pacific Coast Railway in San Luis Obispo, was completely disgusted after reading the article in the *Bulletin*. The grades and curves of the narrow gauge were such that the bed simply would not be usable as a line by Southern Pacific, who could build a complete new bed for less money than it would take to make this one usable, he said.[23]

The principal contractor for Southern Pacific construction through the Cuesta, F. A. McMurtrie, had learned his trade in Pennsylvania building railroad line in the Lehigh coal region. Later he was chief engineer for the Denver and Rio Grande Railroad. He threaded

Pavilion at Oceano in 1908. The note on the postcard reads: "S. H. William, president of the Oceano Beach Land and Improvement Company, and party inspecting pier at Oceano Beach." The pavilion saw many dances and forms of entertainment during its years. It no longer exists.

that giant road through the canyon of the Arkansas and into Leadville, and continued it over Marshall Pass to an elevation of 10,800 feet and through the high Tennessee Pass. Then he pushed it through the Black Canyon of the Gunnison over the high mesas beyond and through to Utah.

McMurtrie seemed well qualified for handling construction over the Cuesta, yet the job proceeded much too slowly. It was described as the most expensive railroad building on the coast. It was costing Southern Pacific about $300,000 for each mile in the Cuesta including the tunnels.[24]

THE DEATH OF JOAQUIN ESTRADA was reported in the *Tribune* on May 2, 1893. Senor Estrada had been the original grantee of the great Santa Margarita Rancho, and had sold it in 1869 to General Patrick Murphy.

Estrada was a leader in San Luis Obispo during both the Mexican period and the early years of the American period. In 1850 he had served as County Recorder and in 1858 he was County Treasurer. Until his death at the age of seventy-eight, he made his home at the foot of the Cuesta at a place well-known as Estrada Gardens. Over the years, nearly every group that had outings had picnicked there.[25]

In early May, workers from Camp No. 3 began to appear in town, and word spread that they had left the job as a body. They had demanded wages of $2.00 a day, and when the demand was refused, they stopped work. There were fifty men employed at that camp.

By this time, the workers were getting $1.75 a day or about $45.50 per month for twenty-six days' work. Out of this amount, $18.00 was taken for board, and $1.00 for hospital fees, leaving net pay of $1.02 a day. Shoes, overalls, and shirts wore out rapidly, so a worker's store bill was about $3.50 a month, leaving him about eighty-eight cents net for a day's work.

Wallace stayed with it. Then the boss put him to work in a hole full of rocks with water up to his knees. Somehow, that was too much. He climbed out of the hole and quit. He had worked four and a half days in April and four and a half days in May.

For his time, he was given a time check for $5.69. He complained that he had been shorted, but Erickson told him he had taken out board and hospital fees of $1.00 for April and $1.00 for May. Resigned to his fate, Wallace left camp for San Luis Obispo, where he was directed to a particular hotel to cash his check. The hotel charged him ten percent for cashing the check,

Employees and local people gathered under the covered board sidewalk at the Oceano Hotel and Saloon to have a postcard photo made. This one was sent by E. M. Bonetti to Mr. and Mrs. D. Martinez in San Luis Obispo.

Men working in the tunnels received $2.50 a day—considerably higher, but the risk and working conditions demanded it.

There were plenty of stories about the poor treatment and the low pay received from some of the contractors.

William Wallace, a laborer with Erickson's Camp No. 5, came into San Luis Obispo one day and began telling his story to everyone who would listen along Monterey Street: "I was sent down here from San Francisco by an employment agent named Hanson . . . who told me . . . the work was not hard . . . the pay would be $1.75 per day and board $4.50 per week, leaving me $6.60 a week to provide for clothing and savings."

Wallace said that he arrived by train in Santa Margarita along with others to join the work force at Camp No. 5. The work was hard, but

so Wallace found himself with about $5.00 for his nine days' work.

Others reported similar treatment. For the most part, these men were down-and-outers, and very few were matches in a contest with their bosses.[26]

A reporter named Carter from Santa Margarita became a regular visitor along the wagon road that followed the rail bed. His writing was sometimes fuzzy, but he succeeded in providing some feeling for what was happening along the Cuesta.

"Your tramp goes often for the sole purpose of feasting his eyes on the great reality," he wrote one day in April 1893.

Up at tunnel number two one morning he

found the foreman, Remick, and his crew working in and out of the tunnel. "There is the click of hammers on drills, the smell of powder, the glimmer of candles in the visible darkness, the barely discernible figures in the gloom—the carpenters, a car, a mule, a group of engineers and assistants."

He recorded activity along the trail this way: "We meet gang after gang of men and teams, all very busy. The cuts through the points of spurs of the mountains are but little less work than the tunnels."

Near Erickson's Camp, he said, "Here, we see many wagon loads of stone, sand and cement on the move to say nothing of great piles of material on the ground. There are many familiar faces among the teamsters. Through all this part of the work, there are no bridges. It is all culverts, and a great space to be filled with earth.

"There must be fully 1200 men employed, directly and indirectly, on this great work," Carter estimated, "very few of whom can be seen from any of the ordinary public roads."[27]

❦

In mid-May of that year the San Luis Obispo Mission Church asked for bids from local contractors for the addition of a new wing. The improvements called for a brick "ell extending from the present church building toward Chorro Street . . . which will be 25′ x 40′ making additional seating capacity of at least a hundred."

"We notice that in some sections of the country," the newspaper reported, "the old Missions are being restored so as to renew their appearance as originally constructed, and it is a regret that the same spirit cannot be exhibited here."

F. C. Mitchell was selected as contractor for the addition of the new wing of the church. His low bid was $2,850.[28]

❦

One Friday in May 1893, George Manderscheid, who had been the trusted agent for the Pacific Coast Steamship Company and the Pacific Coast Railway at Port Harford for fifteen years, disappeared.

A short article appeared in the following Thursday's Tribune about his disappearance. The story mentioned that he had left a letter for Mrs. Manderscheid which said that he would be gone for only a few days. He mentioned that he was going to Paso Robles.

Since there was a letter, it seemed safe to assume that there had not been foul play. However, a few people thought "he must be suffering from some brain trouble."

Nearly two weeks passed without any word about the agent. By this time, every possible reason for his disappearance had been advanced through town talk. Until now, he had been considered a man of highest "integrity and industry." But there were unconfirmed rumors that some $1,500 in company funds had disappeared. On the other hand, people said it was highly unlikely that he was in a position to have access to that much company money.

Another rumor assumed that family differences had developed, but friends of both Manderscheid and his wife denied this possibility.

Yet another rumor suggested that the agent had received a strongly worded official communication from his immediate superior. He had found it offensive, and upon impulse, had headed for the San Francisco office of the company to complain or present his case. This version left the agent's integrity intact.

The San Francisco newspapers took hold of this story and left no room for Manderscheid's dignity. They frankly accused him of absconding with company money.

Then the truth suddenly reached everyone. The Pacific Coast Steamship and Railway had hired Morse's Detective Agency in San Francisco to find Manderscheid, and the detective agency placed an advertisement in a San Francisco newspaper offering a one hundred dollar reward for his return. It soon became generally known around San Luis Obispo that the company was really missing some money.[29]

❦

Construction of the new wing of the mission church in May 1893 included some removal of old parts. The Tribune said, "To a relic hunter, the old construction now being torn away would be of the greatest interest and value."

While cutting away the roof of the church where the new wing was to join it, workers found that the ceiling covered an earlier ceiling. They reported that the boards in the original ceiling had been hewn down to the required thinness and smoothness with hatchets or similar implements, and that the nails used were wrought iron.

"The decorations were equally crude," the *Tribune* reported, "the boards having been whitewashed and then rather archaic stars painted on the white surface with some thin blue coloring matter and seemingly without a brush." [30]

Along with the construction of the Southern Pacific railroad bed came the promise of even greater long distance communication with the outside world. A report reached town that telephone lines were almost completed from San Francisco to Kings (Kings City). The *Tribune* optimistically predicted that "within the next two months we will be able to talk directly with our friends in San Francisco and . . . Los Angeles." It was unbelievable.

The telephone line followed about the same course as the Southern Pacific railroad. South of San Luis Obispo, plans were underway for telephone lines connecting San Luis Obispo, Santa Maria, and Lompoc.

For years and years, the people between Soledad and Santa Barbara had felt their remoteness from the world. Soon railroad and telephone lines connecting them to San Francisco and Los Angeles would change life completely. [31]

The Board of Trade of San Luis Obispo, formed in 1887 for the purpose of promoting population, land sales and general prosperity, had not remained active after the money was finally raised for the purchase of land for a Southern Pacific right-of-way. But in 1893 many businessmen (including some of the same people who had been active in 1887) began to feel once more the need of organization to promote their city.

A few of the city's prominent men gathered at the San Luis Obispo Bank on Saturday afternoon, May 27, to discuss promotional ideas and needed improvements. Judge McD. R. Venable acted as temporary chairman. The group decided to organize the San Luis Development Company, and Chauncey Phillips, J. M. Felts, and L. N. Kaiser were elected to serve as an executive committee. Luigi Marre, McD. R. Venable, and George T. Gragg were appointed to a committee to draw up a plan for a "highway" between San Luis Obispo and Avila Beach.

R. E. Jack, J. M. Wilcoxon, and Horatio M. Warden were appointed to assist the newspaper's development in the city and county. Jack, R. A. Loomis, and L. Rackliffe were appointed to investigate the feasibility of improving the water system.

Jack, Phillips, Marre, and Warden, along with J. P. Andrews, H. A. Vachell, and Benjamin Brooks, assumed responsibility to investigate construction of a railroad from Port Harford to the San Joaquin Valley. [32]

In June, the beginning of the tourist season, Southern Pacific announced its intention of providing the fastest possible train service between San Francisco and their own Del Monte Lodge in Monterey. They expected to achieve an average speed of forty-three miles per hour and to run at sixty miles per hour along some of the straight stretches. A mile in one minute was a tremendous breakthrough, and the announcement was dazzling. [33]

On Thursday, June 8, 1893, Southern Pacific's Chief Engineer William Hood and an assistant arrived in San Luis Obispo. They were accompanied by contractors who had crews working along the Cuesta. These men had been following the route for the railroad line into San Luis Obispo, on which work was expected to begin soon.

The newspaper predicted that a planned "viaduct crossing Monterey Street will be a substantial and ornamental work." A depot building, a roundhouse, and a machine works were all part of the plans. [34]

Tunnel number one was now dug to a depth of 1,950 feet, and it still had to be dug another 1,930 feet. With two shifts of workmen, digging proceeded at about ten feet a day.[35]

❦

THERE WAS NO CELEBRATION planned for Independence Day in San Luis Obispo in 1893. Instead, San Luis Obispans attended celebrations in other communities in the county.

Paso Robles welcomed visitors with a temperature well in the nineties and a big barbecue in the park.

Santa Margarita offered a brass band and a day of entertainment. People came up the grade in their wagons and buggies. Some came by Wells-Fargo coach.

Pismo had an estimated three thousand visitors that day. There were speeches, a barbecue, and a ball game. In the evening there was a "grand ball."

On that Fourth of July, a stringer for the *Tribune* living south of Arroyo Grande saddled his horse, Nig, and headed for the Pismo celebration. It was the time of year when the berries in the brambles along the road were ripening. He wrote proudly of how well the fruit and vegetables grew along the Arroyo Grande.

Beyond the town of Arroyo Grande, the stringer traveled the long road through the new town site of Grover, laid out to meet the planned route of the Southern Pacific line. He wrote of viewing the whole bay as well as Port Harford, nearby Pismo, and Point Sal to the south. At the time, nothing blocked the view from the bare town site. He also said that he could see the distant hills of Los Berros and Nipomo.

At the beach at Grover there were bath houses well patronized by the bathers, and the beach was alive with "conveyances" of every kind from a "dog cart to a four-in-hand."

The stringer watched the teams, the bathers in the surf, the clammers, and the children playing on the dunes. It was "the grandest panorama I ever beheld," he said. The developers of Grover called the beachfront Huntington Beach. The stringer couldn't figure out the meaning of the name. He did not know the name of the man who was a principal owner of

Southern Pacific. But that name was soon dropped anyway. The whole length of the beach had been called Pismo too long for people to accept a name change.

The warehouse at Pismo was used as an auditorium for the Independence Day exercises. A grandstand had been constructed, and it was bountifully decorated with evergreen boughs and a large United States flag. President of the Day Mark Harloe delivered an address that brought rousing applause. Then the Honorable George Steele provided the patriotic address of the day. "The crowd was spellbound," the reporter wrote.

Four full beefs were barbecued to feed the crowd.[36]

❦

During the early part of summer in 1893, railroad workers began appearing in San Luis Obispo from the Cuesta saying that they had been discharged. There had been so many ups and downs since construction started that even the smallest negative signs were depressing to townspeople. Prosperity seemed always a step away, and many people felt work might stop again.

But concerned community leaders, the newspaper, and property owners did some investigating and determined that progress was being made.

Work was still underway at tunnel number one. Only so many men could successfully dig at one time in a tunnel, but most of the time there were two shifts of men at work.

The contractors explained that the men who had been discharged were workers outside the tunnels, because work on the railroad bed moved along much faster than the tunnel work. Money came to the contractors from Southern Pacific on a regular basis, and they could use it most efficiently by making progress along the entire line at about the same pace. When work on the beds got too far ahead of the tunnels, they stopped it or slowed it down for a while, which meant laying off some men.

People in San Luis Obispo looked forward to the beginning of work on the depot, the roundhouse and yard buildings in town. This would mean that there would be crews of workers living in town and spending money in town. There were frequent mentions about construction of the railroad bridge across Monterey Street beginning soon, but there were no signs of it.[37]

❦

ON RATHER SHORT NOTICE in July, R. E. Jack, who was now mayor of San Luis Obispo, heard that United States Vice President A. E. Stevenson was making a steamer tour along the coast of California from San Diego to San Francisco.

Jack thought it was quite possible that the ship might stop at Port Harford, and that the vice president might accept an invitation to visit San Luis Obispo. He quickly arranged a notice to be printed in the *Tribune* and called a meeting of leading citizens at the Ramona Hotel.

An invitation was telegraphed to Redondo Beach, the first stop for the ship, and in a return telegram dated July 17, 1893, Stevenson sent this message: "Our party highly appreciates your courteous invitation and will be pleased to be at your service while at Port Harford."[38]

Hurried plans were made and at 7:00 A.M. on July 18, a greeting party boarded a Pacific Coast Railway car that took them to Port Harford to meet the steamship *Corona*. They had hoped to use a steamer tug in the harbor to give the vice president a tour of the breakwater. Since the harbor was a federally financed facility and local people hoped for its further development, the prospect of showing it to the vice president really appealed to them. Unfortunately, the *Corona* arrived in port an hour late, and there was a heavy fog.

So, Stevenson and his party were led from the ship directly to the waiting train on the wharf. In the party were Mrs. Stevenson, their daughter, Mrs. Stevenson's sister and her daughter, Judge W. G. Ewing, his wife and their two daughters, Judge George Burnett and his daughters, a Judge Shope and a Mayor Pickett.

Mayor Jack and members of his party provided a warm welcome for their distinguished visitors. San Luis Obispo's Judge McD. Venable, who was returning from Santa Barbara on the same ship, knew some of the people in Vice President Stevenson's party and made some of the introductions. The guests boarded a special car of the train—a new one that had never been used—one of the cars recently purchased after the fire.

At the new depot at the corner of Higuera and South streets, the vice president debarked to the lively music of the San Luis Obispo band.

Some fifty decorated horse-drawn conveyances stood ready for a gala procession across town to the Ramona Hotel. But the parade was not direct; it went past the mission and out Chorro Road where, across the green fields in the distance, the vice president could glimpse railroad construction on the hairpin turn and in the direction of Stenner Creek.

Back in town again, there was a continuous display of bunting and other decoration along the parade route. All the bunting in town had been gathered and decorations placed within a few hours, in a spontaneous expression of excitement.

The Ramona Hotel was crowded with people who cheered as Stevenson stepped down from the carriage, climbed the steps of the hotel and entered the lobby. The ladies of San Luis Obispo had covered the lobby with flowers. When little Ernestine Ortega greeted the vice president with an armful of sweet peas, he reached down and gathered her into his arms along with the flowers. The crowd was delighted.

Ramona Hotel Manager Fredericks stood ready once more to "prove the capabilities of the house." The lunch was light but beautifully prepared. Souvenir menu cards were distributed to all who were present.

Following the meal, the vice president and his party walked out on the balcony of the hotel to greet the waiting crowd. During the next half hour, Stevenson and each of the men in his company spoke. "All of the gentlemen are brilliant, polished and practiced speakers, and all were speaking in a vein appropriate to an after-dinner occasion," the *Tribune* reported.

Back in the lobby of the hotel, Vice President Stevenson greeted the long line of citizens one by one with a handshake and a few words of conversation.

At last, there was the return trip of escorting vehicles to the train station, the train ride to Avila, and the parting of the *Corona* from Port

148

Hauling oil by mule in Santa Maria.

Harford enroute to San Francisco.

It had been a great day in the history of San Luis Obispo.[39]

After the big fire in 1887 that burned the Andrews Hotel to the ground, the property on the northwest corner of Monterey and Osos streets remained undeveloped for several years. Then in July 1893, J. P. Andrews, the owner, announced plans for a two-story brick building at that location. The ground floor was clearly designed for a bank, but Andrews was non-committal about plans when a *Tribune* reporter sought information.

This building at the corner of Monterey and Osos in San Luis Obispo was constructed by J. P. Andrews and partners in 1893 for use as the Andrews Bank. It opened for business January 2, 1894. This is the same corner where the Andrews Hotel had been built in 1885. It was destroyed by fire in 1886. In back of this building at the corner of Osos and Palm streets, Andrews later built a less auspicious solid brick hotel. The upstairs of the bank housed San Luis Obispo's first public library.

The upper floor was to be for the town's public library. In exchange for a lump sum of money, the library was to have use of the upstairs for the next twenty years. The entrance to the library would be on Osos Street, up one flight by an "easy stairway."[40]

While plans were being readied for construction of the Andrews Building, there was also interest in the unique developments of a local telephone and telegraph company. The company had set up temporary headquarters in San Luis Obispo while constructing a long distance line between Los Angeles and San Francisco. A line now existed between San Luis Obispo and Santa Maria, and between Lompoc and Santa Barbara.

"This section of the State has been a 'gap' which is at last closed," the *Tribune* reported.[41]

It was big news in San Luis Obispo when word reached town during July that George Clements Perkins had received the appointment to fill the uncompleted term of the late U.S. Senator Leland Stanford. Leaders working for change and progress in this part of the state felt some vested interest in this appointment.

Perkins had been president and was a major stockholder in Goodall, Perkins and Company, the prinicpal organizational owner of Pacific Coast Steamship Company and the Pacific Coast Railway. His name also appeared as president of the West Coast Land Company during its early operations. The fact that he had served as California's governor for three years beginning in 1879 completed his credentials for the new appointment.

In a letter to Perkins, Governor Markham said, "I have given the most careful consideration to the appointment . . . to succeed the late

Senator Leland Stanford.... Believing that your very successful business career and your long experience in public life... have fitted you well for performing... this high position, I have concluded to tender the appointment to you..."[42]

🙟🙟

One of the mining companies working in Edna to remove bituminous rock began searching for a more economical way to transport their product to the metropolitan areas for marketing. Finally, the company purchased Pismo Wharf. It was not in very good condition, but they rebuilt it and extended it into navigable water.

The wharf soon became available to serve other commercial purposes. A man named Kimball who had sizeable lumber interests in Mendocino County joined with W. F. Stevens, who was living in Pismo, in establishing a lumber yard. Kimball also operated six large "steam schooners"—the *Noya, Daisy Kimball, Protection, Albion, Scotia,* and another unnamed vessel. He planned to put the *Protection* on a regular run between Pismo and San Francisco Wharf Number 1 hauling both cargo and passengers.[43]

In August an announcement began to appear regularly in the *Tribune* stating that steamers would leave Pismo Wharf for San Francisco and wayports every Saturday at 2:00 P.M. and return from Mission Wharf Number 1 in San Francisco to Pismo every Wednesday at 2:00 P.M. It was an overnight trip from port to port.

So, business in San Luis Obispo County seemed to build by a pyramiding process, although not all the building blocks stayed in place.[44]

🙟🙟

The blue skies and warm days of summer provided distractions from railroad and wharf building, land developments, and plans for cities.

At both San Luis Obispo and on the beach at Pismo during August, crowds gathered on two successive Sundays to see Charlie Vaughn, a young man from San Luis Obispo, and Professor Roundtree, a traveling entertainer, make balloon ascents and parachute jumps.

The balloon ascents were sponsored by the Arabian Remedies Company. The object of the entertainment was to attract a large crowd to an open field where the company offered its "panacea... to a disease laden world." First the professor made the ascent in his balloon with two parachutes. It was a beautiful sight against the blue sky. At about two thousand feet elevation, the balloonist dropped away from the balloon, his parachutes opened, and he came swinging and swaying slowly to the ground to the applause of a thrilled crowd.

Later the same day, Charlie Vaughn made the ascent as the balloon rose above the afternoon shadows. He stayed with the balloon until it was 2,800 feet high, then he descended in his parachute to thundering applause.[45]

The weather on Sunday, August 6, 1893 was beautiful. At Pismo Beach, there were many activities to claim the attention of visitors. Professor Roundtree performed his balloon ascent and parachute jump and sold his medicine. The sea was as calm as a mill pond, fishing and clamming were at their best, and there was a great deal of shipping activity on the wharf.

The steamer *Protection* was docked. Men were unloading lime and cement. Wagon teams were hauling construction materials to San Luis Obispo for use in the construction of J. P. Andrews' new bank building.

Products brought on board the ship included live hogs, horses, grain, clams, and bituminous rock. Shipping rates were half those of the Pacific Coast Steamship Company operating from Port Harford at Avila.[46]

🙟🙟

On Monterey Street in San Luis Obispo that summer in 1893, it was easy to see that people were getting ready for great things to happen. The most evident change underway was the construction of the Andrews Building. A Los Angeles contractor had been employed, and work started on the new brick building in August.

Across Monterey Street from the Andrews Building and nearer Morro Street, Loobliner's modernized the front of their store and painted the building. At the corner of Chorro and

Monterey, the Quintana building needed renovation, and Mr. Quintana reported that he was making plans. This building extended into the still crooked Chorro Street, and many people hoped Quintana would plan frontage changes to set the building back so Chorro Street could be straightened out. There were also other businesses along this block that needed to be set back.[47]

☙❧

San Francisco newspapers continued to report occasionally that railroad work between Santa Margarita and Ellwood had stopped or been slowed or was threatened in some way, and the *San Luis Obispo Tribune* and other newspapers tried to counteract such stories, which they always seemed to find untrue. In August 1893, it was repeated in San Francisco that Southern Pacific had called upon their contractors to discharge a thousand workers, and the *Tribune* tried to point out the facts:

" . . . There has never been more than about twelve hundred men along the 'gap.' Outside of the tunnels the work is largely grading and when a man with the aid of his team of four or six horses and the patent self-dumping horse shovels move(s) a cubic yard of earth at one effort, there isn't a need for many men.

" . . . The facts are that the time when the work can be completed depends . . . on the progress made in the tunnels, and . . . only a certain number of men can work at one time. That maximum number has always been employed and is now."

Of the seven tunnels under construction, the *Tribune* reported that the largest would be 3,700 feet long; the second, 1,500 feet; the third, 800 feet; the fourth, 400 feet; the fifth, 270 feet; the sixth, 450 feet; and the seventh, 670 feet.[48]

The stonework on the many culverts across the Cuesta were marvels of hand work, and as crews moved closer to San Luis Obispo, many people hitched up wagons and went out to look for themselves.

In some situations the work involved appeared "ridiculously out of proportion to the obstacles to be overcome." For example, on the Lowe place at the edge of town, there was a little gulch which even during heavy rains didn't carry much of a stream, but in order to span the gulch with a railroad bed, the contractor had to construct a solid granite culvert 127 feet long that ranged in height from four to five feet.

Visitors also came back to town reporting their amazement at a culvert across Brizzolara Creek on the Lowe place. "This creek is quite a noisy little stream in the times of heavy rains and floods," a reporter said. " . . . A bridge with a span of eighty feet must take the [rail] road over the creek." Excavations were made as much as twenty feet below the bed of the stream to lay "a solid mass of granite block and cement, say twelve by twenty-five by fifty feet."

The culverts to be constructed in or near the city of San Luis Obispo would be on the Hathway place, and a big one in the San Luis Obispo Creek just south of the Ramona Hotel. Then the contractors would put in the foundations for a railroad bridge over Monterey Street.[49]

One day in August 1893, a *Tribune* reporter riding along the road in the Chorro Valley noticed unusual activity near the end of the planned horseshoe turn coming off the Cuesta. Upon investigation, he discovered that Southern Pacific planned a small station not far from Chorro Creek. It was intended to serve the farmers of the Chorro Valley. The reporter referred to it as "the town of Chorro."

The railroad had some seventy-five men and numerous wagon teams, plows and horse shovels clearing and leveling a spot on the hillside. From that point on the horseshoe turn, the railroad moved in the direction of Stenner Creek where a 1,500-foot-long steel bridge was planned.

"Imagine the approach to this City," the reporter wrote, "with the train emerging from the tunnels, sweeping down the grade through the Potrero, rounding the sharp curve . . . with the Chorro station immediately below it, then rounding the great loop and turning directly back and heading south with the pretty town [San Luis Obispo] lying in its path, and the wide landscape of mountain and valley, rock and river, fertile fields and masses of orchards on every hand. No traveler who ever passed through but will hold the scene in his memory forever."[50]

CHAPTER XVII

Work All Along The Line

ord about a "flag" stop to be called Chorro had no more than been passed around town when it was announced that the stop would be called Goldtree instead. Isaac Goldtree owned the piece of land at the horseshoe turn in the Chorro Valley, where the railroad was interested in laying about one-half mile of sidetracks to accommodate farmers in the valley and up the coast. Goldtree generously provided railroad right-of-way for the purpose.[1]

Isaac was one of the brothers in the Goldtree Brothers General Store which was established in June 1883 on the northeast corner of Higuera and Chorro streets. As had other successful merchants in San Luis Obispo, they had often wound up trading credit accounts in merchandise for land throughout the county. Consequently, they came to own tracts of land in various locations.[2]

When Southern Pacific stopped construction of the line at the new town of Templeton in 1887, then later continued building to Santa Margarita, it created competition between the two towns because each had a vested interest in trying to remain the terminus of the line for as long as possible. The end of the line was generally a hub for business activity. Farmers brought their goods to the closest town and spent their money with businesses in the community, and travelers often stayed overnight at the end of the line before continuing their journeys by stagecoach. So it was not unusual that some of the people in the northern towns resented the continuation of the line toward San Luis Obispo, or that San Luis Obispo promoters didn't get support from other communities in the county during their long endeavor to raise money and obtain rights-of-way. Consequently, San Luis Obispo wound up feeling strongly independent about their achievement.

Some of these same promoters began a second big endeavor. In anticipation of the arrival of the rail line, and the opening of the town to overland travelers, they quietly held a few meetings to form a local land development company. They signed papers on August 24, 1893 to establish and incorporate the San Luis Obispo Investment and Development Company. Those who signed the incorporation papers were: R. E. Jack, cashier, San Luis Obispo County Bank, and owner of 46,000 acres of land; McD. R. Venable, president, Commercial and Savings Bank, and county judge; H. M. Warden, a large landowner in the Los Osos Valley and in town; J. M. Felts, county assessor; C. H. Phillips, manager, West Coast Land Company; H. Brunner, manager, Commercial and Savings Bank; Benjamin Brooks, lawyer, publisher, and editor of the *Tribune*; C. R. Callender, real estate broker; Senator George Steele, a large landowner; the Goldtree brothers, general store owners and landowners; the Crocker brothers, general store owners and landowners; the Sinsheimer brothers, general store owners and landowners; W. Sandercock, a drayage company owner and a contractor on the Cuesta; Luigi Marre, hotel owner at Port San Luis and large rancher; and John Price, large ranch owner.

Jack, Venable, Warden, Felts, and Phillips were named members of the Board of Directors, and shortly after the initial meeting plans were made to establish an office on Chorro Street next to the *Tribune* office.[3]

All of these men subscribed some cash for the purpose of promoting the community's resources and the land around it. As county assessor, Felts would keep the company informed about the accessibility of various lands. Benjamin Brooks could be counted on for local promotion and support in the newspaper. Venable was a judge, and the group included lawyers. All had land to sell and talents they could provide to the new organization.[4]

❧

A few minutes before four o'clock Friday morning, September 8, 1893 in Cayucos, Edward Zoppi was awakened by a strange crackling sound on Ocean Street. When he looked out the window, he saw fire bursting through the rear of Waterman's Saloon and Samuel's Store. E. E. Warren, Zoppi's neighbor, was awakened by the same sound, and the two men hurried to the church together where they rang the bell continuously. Soon all the men in Cayucos came running, half-dressed and cold, to answer the alarm.

There was a loud explosion in Samuel's Store, and everyone knew the dynamite powder stored there had gone off.

Although it was already too late to try to save either the saloon or Samuel's, the townsmen tried to wet down the roof of the Cosmopolitan Hotel with wet sacks and water from Cass and Company's tank. But the flames lapped closer and closer and the heat became so intense that the fire fighters retreated from the roof, and the old wooden hotel soon went up in flames.

Cayucos had an unusually wide street, so the flames did not jump across to Cass's warehouse or the wharf. The men wet down the buildings and covered the roof with wet sacks to guard it against flying embers. Fortunately, there was little wind, and such as there was carried embers in the opposite direction.

In a valiant effort to save the Exchange Hotel, a group of men tore down Dean's barbershop and some outbuildings between the hotel and the path of the fire. A bucket brigade formed between Cass's water tank and the raging fire. In the end, the entire business street of Cayucos, one block long, was destroyed except for the Exchange Hotel. No damage was done to Cass and Company buildings next to the wharf.

Word about the fire in Cayucos spread quickly up and down Monterey and Higuera streets in San Luis Obispo the next morning. Telegrams were sent by friends and relatives and word soon came back confirming the fire. Local banks and insurance companies had interests in Cayucos that sent a number of men out the Chorro Road. Judge Venable and R. E. Jack were among the first to hitch up a team and start up the coast.

The final toll included the Cosmopolitan Hotel, the Commercial Bank, a couple of saloons, the Odd Fellows building, Samuel's Store, P. Taminelli and Company's General Store, the Bank of Cayucos, E. E. Warren's Drug Store and house, Dean's barbershop, and a stable.

There was a great deal of speculation about how the fire might have started, but no evidence to prove anything.[5]

❧

In September 1893, a new subdivision was laid out at the edge of San Luis Obispo across from the county hospital on 320 acres that had been all vineyard—Black Hamberg and Chassela grapes. The Goldtree brothers owned the tract, and the recently organized San Luis Obispo Investment and Development Company was expected to handle the sale of lots.[6]

❧

Most people in San Luis Obispo who had an opinion were pleased because Southern Pacific planned a trestle across Monterey Street, the main wagon road to the Cuesta, and another across the wagon road (now Johnson Avenue) that led to the county hospital and the planned Goldtree tract. The passage under the railroad bridge on the hospital road would be sixteen feet wide and nine feet high—more than ample for wagon traffic out that way in 1893!

Masonry work was already underway for the railroad bridge over the hospital road, and teamsters with their wagons were doing excavation work for the purpose of laying a rock bed upon which to build the culvert at the planned Monterey Street bridge.

In mid-September, Southern Pacific Railroad's principal engineers visited San Luis Obispo. They included William Hood, chief engineer; J. A. McMurtrie, contractor on the Santa Margarita extension; W. F. Marsh, division engineer; and O. Winningstadt, assistant to Hood. A *Tribune* reporter tried to interview Hood about plans for extension of the line beyond San Luis Obsipo, but as usual, Hood would talk only about work accomplished or underway.

The money market was tight, and no officer would commit the railroad company beyond the obvious.[7]

Speculation about the exact route that Southern Pacific would follow south of San Luis Obispo provided land developers and dreamers continuous food for thought. It also laid the basis for disappointment for some who held land in the wrong places.

The *Arroyo Grande Herald* encouraged its subscribers to believe that the Southern Pacific would follow about the same route as the Pacific Coast narrow gauge from San Luis Obispo to Arroyo Grande and finally to Los Olivos. The *San Luis Obispo Tribune* was certain that Southern Pacific would buy the Pacific Coast railway through a stock exchange. Pacific Coast stock was down to eight cents a share, and some investors hoped an exchange for Southern Pacific would prevent big losses. As people were eventually to discover, Southern Pacific would stay close to the coast south of San Luis Obispo.[8]

The *San Francisco Chronicle* succeeded in getting an interview with Colonel Charles Crocker about plans for construction of the line to Ellwood. Crocker said that he was looking for a way to market bonds issued by the Pacific Improvement Company for the purpose of completing the coast line. So far, no market had been found.[9]

In October, the work on abutments for the railroad bridge crossing Monterey Street near the Ramona Hotel made local people very much aware of railroad construction activity. In some ways, completion of that bridge seemed to spell completion of the line to San Luis Obispo.

Rock for use in construction of the bridge was

Sunday crowds from San Francisco, San Jose and the bay area arrive at Santa Cruz depot for a day at the beach.

taken from the Fernandez Ranch on San Luis Mountain. It was hauled by wagon from the mountain along Monterey Street to a place near the hotel.[10]

On the Cuesta, work at both tunnels number one and number two continued.[11]

Construction at the tunnels slowed down and speeded up over and over again, but at the end of October 1893, Higbee and Bernard as well as Erickson, the two principal subcontractors, received word from Southern Pacific Railroad to proceed full speed with both tunnels and grading. So, new workers were sent from San Francisco to Santa Margarita and from there they were hurried to the construction camps on the Cuesta.[12]

An announcement was made in the *San Francisco Examiner* by H. E. Huntington, first assistant to Collis Huntington, that there would be no more delay in construction of the coast line road. "While the section between Santa Margarita and San Luis Obispo is the hardest . . . the stretch between San Luis Obispo and Ellwood is anything but easy," he announced. "There are a great many deep canyons that will require high trestles . . . the road may possibly be through to Los Angeles in a year, but that is problematic . . . the seashore line is a pet idea of President Collis Huntington."[13]

PEOPLE WELCOMED THE RAIN that fell on Tuesday, October 24, 1893. The roads and streets were terribly dusty and the rain was not heavy, but it settled the dust and provided a clean earthy smell. (Some people attributed their influenza, grip and other ailments to a need to clean up the air.)[14]

The evening mail arrived by coach at the post office each day at 7:20 P.M., and people gathered in line beginning at the post office window and extending out into the street. One young lady in the post office was responsible for separating and distributing the mail as quickly as possible after it arrived.

In general, ladies and girls were given first attention, and the local men accepted this condition graciously. However, one time a stranger in town waiting for mail wrote a letter to the editor of the *Tribune* complaining that he simply didn't understand this local "wholesale abrogation" of rights by the men. His concern did not change the deeply ingrained practice, and the "ladies first" motto continued in San Luis Obispo.[15]

It took a while for the people of Cayucos to recover after the big fire there, but by November 1893, thirteen new buildings were under construction, and people were feeling good about their town again.

However, some Cayucos citizens strongly advocated the need for a poundmaster to keep cattle, horses, hogs, and goats out of the street. Some people simply would not corral their animals properly.

Some voiced disapproval of the treatment of animals by the local butchers. "Our butchers," someone was quoted as saying, "are in the habit of buying young calves all the way from two to eight days old." Before slaughtering these animals for shipment to San Francisco, they "keep the poor little animals closed up in a pen, awaiting the arrival of the steamer, without food or water. The poor creatures . . . [bellow] day and night, to the discomfort of the people in town."[16]

During the second week in November 1893, more progress was made in digging tunnel number one than any other previous week. The crew dug a record of seventy-two feet, leaving only six hundred feet to complete. In tunnel number two only three hundred feet of digging remained. Work was also well underway in tunnels six and seven.

There were predictions that all seven tunnels would be complete by February 1894.[17]

The line from Santa Barbara in 1893 turned inland at Ventura and ran to Saugus, then curved in a southerly direction through the San Fernando tunnel before reaching Los Angeles. This route took advantage of track already in existence along the inland route.

The *Santa Monica Outlook* pointed out that it was eighty-two miles from Ventura to Los

Wide street and street car line in early Santa Maria.

Angeles along that line, but it was only forty-five miles from Ventura to Santa Monica and only seventeen additional miles from Santa Monica to Los Angeles—actually a much shorter distance. The *Outlook* predicted that the coast line would one day run to Santa Monica.[18]

A group of officials from Southern Pacific Railroad appeared in San Luis Obispo on Friday, November 19, 1893 and made a brief inspection of the planned route of the rail line through the town. They paid one brief visit to C. H. Phillips' office. Otherwise, their visit was almost secretive, and all of them left town immediately except William Hood. He stayed over, and several of the town's prominent citizens paid him a visit at the Ramona Hotel that evening.

The buildings which would be needed in town by Southern Pacific were now being considered. San Luis Obispo would become the end of the division. It would have shops, warehousing, and a brick passenger depot. Hood inspected the brick produced in the San Luis Obispo area and indicated that it might be used.

A switch running from Monterey Street to the creek in the rear of the Ramona Hotel was planned to accommodate passengers stopping at the hotel.[19]

A *San Francisco Chronicle* reporter accompanied some railroad officials by rail to San Luis Obispo County in late November 1893. He reported seeing gangs of workmen along every mile of the unfinished rail line. He watched work in the tunnels and saw men wielding picks, shovels, hammers, and drills. He estimated seeing some thirteen hundred men at work for the various contractors and noted a dozen different clusters of white tents along the thirteen-mile route. Here and there in the larger camps, there was a tent supply store.

The reporter spoke of the wide horseshoe turn coming into the Chorro Valley and the expanse across Stenner Creek that would require construction of a 900-foot steel viaduct. Upon reaching San Luis Obispo, he learned that there would still be a gap in the track of 110 miles between San Luis Obispo and Ellwood.[20]

At the beginning of December 1893, railroad crews were working outside San Luis Obispo at the north end in the Arlington Tract. Work had been underway on the railroad bridge sites across Monterey and across Johnson streets for some time. Tunnel work was still underway on the Cuesta. The light of day through tunnel number two was expected before the end of the month, but tunnel number one, known as the "big tunnel," wouldn't be finished for several weeks.

Local people were walking and horseback riding along the railroad bed nowadays to see the progress. The opening of tunnel number two was expected to draw a real crowd.[21]

In early December, an advanced guard of railroad construction workers began surveying and driving stakes to identify the location for placement of water and sewer pipes in San Luis

Obispo. Soon afterwards workers began digging trenches.[22]

One group of land investors in San Luis Obispo referred to themselves as the "Syndicate," and their first effort as a group now came to light with railroad construction activities in town.

They subdivided a portion of Terrace Hill, one of the community peaks, and offered small lots at very low prices. This location was promoted as a "thermal belt," with an unparalleled view of the city. It was expected, according to the publicity writer for the tract, that the property would be very much in demand. It would be sold on a "first-come, first-served" basis.[23]

A reporter from the *Santa Maria Times* visited San Luis Obispo in early December 1893, asking questions about the success of San Luis Obispo in raising money for railroad right-of-way land. At this late date, a few Santa Maria business people were now concerned about being bypassed by Southern Pacific. It was known now that from San Luis Obispo the line was scheduled to cut sharply to the coast, running to Pismo Beach, the new town of Oceano, and then to Guadalupe.

But some Santa Maria businessmen were still hoping that they might somehow collect funds for right-of-way and convince the railroad to come through Santa Maria. As in so many efforts at cooperation during these years, the leadership was not strong enough to deal with the problem, and it was much too late to begin.[24]

In early December the *Tribune* reported, "The right-of-way through the town and clear to the southern boundary where the [railroad] shops are to be located, has been occupied by the railroad forces." The people of San Luis Obispo watched a constant stream of men and wagon teams loaded with ironstone sewer pipe travel along the right-of-way to construction

locations. A small army of men and teams cut away the slope at the east end of Morro Street where construction was planned.

The December weather, as so often happens in San Luis Obispo, remained dry. Construction contractors were jubilant and made progress while they could.

People asked each other how they could accept all of this change with such equanimity. Although they watched the work in town, took buggy and horseback rides out to the various camps along the Cuesta, and kept well informed of general progress, they could no longer be aroused to any great extent. They had waited so long, and now it was happening.[25]

THROUGHOUT THE YEAR 1893, the building for the new Andrews Bank at the corner of Monterey and Osos streets had been under construction. As the year ended, it was nearly ready for occupancy. The large stockholders included J. P. Andrews, with an investment of $50,000; Pat Moore, $20,000; R. Hutchinson, $12,000; J. W. Smith, $10,000; Henry Bosse, $10,000; Timothy Murphy, $10,000; and Pat Murphy, $10,000.

Andrews was elected chairman of the board, and Smith was elected secretary. $158,500 had been subscribed by the stockholders for the beginning operations of the bank. Its doors were opened for business January 2, 1894.[26]

On Sunday evening, December 10, 1893, San Luis Obispo townspeople suddenly faced what seemed sure and terrible tragedy. About nine o'clock in the evening someone noticed smoke rising from the roof of the Ramona Hotel.

The ringing of the fire bell was described as "constant, long continued and agitated." At the time it rang, the streets were quiet. There probably wasn't a team on either Monterey or Higuera. In fact, it was almost bedtime for most folks.

To complicate conditions, there was an unusually dense fog that night, as volunteers galloped their horses to the fire station. Cries of the "fire boys" could be heard all around town as they harnessed horses to the fire rigs and raced along the rutted dirt streets toward the Ramona. Later, Captain Pritchard told people that he could distinctly hear the orders conveyed among the firemen at his residence two and a half miles away.

The town's one steam fire rig was on the hotel grounds within fifteen minutes after the alarm struck, and fortunately, the water supply was ample. At first the flames appeared to be out of control, but the men were able to get their equipment close to the fire and soon had two streams of water trained on the blaze. Within half an hour, the flames were extinguished, and the fire fighters were decidedly the town's heroes all the next day.

An investigation by light of day on Monday led to the conclusion that the fire was the work of an incendiary. It had started on the outside of the building, burned through the wooden clapboard and gained headway quickly within the hotel. A good draft had carried the flames to the roof and under the floor of the hotel.[27]

Wesley Burnett had been in San Luis Obispo most of the day on business and did not begin his return trip to his ranch across the Cuesta until about five o'clock, one evening in mid-December 1893. It was already nearly dark.

He succeeded in finding his way along the Cuesta, and he was just a few hundred yards past the first saloon when he met the stage from Santa Margarita in the darkness. His horse became frightened by the noise and snorted and jumped uncontrollably. Suddenly, horse, buggy, and Burnett plunged over the grade.

It was so dark the people aboard the stage missed the entire accident. Bruised and unconscious, Burnett lay helpless some forty feet below the road. Nearly two hours passed before he regained consciousness. In the dark, he could make out a man with a lantern. He called out, but his voice was weak. After a time, the man located him and assisted him back to the road, then accompanied him to the saloon. From there, someone drove him to the Laughery Hotel in San Luis Obispo.

Burnett had bruises on his chest, face, and left arm. His buggy was smashed to sticks, and his

Capitola, a beachtown, enjoyed early access to the railroad. This 1908 postcard depicts the small depot at this location.

horse's leg was badly injured. Somehow, the proximity of the accident to the saloon was thought by some folks to have played a part in the accident, and Burnett never proved the contrary.[28]

While the Andrews Bank building was being built, subscriptions were being solicited for the city library which was to be on the second floor. The sum of $2,500 was raised. W. W. Stow, former legislative representative and public relations man from Southern Pacific Railroad, gave $1,000 for library books, apparently re-serving the privilege of selecting them. Stow was married to one of the Hollister daughters. He and his wife shared property in the Chorro Valley with other Hollister heirs.[29]

By the end of the year 1893, the town of San Luis Obispo had realized many improvements and was bustling with activity. Future economic prosperity seemed assured. All waited in anticipation of the first train's coming across the Cuesta and rolling into town.

Southern Pacific broad gauge depot at San Jose in 1912.

CHAPTER XVIII

Opening The Tunnels

New Year's Eve fell on Sunday in 1893, and Charles Zinman, an upholsterer in San Luis Obispo, along with Jacob Heister, a new man in town who had recently opened the small saloon at the corner of Chorro and Higuera, hitched a wagon and rode out to Laguna Lake to hunt for duck. It was a nice day, and the prospects for shooting duck appeared excellent.

Heister was almost immediately successful. As a group of ducks rose from the surface of the water, he fired his shotgun and a bird fell. The men did not have a boat, but they found a small skiff filled with water nearby. They bailed it empty, and Heister began the precarious task of paddling it in and out of the heavy growth of tule. At one point, the tule was so thick and high that Zinman, on shore, could not see his companion or the boat. He ran back to higher ground trying to sight him—moving first one direction and then another along the shore.

The Laguna was known by local people to be dangerous. Ages of washing from surrounding hills had filled it with soft silt and slime of unknown depth. A variety of water weeds and grasses grew rank in the swampy waters.

Still unable to sight his friend, Zinman's worst expectations were suddenly confirmed by calls for help from Heister somewhere out there in the thick growth. Zinman waded in the direction of the sound but almost immediately found himself sinking as if in quicksand, grasses weaving about his body and fern paralyzing and using his strength. He grabbed at the tule and pulled himself toward the bank. Safe

Tunnel number one. This scene shows workers, local dignitaries and wives on hand for the completion of the longest tunnel along the Cuesta grade. The light of day appeared as a small opening at the top of a large pile of loose rock, and workers began scrambling through to the other side.

but exhausted, he rested there until he suddenly realized that he could no longer hear Heister's calls.

Zinman dashed for the wagon and whipped the horse all of the way to town to get help. Upon returning, he and some men who had accompanied him met Alex Trimble and Leland McCabe, who had been hunting on the opposite shore. They had heard Heister's calls for help and had seen Heister in the boat one moment, and in the next, an empty boat.

Nearly two hours passed before the group located Heister's body. He was a native of Germany, in his mid-thirties, and had not been well-known around town. Coroner Nichols noted that he had an excellent physique.

Heister had arrived in San Luis Obispo by several steps. He had worked in Seattle for a while where he had a wife and child. There were problems at home, and Heister left his wife and went to San Francisco. He joined one of the gangs employed in San Francisco to work on the railroad tunnels on the Cuesta. He soon became head cook for the railroad gang at camps two and three. He worked hard and saved his money.

With his savings, he rented a building in San Luis Obispo and opened a saloon. Upon investigation, the coroner found that Heister had several hundred dollars.

Now he was dead. He had drowned at about 10:00 A.M. on the last day of 1893 in Laguna Lake near San Luis Obispo. He was young, strong and in good health. Undertaker Bowen took charge of the body, and Dr. Van Cleve of the Garden Street Church officiated at a small service. A few people attended the service out of respect for a man who hadn't had time to make many friends. The reasons for both his life and tragic death seemed a mystery to local folks.[1]

⚬❦⚬

By the end of 1893 tunnel number two was cut all the way through. The other shorter tunnels were uncompleted, but no one was excited about them. The steel bridge across Stenner Creek was viewed as the biggest project immediately ahead,[2] but the most interest was in speculation about what date the light of day would be seen from both ends of tunnel number one. On the last work day of 1893, the tunnel was within 267 feet of completion. During the first week of 1894, crews removed another 73 feet of soil. Marsh, the engineer in charge of that tunnel, was predicting a breakthrough by January 24. On that day, he expected to walk the length of the tunnel from opening to opening.

The big event actually occurred on Saturday, January 19, 1894. Crews from both ends of tunnel number one met each other, cheered, and exchanged sides. They had opened a small hole all of the way through. What a sense of victory ensued!

The next day a number of citizens walked and rode horseback along the railroad bed from San Luis Obispo to the tunnel. They walked into it and climbed up the embankment to the hole near the ceiling that led to the other side—the first citizens of the county to go through the tunnel. Mr. A. A. Fox had the distinction of being the first to take a "four-footed critter" through. His dog, unimpressed, reluctantly climbed the embankment and crawled through the hole with his master.

A mass of rock still had to be removed, and the timber work in that part of the tunnel had not yet been completed.[3]

Ties and rails were arriving by the carload, and the first big engine would soon pass through the tunnel to deliver materials farther along the road bed.

There was no talk about work south of San Luis Obispo to complete the coastal gap. Financial conditions were bad, and no new contracts for railroad construction had been made. Some people felt rather desperate about their land purchases south of town. One purchaser in the Grover subdivision wrote to Charles F. Crocker, the vice president of Southern Pacific Railroad Company. He asked if there were any truth in the rumor that the planned route had been changed. Crocker wrote back to say, "I personally do not know of any change proposed in the route of the Southern Pacific Railroad in San Luis Obispo."

Crocker referred the letter to William Hood, who sent a second letter. Hood's letter said, in part, "...Colonel Charles F. Crocker would probably give me the order to change the proposed line...if such change were contemplated and as he has answered you that he knows of no proposed change, I can say nothing to strengthen his statement to you."

Without doubt, Hood was master of the "no comment" reply.[4]

⟋⟍

IN LATE JANUARY, THE *Tribune* published a list of the books to be given to the new San Luis Obispo library by W. W. Stow. Stow told Henry Brunner, who had undertaken the establishment of the new library, that if any book on the list were given by someone else, he would substitute another one for it.

Rent for space on the second floor of the Andrews Bank Building had been paid in advance for twenty years. Now, the library was seeking donations of books.[5]

⟋⟍

With the completion of tunnels number one and two, local interest was soon caught up in plans for the construction of the steel bridge across Stenner Creek. This project was close enough so that people could view it after only a short drive out the Chorro wagon road (later Highway 1) and along a trail beside Stenner Creek.

It was a 935-foot long steel bridge that was being manufactured by the National Bridge Company in Pittsburgh for delivery and assembly at the Stenner Creek site. The contractor thought that it could be assembled in from three to five weeks. Massive granite piers were being placed to support the structure. It was necessary to dig twenty-five feet below creek level to hit bedrock. By February 1, 1894, pits for twenty-four piers had been excavated and granite had been placed as base for three of the four major piers.

Tunnels one and two were not only finished, but cleaned out, timbered and ready for permanent track. Tunnel number seven was also finished, and the other tunnels were nearing completion. Work crews in the various tunnels

were now caught up in competition with each other and took pride in breaking records.[6]

⟋⟍

OFFICERS OF THE COMMERCIAL Bank in San Luis Obispo found themselves in trouble in early February.

Judge McD. R. Venable, L. M. Kaiser, and H. Brunner, all officers of the bank and prominent men about town, represented the county in collecting money from the state for welfare use. The amount due to the county for this purpose at one point was $2,202, but the bank gave the county only $1,800, leaving an unpaid balance of $1,121.

Warrants for the arrest of these men were issued upon the complaint of C. A. Farnum, the County Auditor. The warrants claimed that they "willfully, unlawfully, feloniously and fraudulently" embezzled the unpaid balance to their own use.

After appearing in court to hear the charges against them, the men were allowed to remain free upon their own recognizance. They refused to discuss the matter with a *Tribune* reporter, and the *Tribune* story about it editorialized to the extent of saying, "Probably the difficulty is properly charged to the fund to which it belongs, a matter with which the bank has no concern."[7]

⟋⟍

Tunnel number three was dug through during the first week in February 1894. Four tunnels were now dug all the way through. There were three to go.

As work on the tunnel was finished, the crew was utilized for preparing railroad bed. During February, work crews were used to straighten and clear the bed for laying track between Santa Margarita and tunnel number one. During that month, too, graders worked on the stretch of bed between the last tunnel, number seven, and the place where Stenner Creek Bridge would be located.[8]

As some subcontractors completed the jobs for which they had been hired on the grade, they stored their wagons, scrapers and tools on back lots in San Luis Obispo. Among other things, an electric light plant that had been in use in one of the tunnels was brought to town in February 1894. Contractors had high hopes that they would soon be offered new contracts for continuing the line south of San Luis Obispo to Ellwood.

Speculation about continuation of the line continued. Some said there would be time enough for issuing new contracts after all work into San Luis Obispo was finished. Others pointed out that the contractors had thus far been fortunate not to experience serious delays because of rain. There was one prediction that decisions would be made in a hurry after Collis Huntington had inspected the work. Southern Pacific annual reports for that year indicated that work on the Cuesta was insignificant compared to other concerns of the company. The company was experiencing financial setbacks, and officials' attentions were focused on other more important activities.[9]

⌒✖⌒

ON TUESDAY MORNING, February 20, 1894, Commercial Bank officers McD. R. Venable, L. M. Kaiser, and H. Brunner appeared in court on the charges of embezzling that had been brought against them by County Auditor C. A. Farnum.

The men were not at all surprised to discover that the courtroom was crowded by curious townspeople. They were probably facing the most embarrassing time of their lives in this small community, but the circumstances of the whole event were such that they were apparently confident that their names would soon be cleared.

The problem leading to this courtroom scene had begun nearly two years earlier.

In June 1892, the county placed a claim with the state for $1,120.70, an amount which state statutes permitted the county for the care of aged indigents. P. Ready, chairman of the Board of Supervisors, sent the claim to the state controller's office. The claim was audited and allowed, but the state lacked funds to pay it at that time. Later, the state issued a warrant for the amount requested, but no demand was

made for it, so it remained in the state controller's office.

In the meantime, Ready vacated the office he held, and was succeeded by Mr. Mitchell as chairman of the supervisors. Mitchell was unaware of the earlier transaction. Later, a claim under the same statute was filed for the year 1893, and Mitchell gave this claim to the Commercial Bank for collection. At the same time, Mitchell gave the bank power of attorney to receive "this claim and any other monies which might be due then or thereafter . . ."

The bank filed Mitchell's claim through its correspondents. It turned out that the state didn't have funds to meet the 1893 claim, but the correspondents received the earlier claim of $1,120.70 and sent it to the Commercial Bank.

The bank officers thought an error had occurred. They did not know about any previous claim, but their correspondents in Sacramento assured them that the amount was legal and accurate.

The $1,120.70 was placed to the credit of the county treasurer in an account titled "E. L. Warner, treasurer, special," and Warner was advised of this act. The bank took no other action, and the money remained at the disposition of the treasurer.

McD. R. Venable, though president, did not participate in the bank's operation, so he wasn't aware of the accounts or of the particular procedures existing between the county and the bank.

Henry Brunner, the vice president, was in Europe when the request came from Mitchell. L. M. Kaiser acted routinely by calling on the Bank of California in San Francisco to pursue the matter. The San Francisco bank followed up by assigning the collection to D. O. Mills and Company in Sacramento.

The county treasurer knew about the special account. He had not only received the written notice about it from Kaiser but Kaiser had spoken to him in person about it. He simply did not relate the money to the claim by Ready back in 1892. Neither did Auditor Farnum.

So, at long last, the bank officials were cleared of wrongdoing. Judge Egan said, "I am entirely satisfied that there was no embezzlement of the money, that Mr. Kaiser did as was required to

An illustrator from the San Francisco Examiner visited San Luis Obispo to sketch this busy scene on Monterey Street during a gathering of lodges in California.

do, followed the usual course of business and did all that a businessman would have done under the circumstances. It does not appear . . . that any public offense was committed . . . the defendants are discharged."[10]

❧

In full expectation of great things happening very soon, a new ordinance was established in San Luis Obispo requiring all houses and buildings to have numbers. Even though nearly everyone knew every structure in town, the railroad was expected to bring many strangers to the city. Formal addresses like those used in large cities would help new people get around.

Mr. A. E. Dart promoted the ordinance somewhat because he had purchased a line of nickel-plated house numbers which he would put on any building at twenty-five cents for each number. It took people a long time to accept the

ordinance as important, and most people didn't spend the money for house numbers for several years.[11]

❧

The *San Luis Obispo Tribune* announced plans to distribute a souvenir railroad edition around May 1, 1894, to celebrate the expected arrival of the first Southern Pacific trains in San Luis Obispo.

The newspaper proposed to issue about ten thousand copies. The issue would carry information about the resources of the county written by people in town who were most authoritative. It would also publish photographs of principal structures along the railroad route, including Stenner Creek Bridge and tunnel number one, as well as scenes, farms, and houses in the county.

Articles to be published were written by

Myron Angel, C. O. Johnson, Horace Vachell, J. V. Webster, E. W. Steele, C. H. Phillips, and others. The *Tribune* also planned articles about important residents in the county.[12]

❦

By the end of February, digging of all seven tunnels was completed, although clean-up, grading, and support work was still underway in some of them. The permanent roadbed was now laid between Santa Margarita and the middle of tunnel number one.

Grading between tunnels proceeded quickly because there wasn't much distance between them. Grading between tunnel number seven and the location for the Stenner Creek Bridge was about two or three weeks away from completion. Track laid to the bridge site would enable that job to move along quickly.

Collis Huntington was expected to arrive in San Francisco after a long time in the East. This news led to speculation that decisions would soon be made about construction south of San Luis Obispo.[13]

SOUTHERN PACIFIC TERMINUS. 3RD AND TOWNSEND. SAN FRANCISCO. CAL.

Early railroad depots at San Francisco and Los Angeles.

SOUTHERN PACIFIC STATION. LOS ANGELES. CAL.

CHAPTER XIX

The Steel Bridge Across Stenner Creek

In the March 3, 1894 issue of the *Tribune*, this brief news item appeared:

TUNNEL NO. 1
THE FIRST TRAIN PASSED
THROUGH LAST NIGHT.

It Was Loaded Down With Railroad Men and Material for Track Laying.

Last night the first train passed through Tunnel No. 1 with a train of cars loaded with steel and ties. The crew consisted of Engineer Allen, Fireman Hawkins, Conductor Draper, Brakemen Taber and Carnes.

Messrs. Estabrook and Linnell, the agents of the Southern Pacific Railroad Company, were on the head end of the train with bullseye lanterns. Mr. Marsh, the engineer of the construction, piloted the train through the tunnel.

But there was still much work to do! [1]

One day in mid-March 1894, Dr. Nichols received a message at the hospital to come up the grade to Higbee and Bernard's camp near the mouth of tunnel number six, and when he arrived, he was hurried along the railroad bed to the body of Patrick McMahon.

It was a dismal sight. McMahon was a strong young man who worked as a teamster for Higbee and Bernard, the construction contractors. A number of men had met accidental death or injury on the Cuesta, but none of Higbee and Bernard's men. Now, as they were completing their contract, this accident had occurred.

McMahon was killed when he fell from a large wagon loaded with lumber while guiding a four-horse team down a steep grade along the rail bed. A man at the back of the wagon was attending to the brake. As they turned a corner on the narrow bed, the wagon started to slide. McMahon tried to straighten the team, but the box on which he was seated toppled, and he was thrown forward between the horses all of the way to the ground. The wagon passed over him and tipped over the grade, rolling twice in its descent. McMahon's neck was broken, and he died almost immediately. The horses escaped injury.

Dr. Nichols found a letter from McMahon's mother in the man's pocket. It was a loving letter which was read to the jury at McMahon's inquest. The foreman agreed to communicate with the young man's mother immediately. [2]

This illustration of the construction of the Stenner Creek railroad bridge appeared in the San Luis Obispo Tribune Souvenir Edition distributed in May 1894. Southern Pacific track made a great U out of the Cuesta into the Chorro Valley and then across a great canyon and Stenner Creek. The Stenner Creek bridge arrived from the factory ready to assemble like a huge tinker toy. Crossing Stenner Creek was the last major obstacle before track could be completed into San Luis Obispo.

Among those invited to a dinner party at the Ramona Hotel given by Messrs. Higbee and Bernard was Benjamin Brooks, the editor of the *Tribune*. The occasion was a celebration of the completion of the construction of the tunnels.

Dr. G. B. Nichols, who operated the small Southern Pacific Company hospital, was invited. All of the subcontractors were also there.

The celebration began in Santa Margarita. The guests boarded locomotive number 1646 for a ride through all seven tunnels. Conductor Batler was in charge. Afterward, everyone met at the Ramona Hotel.

William Hood, Chief Engineer for Southern Pacific, was there, but he stayed in the background throughout the evening. Before dinner, there were many toasts. Bernard and Higbee toasted the press generously—the company had been treated well by the *Tribune*.[3]

A new man named C. C. Serouf appeared on the Cuesta. He was in charge of laying track, and his work was now beginning in earnest. He expected to lay two thousand feet each day.

Two four-horse teams loaded with camp stoves had arrived at a construction site near the depot in San Luis Obispo. This helped local people identify the location chosen for the railroad turntable.[4]

The anticipation of the Southern Pacific line's reaching San Luis Obispo was reason enough for Ben Brooks to wax poetic occasionally. He had played a significant role in the community through its years of dickering with Southern Pacific, organizing and encouraging the community to contribute to the fund for purchase of right-of-way land, serving on committees, and commending individuals for their roles in the campaign to close the gap.

Now it was time to encourage settlers from everywhere. He anticipated that the *Tribune*'s Souvenir Railroad Edition would get distribution in the East by Southern Pacific. Through an exchange of the *Tribune* with other newspapers, an occasional article about San Luis Obispo was printed in other papers.

So, Brooks wrote, "... little is known of our wonderful and lovely climate—a climate that will allow a laborer to work all the year around without his coat, a climate wherein one can pick the loveliest flowers all the time, where ice and snow are things only heard of as in fairy tales, and where nature ... gives a living to any laborer who is worthy of his time.

"For many years our county ... has been shut out from communication with the outside world by the lack of a railway ... We wonder if anybody yesterday heard the locomotive's whistle plainly telling us that in a few weeks ... San Luis Obispo will be connected with the outside world."

Work was moving ahead quickly at the depot grounds. Brooks counted about eighty workers at the site of the depot and the turntable.[5]

IT WASN'T UNTIL MARCH 1894 that leaders in Arroyo Grande reluctantly abandoned the hope that the Southern Pacific line south of San Luis Obispo would follow the Pacific Coast narrow-gauge line through their town. In facing this issue, they now considered means by which they could maintain a solid business contact with the railroad. It was going to be necessary to maintain good road between Arroyo Grande and the expected Southern Pacific stops at Pismo and the developments at Grover and Oceano.

Among the ideas discussed was the use of electric streetcars from Arroyo Grande to the beach towns, and there was discussion about utilizing the power of the Arroyo Grande Creek to generate electricity to operate the electric streetcars.[6]

From the beginning, Chorro Street in San Luis Obispo was little more than a crooked horse trail between Monterey and Higuera streets and past the mission. The buildings that existed along the block in 1894 were now a continuous obstruction at the town center between the principal business streets. It was seriously difficult for two wagons coming from opposite directions to pass one another. At the time, a narrow bridge across San Luis Creek also limited passage.

Now, during these times of gentle boom and high expectations about the future, there was

An early passenger train steams across Stenner Creek bridge into San Luis Obispo.

a strong movement to widen and strengthen Chorro Street along that block.

Taxpayers were disposed to improvements, but the landowners along the block "entertained exaggerated notions" of the value of their property.

To widen Chorro required purchase by the city of two pieces of land. One fronted on Higuera Street about ten feet and extended along Chorro Street about eighty feet. The second piece fronted on Monterey about eighteen feet and ran along Chorro about one hundred and fifty feet. The city finally negotiated the purchase of the first piece of property at the somewhat inflated price of $3,750—$2,500 for the land and $1,250 for damage to the building.

"It was a huge price," Brooks commented, "but it went, chiefly because no other price would be agreeable to the owner, and also because the course of the creek ran through the property so that the widening seriously injured it."

Messrs. William Sandercock, Robert Pollard, and J. W. Barneburg had been appointed commissioners to appraise damage done and establish the price paid by the city. Transfer of the land to the city occurred only after much litigation and finally, condemnation. When the exchange was finally accomplished, it was noted that "in a short time the old landmarks will be removed," and that block on Chorro Street could at last take its proper place as a business street.[7]

Construction activity on the Southern Pacific rail line was never more intense than during March 1894. Hundreds of men prepared the rail bed between the last tunnel and Stenner Creek. Not far behind, other work gangs laid the track. Steam engines now pulled carloads of supplies and materials to the end of the finished line and were sighted and reported by excited travelers in the Chorro Valley.

The newspaper received a report that the trains were hauling as much as 120 cars of gravel each day.[8]

In late March 1894, word came down the grade that the structural parts for the steel bridge to be assembled across Stenner Creek had arrived from Pittsburgh. It occupied fifty or more freight cars scattered along the tracks from the mouth of tunnel number one all the way back to Templeton.[9]

THE UNUSUALLY DRY weather from the summer of 1893 into March 1894 maximized working time for railroad construction, but it was discouraging for the farmers.

Farmers around Shandon and Creston were suffering seriously with the drought condition during this period, and some were making plans for a cattle drive north to find water and grassland. Except for a few favored locations, the land was parched and the grass gone. For some folks, the failure to get a crop this year would mean leaving the county. Quite a few farmers were already overextended financially, having borrowed against their land to plant wheat and other crops which did not look promising.[10]

In March 1894, a new Masonic Temple building was nearly completed on Marsh Street, some of the obstructions along Chorro Street had been cleared on each side of the narrow bridge at Monterey Street, the County Bank had overhauled the exterior of its premises, and construction activity was underway at the railroad bridges over Monterey and Johnson streets as well as at the depot site. San Luis Obispo had never in its history seen so much activity within its limits. It was a town about to be reborn![11]

In 1894, lots were being sold in a subdivision called El Moro at a site in the Los Osos Valley. The subdivision map proposed two wharves, a large hotel site, and a branch railroad to connect with the "overland line." It was not until after World War I that Walter S. Redfield and Richard Otto resumed the development of this property and renamed it Baywood Park. In 1980, many of its streets remain unpaved, but it continues to grow as a residential community.[12]

Deputy Collector Noah of the Internal Revenue Department returned in the early part of 1894 from Los Angeles, where he had been informed about procedures for registering Chinese under the new federal law providing for a certificate of residency under penalty of deportation.

Ah Luis, the "acknowledged chief" of the Chinese in San Luis Obispo, announced that the local Chinese would all register as quickly as possible. Mr. Arnold, the photographer, was already busy taking the required identification photos to be attached to residency certificates.[13]

J. M. Baumgartner, a former newspaperman involved in Democratic politics, was named a deputy for Internal Revenue with the special duty of registering the Chinese in San Luis Obispo County. He started in the northern part of the county and worked his way south. During this time, some Chinese worked as cooks and laborers on the ranches. In the towns, they operated laundries and worked in the hotels.[14]

When the Pacific Coast Railway built its narrow-gauge track during the 1870s, Chinese work crews were employed. As reported in this book, Chinese workers were again used to some extent in the construction of the Southern Pacific coast line track through San Luis Obispo County. For example, in May 1886, the *Tribune* reported "1500 Chinese coolies" were at work laying track south of Soledad. After the line reached Templeton, a long delay in construction occurred, but in October 1888, work started again, and the *Tribune* announced that "150 Chinamen, 100 white laborers, and 50 bridge carpenters" were at work. The next month, November 1888, the newspaper again reported "long lines of Chinamen" stretched along the ravine, "their shovels flying in the air with monotonous regularity."

When work stopped again at the end of 1888, many Chinese remained in San Luis Obispo and found other kinds of work.

Work on the Cuesta did not begin again until October 1892. At that time, work camps were established at each end of the location for tunnel number one. From this time, there were continuing references to various work crews, but all were clearly references to Caucasians. Camps were constructed to accommodate them, but there were also reports of discontent among the workers. Were there Chinese workers in the tunnels and along the railroad bed on the Cuesta? In April 1893, Chief Engineer William Hood flatly denied any use of Chinese except as cooks during the work on the Cuesta. But he added that "we may have yet to employ Chinese laborers."

In 1894 Baumgartner registered 261 Chinese in San Luis Obispo County. This number was unusually large in such a sparsely settled area, and although the written record does not show it, these census numbers may indicate that more Chinese worked on the Cuesta than was recorded.

At the beginning of April 1894, General Patrick Murphy, owner of the Santa Margarita Rancho and founder of the town of Santa

Margarita, announced that he was subdividing sixty-four acres of land adjoining the city of San Luis Obispo into lots ranging in size from one to ten acres. J. C. Ortega was serving as sales agent for the property. Murphy was also selling lots he owned in the Mission Vineyard Tract in San Luis Obispo.[15]

❦

Months before the first trains arrived in San Luis Obispo folks there found pleasure in the fact that they could spot the work trains as they rounded the turn into the Chorro Valley.

Information was difficult to sort out, and rumors, more than evidence, affected the daily conversation and feeling of people living in town. They had always heard that San Luis Obispo would be a division town for the railroad, but it wasn't always clear, even to *Tribune* editor Benjamin Brooks, what this might mean.

Now, some people were in positive awe of the magnitude of what seemed to be happening. The roundhouse, people were saying, might be large enough to house twenty-six engines. Nothing quite so technically and economically important had ever existed in San Luis Obispo. It would soon be a railroad town! Strangers were appearing in town quite regularly now. The hotels were full at times. People were looking over the territory, considering land purchases and business opportunities.[16]

Myron Angel spent several months in Washington, D.C. in 1894 and found the opportunity to speak out on several occasions in behalf of his home county.

For years, the harbor at Avila had received an allotment of $30,000 annually for maintaining a breakwater, dredging, and whatever was necessary to accommodate ships carrying passengers and freight. During his visit, Angel accidentally discovered that this usual allotment was being overlooked by the Congressional Harbor and River Committee, so he hurriedly arranged appropriate appointments and represented the county before members of the committee.

Angel's real purpose for being in Washington probably involved some personally high stakes. He sought federal assistance in the de-velopment of Morro Bay as a harbor and probably sought right-of-way across government lands for his dream of a rail line from the interior of California to the sea.[17]

❦

In April, just when San Luis Obispo County business interests most wanted to show off the area at its best, they were faced with the driest weather in years. The hills and pasture land were brown, grain crops were failing, too many local farmers were in debt from overextending their planting, and there was no rain.

Real estate interests, readying for a boom with the arrival of the railroad, searched for whatever information they might use to prove that the drought conditions were uncommon.

The *Tribune* published a rainfall chart on April 5, 1894 showing annual rainfall from 1869 to 1893. The evidence was clear. San Luis Obispo had experienced both feast and famine during the previous twenty-five years.[18]

❦

Track was completely laid to Stenner Creek by April 6, 1894, and long trains pulled by two and three engines carried one hundred carloads of gravel every day from pits on the north side of the grade. Workmen spread the gravel between the tracks and along the bed to stabilize the track and minimize erosion.

After all the weeks that structural parts for the bridge at Stenner Creek had lain ready for use on flatbed cars, it was discovered only at the time that work began that some parts had not arrived. So, the bridge was delayed while a search for waylaid freight cars was undertaken. Some were found in faraway New Orleans, and the rush began to get them to the West Coast and to the construction site. Promised commissary cars to feed the labor gangs were also delayed. Finally, all the variables for assembling the bridge were brought together, and work began.

In order to get some sections of the bridge in place, a sidetrack was constructed alongside the line of the bridge down to the bed of the creek, a drop of ninety feet. A stationary engine let loaded flatcars down to the creek bottom over a stretch of about five hundred feet of slope. Then

Rios-Caledonia adobe at San Miguel served as home and hotel. Now restored and open to the public, it dates to the Mexican period when Petronillo Rios, grantee of the El Paso de Robles Rancho, owned it.

each piece was hoisted by a kind of derrick into the desired position, and a crew riveted it into place.

The parts were numbered, and their assembly was handled somewhat like that of a large pre-planned tinker toy.

Ben Brooks, along with a lot of other towns-people, went to the site often to observe the substantial change that occurred each day. One day, he found Tommy Thomson, the contrac-tor, standing on top of a boulder observing work on the bridge. "I have contracted to complete the bridge in twelve days but I do not believe it can be done," Tommy told Brooks. There was a twinkle in his eye when he said it.

Meantime, grading from the south side of Stenner Creek into San Luis Obispo was under-way. There was some delay at the crossing on Monterey Street, but a large crew of workers was assigned at this point and work proceeded fast.

Work was also underway on the turntable and the depot, but the movement of trains into San Luis Obispo would not be held up for completion of the depot, warehouses, round-house, or other shops.

"It will take a long time for our people to get used to the innovation," Brooks said. "We have been so long used to being out of the world that it would probably affect us unfavorably and shock our nervous systems to have close con-nections with San Francisco pulled on us too suddenly."[19]

THERE WAS A VIGOROUS campaign in April 1894 for the San Luis Obispo City Board of Trustees. Those elected for new full terms were C. H. Reed, 343 votes; E. P. Unangst, 326 votes; W. A. Henderson, 326 votes; F. W. Vetterline, 231 votes; R. E. Jack, 220 votes; and R. E. Lee, 190 votes.[20]

In the fall of 1893, the school trustees at Nipomo had been forced to make a quick de-cision about hiring a school principal. They had received only one application for the posi-tion, so they hired T. B. Morris, recently from Iowa, to fill the post.

There was no formal investigation of Morris, but he seemed to be doing nicely as a teacher and in conducting the affairs of the school. He was also active in the church and Sunday School and was music instructor in the town band. From his position as principal of the school and his work with the band, he earned $108 per month. This income was considered exceptionally good at that time.

Suddenly, one day in April 1894, the trustees announced that they had asked for and received Morris's resignation, and that he was leaving town. Some people were truly chagrined by this act of the trustees and demanded that it be explained.

Morris's indiscretions had first come to the attention of Frank Dana, clerk of the Board of Trustees for the Nipomo school. A few parents had talked to Dana privately, and Dana talked to Morris. Dana said that he had seriously reprimanded Morris, and the principal had agreed to mend his ways. Dana expected Morris to work until the end of the term and then retire quietly without scandal.

At the next meeting, Dana spoke to the board about hiring a new principal and stated his reasons. Board members L. L. Holt and G. Munoz were not as patient about the matter as Dana. They conducted their own investigation of the matter and decided that the board should ask for Morris's resignation immediately.

They confronted Morris with the information they had gathered, and he readily resigned, thanking them for their tolerant handling of the matter.

"Our little town was somewhat surprised that Professor Morris...was requested to resign," the *Arroyo Grande Herald* reported. But all soon agreed with the board's firm action. Professor Morris's indiscreet conduct with some of his female students was not be be tolerated.[21]

A new office for the telephone company was established on Higuera Street in April 1894. "Mr. H. S. Tittle and his 'hello' girl and message boy are installed herein," the *Tribune* reported.

The division superintendent, H. Keyser, was in town arranging details for operation of the new office. He was expecting a line from San Francisco to reach San Luis Obispo soon. Financial problems had prevented expansion of company lines a year earlier, but poles had been placed over a large stretch of the distance.

"Shortly," the *Tribune* noted, "we may... be able to talk . . . with friends in San Francisco, Los Angeles, San Diego . . . with as much ease . . . as with those in the next block."[22]

The prospect of new growth set in motion a whole set of problems for San Luis Obispo. The water supply presented one of the most serious problems. The water company was privately owned, and it was not making provision for the future.

City fathers hoped that new underground springs along the Cuesta might be discovered during digging of the railroad tunnels, but that did not happen. Now, they wanted the water company to buy up any sources of water within a practical distance. The owners of the company wanted to sell their operation to the city, and this gradually appeared to be the only practical solution for the future if the city wanted abundant water. Without water, the growth desired by the businessmen and real estate promoters would be impossible.[23]

Work at the Jordon bituminous rock mines near Edna proceeded on a fairly large scale in 1894. The company had twenty-two employees removing tar deposits, melting down the material and bagging it. The bagged tar was hauled to Pismo wharf on large wagons and loaded on one of Jordon's steamers for shipment to San Francisco.

One report said that there were fifty mules and horses on the road constantly between the tar pits and Pismo wharf. As long as the boats were arriving regularly, Jordon had hoped to get some freight business from local farmers, but people were too long accustomed to the facilities and services of the Pacific Coast Railway and Steamship Lines, so that idea didn't work out.[24]

Dr. Nichols anticipated the possibility that there would be some people emigrating to San Luis Obispo for their health. As the town's coroner and doctor for the Southern Pacific, he enjoyed financial success and continued to prepare for more.

In 1894 he bought an eighty-seven by one hundred and fifty foot lot on Monterey Street that had several buildings. He added a new building with an office, waiting room and operating room. He restored the rooms in the small buildings for the use of patients who needed continuous care, and this was the beginning of his own private hospital. San Luis Creek ran behind the property.

One of his first live-in patients arrived at the new location in mid-April. It was Mat Reardon, a worker on the Stenner Creek Bridge. Reardon had been standing on the uppermost steel girder, guiding another section being hoisted into place, when he lost his balance and fell from the

Amtrak passenger train crossing the Stenner Creek bridge on its daily run between Oakland and Los Angeles.

girder onto a stack of loose lumber thirty feet below. When fellow workers reached him, he was unconscious. As quickly as possible, he was lifted to a wagon and hauled to town. He had no broken bones, but Dr. Nichols ordered him to bed for a few days.[25]

❧

Paul Rudy, an employee of the electric light works in San Luis Obispo, had been in San Francisco doing business at the headquarters office of the utility company. He was returning aboard the steamship *Eureka*, which was due at Port Harford in the early morning. He had retired to his stateroom when he heard the bell ringing which signalled the engineer to stop the ship.

It was about eleven o'clock Saturday night, April 21, 1894. At first, Rudy thought the boat was coming into San Simeon wharf, but the noises he heard led him to feel that something unusual was happening. He pulled on his overcoat and climbed to the deck as quickly as possible. Other passengers were already on deck and extremely excited. Some had put on life preservers. There was no explanation for the ship's stopping in the dead of night at sea.

Looking around, Rudy could make out a light on shore and soon decided that this was the lighthouse at Point Sur, and the ship was not far from shore. Clouds hid the stars but moonlight filtered through to light the night. Rudy could make out the shore line and a

silhouette of mountains, but there was nothing visible to occasion alarm.

He estimated that the lighthouse must be about one-half mile away, and the sea was not especially rough. Now, crewmen were lowering boats into the water. Any person who might know anything was too busy to talk. Passengers were kept back from the boats as crew members boarded and rowed into the darkness.

There was an interminable wait and much speculation. Had someone fallen overboard? Was there another boat in the distance?

The boats returned overladen with people, half-dressed and soaking wet. They were passengers from a ship in distress. They were hurried below deck to empty bunks, blankets, and hot drinks. Women passengers aboard the *Eureka* offered aid to the stewardess. "With the first boat that came aboard, we learned . . . what . . . happened."

The *Los Angeles*, a steamer bound for San Francisco, had struck a rock about 8:45 the evening before. The third officer was in charge, but failed to realize the ship was off course. Captain Leland was on deck almost instantly when the vessel struck, and he knew immediately that the ship would sink.

Some passengers had already retired for the night, but they were hurriedly awakened and taken to the boats without attention to their dress. Captain Leland stayed with the *Los Angeles* until all passengers and members of the crew were off the ship. Soon, it sunk. Only the two masts and part of its stack remained above water.

"So it was the business of the *Eureka*," Rudy later reported, "to cruise around until all of the life-saving boats" floating aimlessly on the waves had been found.

"Back and forth, we traveled all night listening and peering into the darkness," he said. "One boat after the other was secured, and then a raft was picked up." The last boat was found the next morning with eight or nine passengers on it. It had been drifting about in the wet and cold for twelve hours. One young mother clinging to her five-month-old baby was nearly dead.

The *Eureka* took its unexpected load of about forty passengers to Monterey where they could continue their journey by train.[27]

The Train To San Luis Obispo

In late April 1894, Benjamin Brooks gently brought to the attention of his readers and the city fathers the prospect of a celebration of the arrival of the first train.

The long strained hassle with Southern Pacific Company during the previous five years had adversely affected whatever goodwill existed in the community toward the railroad, so to get everyone to smile one more time was not easy.

Brooks suggested that now was the time to invite officials from Santa Maria, Santa Barbara and other nearby communities. He did not suggest that invitations be sent to railroad officials, but he felt that if a celebration were planned, some Southern Pacific officials would surely come to see what had occurred along the Cuesta. In fact, he mentioned that the officials would probably come to inspect completion of work in San Luis Obispo and that this date might be the one to choose for a celebration.

In San Miguel, Mrs. Frank J. Burns, proprietor of the Central California Hotel, took a much more direct approach. She wrote Richard Gray, an official of the company, and asked him who was coming and when the line would be completed.

The answer she received was noncommittal and typified the letters usually received from Southern Pacific. It read:

Dear Madam:

Replying to yours of 12th inst. The date of completion of the line to San Luis is indefinite. Have not heard of any suggested excursion; therefore, am unable to give you any information about it at present.

Yours truly,
R. Gray[1]

Southern Pacific issued a circular for distribution dated May 5, 1894, announcing the opening of their coast line between Santa Margarita and San Luis Obispo with stops at locations referred to as the Cuesta (the highest point on the line), Serrano, Goldtree, Hathway Avenue, the Ramona Hotel, and San Luis Obispo.

The circular first reached San Luis Obispo in late April. Stenner Creek Bridge still was not finished, but it was scheduled for completion within the week. The rails from Stenner Creek into San Luis Obispo also had to be laid, a distance of about three miles. However, with the bed prepared, laying the rails was expected to be finished rapidly.[2]

On Thursday evening, April 26, 1894, there was a meeting of San Luis Obispo citizens at City Hall to discuss the celebration of the arrival of the first trains in town. It took the same men who had acted as leaders for years to call the meeting. They were Chauncey Hatch Phillips, Robert E. Jack, and L. Rackliffe. They drew up a list of businessmen in town and asked them to serve as a committee to plan a program.

At the meeting, C. O. Johnson was elected chairman; L. M. Kaiser, treasurer; and Benjamin Brooks, secretary. The group agreed to meet again the next evening to hear a report from the executive committee about program plans.

At the meeting the next evening, Chairman Johnson reported that the subcommittee planning the program had now heard by telegram that the first regular Southern Pacific train would arrive in San Luis Obispo at 6:05 P.M. on May 5 and that a special train carrying Southern Pacific officials and guests would arrive earlier in the day, possibly before noon.

The program submitted to the group included a barbecue from 2:00 to 5:30 in the afternoon. The committee suggested a reception beginning at 4:00 P.M., followed by a banquet and promenade concert at the Ramona Hotel. They named people to serve on invitation, reception, barbecue, finance, decorations, and music committees. A representative of the San Luis Band tendered its services on the spot, and there was happy applause by all who were present.[3]

At a third meeting held the next evening, subcommittees announced their plans. Mr. Kemp, chairman of the reception and ball committee, announced that the San Luis band would play as the first train arrived in town and again for a concert after the reception at the Ramona Hotel.

Mr. Farnum told the group that his committee would bring the big gun to the depot grounds and fire a national salute upon arrival of the train. The committee also planned to purchase about twenty rockets and decorations for various buildings in town.

The banquet and invitation committee reported sending invitations to San Diego, Los Angeles, Ventura, Santa Barbara and other points south. They also intended to send invitations to cities north of San Luis Obispo. They expected to make the banquet self-supporting, including payment of guests' meals, by charging about five dollars per person. An oration was planned on the porch of the Ramona Hotel at 5:30 P.M., and the Honorable Charles H. Johnson was the group's choice for that honor.

Johnson had arrived in San Luis Obispo County in 1852 to serve as Customs Inspector at Port San Luis. He settled in San Luis Obispo permanently in 1856. He was the first president of the Board of Trustees in San Luis Obispo and served as a California State Assemblyman beginning in 1860. In later years, Johnson contributed historical articles to the *Tribune*, preserving for future readers much information about the early town. Now, in his later years, he was respected and honored on many occasions.

The decoration committee planned to make both the exterior front and the interior of the hotel "gala." Ladies of the town would bring flowers and all ladies available were invited to

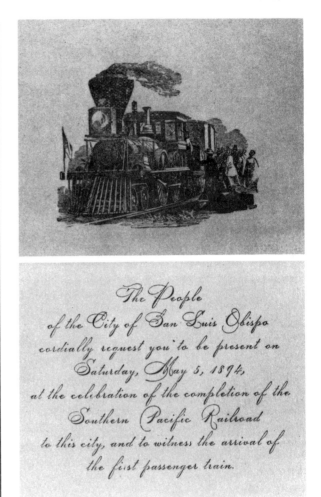

The arrival of the first passenger train in San Luis Obispo was an occasion for the greatest celebration ever undertaken by the community. This invitation was sent to out-of-town dignitaries between San Francisco and Los Angeles. For three days, the people of San Luis Obispo celebrated this marvelous event with visitors from all over the state.

be at the Ramona at 2:00 P.M. Friday afternoon to participate in decorating and arranging flowers.

The barbecue committee needed an appropriation of about $330 to buy food.

The finance committee was confident that it could raise the necessary funds to support all of the planned events. It had already obtained about $450 through solicitation and expected to get a total of about $600.

There was quite a lot of quibbling among members of the committee planning the ball about who would pay and who would not. Some people wanted to let everyone who participated in arrangements for the celebration attend without charge, but charge all others. It was finally decided to charge one dollar per couple for the ball and light supper, with committee members stationed at the door using generous discretion about charging out-of-town visitors.[4]

On May 1, 1894, Brooks said that he considered it impossible for Southern Pacific Company to complete a finished rail bed all the way to the depot by the planned date of May 5.

A great deal of riveting was still needed to complete the Stenner Creek Bridge, although all parts were now assembled and in place. Three miles of track remained to be laid between the bridge and the Ramona Hotel, the planned center for the celebration, and it would be many months before the depot, roundhouse and shops would be completed.

With only five days to go, Brooks wrote, "We are not disposed to suggest that there will be any difficulty which the forces of the Southern Pacific cannot surmount in reaching their proposed destination in the time allowed. We simply think that we will be treated to some very active demonstrations of their skill if they get to the goal on the fifth of May."

The next day some local dignitaries and a few subcontractors quickly took Brooks to task for making statements that might discourage progress or dampen plans for the celebration. In the next day's issue of the newspaper Brooks quickly attempted to allay fears.[5]

On Wednesday evening, May 2, 1894, another meeting of all railroad celebration committees was held in order to review progress and synchronize plans.

There had been substantial telegraphic communication between Robert E. Jack, the invitations chairman, and officials of the railroad. There did not seem to be any way of being sure who would attend the celebration. At this time, the committee expected J. A. Fillmore, the manager of the Pacific system, and perhaps others he might designate or invite.

Jack received a letter from Southern Pacific president Collis Huntington. Jack had had contact with Huntington many times during his long personal struggle to gain a railroad line to the city.

Huntington wrote, "While I would be delighted to see and shake hands with your people yet I do not feel that I can accept your invitation just now. I do want the opportunity, though, of telling your people that probably I am just as glad that the Southern Pacific has reached your city as the good people of San Luis Obispo are. As you know, the building of the line from Santa Margarita through has cost a very large sum, and the earnings for some time to come cannot be otherwise than small, but, as I have said, I am glad it has been done, even if there is nothing in it for us for years to come."

Major A. C. McLeod asked the general committee to meet one more time Thursday night to finalize arrangements. The committee members included McLeod, chairman, C. H. Reed, E. P. Unangst, W. A. Henderson, Smith Skow, F. C. Mitchell, R. E. Jack, W. L. Beebee, L. Rackliffe, L. M. Kaiser, Judge George Steele, E. W. Steele, Benjamin Brooks, B. Sinsheimer, Judge V. A. Gregg, Dr. W. W. Hayes, Judge McD. R. Venable, J. Crocker, I. Lasar, Dr. T. Norton, J. M. Wilcoxon, J. P. Andrews, E. Graves, T. T. Crittenden, William Sandercock, P. B. Perfumo, P. Quintana, August Vollmer, J. M. Felts, Joseph Frederick, J. W. Barneberg, F. A. Vandoit, Henry Brunner, S. W. Wilson, and J. A. Goodrich.

Ladies of the committee were asked to meet at the Ramona Hotel on Friday afternoon. They included Mmes. R. E. Jack, Benjamin Brooks, W. W. Hayes, McD. R. Venable, B. Sinsheimer, J. D. Armstrong, J. A. Goodrich, G. B. Nichols, L. M. Kaiser, T. Norton, A. Sinsheimer, George Steele, Henry Brunner, C. A. Farnum, and T. T. Crittenden. A last meeting of the executive committee was planned for Friday evening, May 4, at City Hall.

San Luis Obispo residents witnessed what seemed a miracle in engineering "know-how" and organization on Thursday, May 3. Contractors, subcontractors and foremen agreed to lay 10,000 feet of track in a single day. This brought numerous citizens out to observe the activity. When the crews arrived for work near the Stenner Creek Bridge, every move had been planned for the day. All the rails, ties, fishplates, spikes, and bolts were on hand at Goldtree at the horseshoe bend. Every section of track to be laid had been carefully considered so that the necessary material would arrive at the right place at the right time. In some sections of the road, curves and tangents were involved requiring rails to fit accordingly.

The first construction train was loaded at Goldtree and sent to the "front" where railroad gangs unceremoniously hustled the rails and other materials from the flatcars. While the gang went to work, the construction train returned for another load.

As fast as rail was laid, small handcars moved along the new track carrying more rails forward. Another handcar carried ties. Gangs of men moved in to lay the ties, place the rails, drive the spikes, and bolt the fishtails.

It was a most exciting and clearly the most dramatic finality to the years of waiting that could possibly have occurred. Men like Chauncey Hatch Phillips, Robert E. Jack, Benjamin Brooks, Charles O. Johnson, and the many others who had invested so much of their lives to see this great event moving toward its end must have been emotionally gripped by every moment of that day. They watched one hundred feet of track go into place every five minutes.

From the standpoint of the contractors, the job would not really be done. They were skipping every other tie and the bed itself was not finished or graveled, but they would have track laid all of the way to the Ramona Hotel by Friday night at quitting time, and there would be a rail bed all the way into San Luis Obispo for the first train to arrive on Saturday, May 5.

Tickets for the ball and supper were on sale at one dollar per couple at the Goodrich General Store and Latimer's Drug Store. The city was overwhelmed with excitement.

As it stood now, three trains were expected. Sometime before noon on Saturday, the special train carrying Southern Pacific officials would arrive. That evening at 6:05 P.M. the first scheduled general passenger train would reach the city. Then on the following Monday, May 7, a train providing special roundtrip rates from San Francisco and all other points along the route would arrive in town. There would be three days of celebrating.[7]

All San Luis Obispo businesses announced

that they would close at noon on Saturday, May 5, in recognition of the arrival of the first Southern Pacific train.

For the people of San Luis Obispo, the most joyous part of the celebration probably occurred the day before the official arrival of the first passenger train. It was "a quiet little festival which they had all to themselves." Beginning early in the morning on Friday, the townspeople gathered along the line of the railroad bed into San Luis Obispo. They gathered on foot, in carriages and in wagons. They were witnessing the greatest change in their community that was to occur in their lifetimes, and there were surprises in store for them.

The track layers worked almost inexhaustably, clearly enjoying the historic roles they were playing. The drama was made all the more intense by the fact that an audience observed the placement of every rail, the driving of every spike, and the placement of every fishtail.

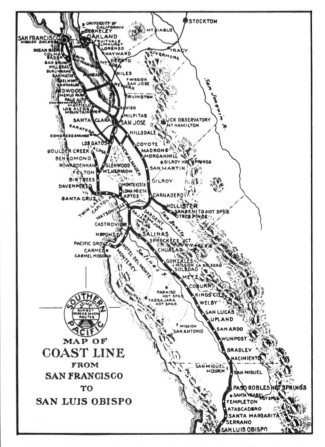

At last, the new Southern Pacific map showing the coast line extension from Santa Margarita to San Luis Obispo.

Southern Pacific passenger train finds its way along the "Road of a Thousand Wonders."

Sometime in the early afternoon, rails were laid to the Ramona Hotel, and the exhausted workers stood to one side. Then there was the quiet waiting for the extraordinary symbol of symbols—the proof beyond all doubt that this dream was reality.

It was 3:25 P.M. The engineer had proper appreciation for his assignment. He had guided the construction engine slowly and carefully the full distance across the Cuesta, to where it was poised at the edge of town. When he arrived at the steel bridge that now crossed Monterey Street, he pulled the rope that sounded the wondrous whistle of triumph. There were cheers and tears and hugging and congratulations and handshaking as the steam whistles of the electric light works, Waite and Ryans, and the deafening siren at the Pacific Coast Railway responded to the very first whistle of the very first Southern Pacific Railroad engine steaming to a stop at the railroad entrance to the Ramona Hotel. Then the cheers started again when the bell at City Hall joined the others.

Then J. C. Castro backed a wagon up to the track and threw back a canvas to reveal a wagonload of beer for the track layers, and workers and townspeople joined in drinking success to San Luis Obispo.

"All about the Ramona," Brooks calmly reported, "it was by way of being a holiday."

Just across Higuera Street from the hotel, preparations for the barbecue to take place the next day were underway. Tables stretched in long lines under canvas coverings and evergreen boughs to protect guests from the May sunshine.

Beginning Thursday night, large fires had been built to make beds of coals. Upon being herded to the site, the cattle were set free in the field, and a half-dozen vaqueros ceremoniously took off in pursuit of each animal, roped him and threw him. The cattle were then slaughtered and butchered at the site. The chunks of beef were hung on racks. The slaughtering and butchering continued throughout the afternoon on Friday. By evening, the people of San Luis Obispo felt prepared to host the state.

Just one major and unbelievable surprise awaited them.

There was no reason not to believe the railroad officials in San Francisco when they notified R. E. Jack that a delegation would arrive in San Luis Obispo about noon on Saturday in time for the main ceremonies that afternoon.

The townspeople also accepted Southern Pacific Company President Collis P. Huntington's word for it when he wrote saying that he would not be able to come to San Luis Obispo.

If the committee planning all of the events for the celebration was a little rattled, it was no wonder. On Friday evening, the night before the celebration, people who were around saw the laying of a sidetrack opposite the Ramona Hotel. The sidetrack was scarcely in place before an engine pulling four private cars moved quietly into place.

Someone in the hotel hurried out to inform the principal committeemen. Someone else got in touch with band members. Very soon, the Ramona Hotel was crowded with townspeople. In a little while, the band was playing and all of the railroad officials who had arrived in private cars gathered in the hotel to greet everyone.

with his assistant, a Mr. Gillette. Culverwell would become resident engineer of the division located in San Luis Obispo.

There were several local dignitaries who had been invited to join the special train north of the Cuesta. They included General Patrick Murphy, owner of the Santa Margarita Rancho; L. Fillmore, Edwin Goodall, and John Howard of the Pacific Coast Railway; George Stone and C. E. Higbee, construction contractors on the Cuesta; and Mr. Shackelford from Paso Robles.

But the man least expected to come, Collis

Taken from Terrace Hill, this old postcard photo shows the first San Luis Obispo depot and many box cars on the side tracks, as well as a general view of the community.

There was William Hood, chief engineer for the company. Hood had made his bid to fame by the use of the "loop" as an engineering method for ascending and descending steep grades by train. Laying track through the Cuesta had required seven tunnels but only one great loop.

Mr. J. A. Fillmore was also on board. Fillmore was general superintendent of the Pacific System for Southern Pacific. J. C. Stubbs, third vice president of the company, warmly extended a hand to townspeople. T. H. Goodman, the general passenger agent in the San Francisco office, was on hand. So was R. S. Culverwell

Potter Huntington, president of the Southern Pacific Company, was also on hand. So was his nephew, Henry Edwards Huntington, who later became a vice president and a member of the board of directors for Southern Pacific. This nephew would one day be most famous for the development of the Huntington Library Museum and Art Gallery.

From the conversation heard that evening, it was learned that the officials planned a trip to Santa Maria on the Pacific Coast Railway the next morning. They intended to leave at 6:30 A.M. and return by 9:30 A.M.

Collis Huntington told the group that he

would then return immediately to San Francisco, but some Southern Pacific executives would remain for the Saturday celebration.

The morning of the celebration arrived, and Brooks wrote, "In the history of San Luis Obispo, when its next chapter shall be written, the page which will stand out in letters of gold will be that devoted to the Fifth of May, 1894."

The first large out-of-town group to arrive traveled by Pacific Coast Railway from the communities south of San Luis Obispo—Arroyo Grande, Pismo, Grover, Santa Maria, Los Alamos, and Santa Ynez.

There was a large reception committee of San Luis Obispans to greet the visitors and to pin souvenir badges and buttonhole bouquets on each person stepping from the train.

Visitors who arrived on the narrow gauge strolled leisurely in the direction of the Southern Pacific rails and the Ramona Hotel at the far end of town. Stores along Monterey and Higuera streets were open until noon, but after that, by agreement, all were closed. Store windows and fronts were colorfully decorated in streamers and bunting.

Among the elderly there were special exclamations about the day. Many regretted that certain old friends had not lived to see it. One old gentleman stood alongside the tracks and remarked, "... I have been waiting forty-two years to see that railroad ..."

This was the largest crowd that had ever gathered in San Luis Obispo, and it seemed to require little entertainment. Members of the reception committee estimated that they had made two thousand badges and boutonnieres, but they ran out long before the crowds stopped arriving.

The railroad officials stayed with their schedule. They left San Luis Obispo at 6:30 in the morning on the narrow gauge for Santa Maria and returned with some of the crowd coming from that direction three hours later. The trip provided Collis Huntington and the other officers of the company an opportunity to observe the route, the service, and the condition of the Pacific Coast narrow gauge. For many weeks, they had been surveying the route of the Southern Pacific between San Luis Obispo and Ellwood.

When they returned, Huntington and some of the other Southern Pacific officials boarded their special train for San Francisco. They invited some local dignitaries to ride with them as far as Paso Robles.

Around three o'clock in the afternoon, the crowd gathered for the barbecue. At 4:15, the boys of the Fred Steele Post shot off "Big Bill," their thirty-two-pounder cannon, to announce that the special train from the north would arrive soon. It was another exciting hour. The special train brought four hundred more guests. The regular train from San Francisco came in at 6:00 P.M. bringing even more people.

The townspeople had simply never seen anything like it. The train was working its magic.

The barbecued meat disappeared rapidly. The Ramona Hotel and all the other hotels in town happily accommodated people staying overnight.

As evening arrived, the crowds at the barbecue and around the hotel grounds watched an exhibition of rockets bursting in brilliant design across the sky. The band members played their hearts out to a most appreciative and well-fed audience.

Then the musicians changed clothes and went to the hotel. It was time for the dress-up part of the celebration. The local gentlemen and their ladies arrived in their carriages and the out-of-town visitors came down the stairs from their rooms. All converged in the ballroom to participate in the grand march and to observe each other's elegant dress and enjoy each other's company.

One of the "supper rooms" of the Ramona was set aside for a special gathering that included Mr. and Mrs. Fillmore, Mr. Goodman, Mrs. and Miss Hosiner, Mrs. J. C. Stubbs, William Hood, George E. Miles, Carroll Cook, O. A. Hale, J. A. McMurtrie, George Stone, J. L. Howard, Captain Goodall, General S. W. Backus, General Patrick Murphy, Captain J. S. Currier, Mr. C. F. Degelman, and a reporter from the *San Jose News*.

Robert E. Jack and Chauncey Hatch Phillips assumed responsibility for entertaining these dignitaries. Phillips was the toastmaster, and many toasts were offered that night. Stubbs,

Another year was required to complete the roundhouse and other structures which gradually turned San Luis Obispo into a railroad town.

Howard and Stone spoke about the unusual features of the new railroad line, and Fillmore gave strong assurances to his hosts about the continuation of the line south of San Luis Obispo.

"It was a fitting close to the great day,"

Brooks told his readers. "San Luis Obispans, some time or other, went to bed happy and satisfied."

It scarcely seemed possible. The train would now run between San Francisco and San Luis Obispo every day.[8]

Epilogue

The railroad building years challenged men with strong leadership qualities, and it is interesting to skim this partial list of names of people who played an important role during that time: Robert E. Jack, Patrick Murphy, George and Edgar Steele, Horatio and Lew Warden, P. A. Dallidet, the Hollister family, Jose Branch, Myron Angel, Drury James, the Blackburn brothers, the Dana family, Edwin P. Unangst, J. P. Andrews, Benjamin Brooks, L. M. Kaiser, Nathan, Morris and Isaac Goldtree, Ah Louis, Ellwood Cooper, C. R. Callender, Charles Johnson, W. W. Hays, William Sandercock, R. A. Loomis, William Evans, Judge McDowell R. Venable, Luigi Marre, Horace A. Vachell, P. B. Perfumo, P. Quintana, August Vollmer, J. M. Felts, J. W. Barneberg, J. A. Goodrich, and John Price. These men were all San Luis Obispans.

There were others from outside the area who became involved—men like Charles Goodall, J. Millard Fillmore, John L. Howard, and George Clement Perkins—all officers with the Pacific Coast Railway and Steamship Company. Then, clearly, those outsiders who had the greatest impact of all—Collis Huntington, Charles Crocker, William Hood, and J. A. Fillmore of the Southern Pacific Company.

But there is one person among all of those who received special attention in the community when the railroad line finally reached the city of San Luis Obispo. He was Chauncey Hatch Phillips.

In San Luis Obispo, Phillips' efforts and achievements were viewed with the greatest respect, and many people felt he had wrought a kind of miracle. The *Tribune* paid him the highest tribute by suggesting that he had all of the qualifications to become governor of California. Phillips modestly declined interest in politics.

"He is a clean man," Benjamin Brooks wrote, "a man of affairs about whom no slanderous tongue can wag, a broad-minded, liberal progressive citizen . . . He has wrought broadly and well for San Luis Obispo County and its progress for the last twenty years; the subdivision of its territory and its present condition with the rest of the world are all largely due to his persistent and most intelligent labors."

Phillips never became a candidate for public office. Instead, soon after the arrival of the railroad in San Luis Obispo, word spread that he was involved in the one and one-half million dollar purchase of the Chino Ranch near San Bernardino. The property included 41,000 acres as well as the Chino Valley Railroad and a sugar beet factory.[1]

Phillips was clearly a man of his times—an entrepreneur and a versatile person—and he left his mark wherever he moved. The West Coast Land Company which he established continued under other management in San Luis Obispo County for many years, but Phillips' destiny took him to other places.

❧

The arrival of the railroad in San Luis Obispo County introduced a new social phenomena among the communities. It was now easier for people to travel longer distances to participate in special community events. When an event was important enough, Southern Pacific could even be persuaded to run an "excursion" train.

One such day was September 29, 1897, and the occasion was the centennial celebration of Mission San Miguel. The Bishop of the Diocese of Monterey was speaker during the formal

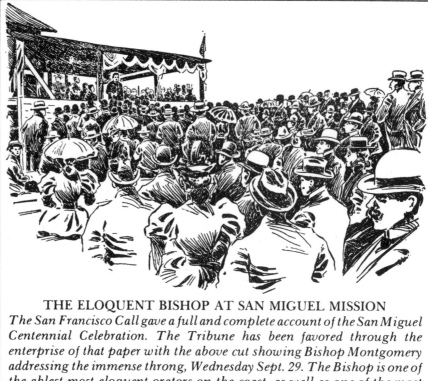

THE ELOQUENT BISHOP AT SAN MIGUEL MISSION
The San Francisco Call gave a full and complete account of the San Miguel Centennial Celebration. The Tribune has been favored through the enterprise of that paper with the above cut showing Bishop Montgomery addressing the immense throng, Wednesday Sept. 29. The Bishop is one of the ablest most eloquent orators on the coast, as well as one of the most popular priests in the United States. Patriotic, broad minded and liberal, it is a rare treat to hear him lecture. Many a person will join with the Tribune in wishing him long life in his noble and great work in behalf of humanity in the diocese of Monterey.

ceremonies, and the day brought an illustrator-reporter from the *San Francisco Call* who duly recorded the event in pen-and-ink sketches for his newspaper.

The event started with a parade from the depot where the crowd gathered to welcome the bishop when he arrived by train. The parade was followed by a band concert in the park, a baseball game between Paso Robles and San Miguel, a tug-of-war between Parkfield and San Luis Obispo, two horse races with enticing purses, literary exercises, a barbecue, and pontifical vespers.

Southern Pacific operated an excursion train from San Francisco, picking up passengers at every stop.[2]

For some time after the trains began running between San Francisco and San Luis Obispo, railroad construction continued in San Luis Obispo. This small mission town was fast becoming a "railroad town." The siding yards, the depot grounds, and the site of the turntable

A San Francisco Chronicle illustrator was present for the centennial celebration at Mission San Miguel, and the Chronicle later provided this illustration for the Tribune showing the mission and some of its out-of-town visitors.

were located on a side hill which required moving and leveling tons of earth. The turntable for reversing the engines for the return trip to San Francisco was necessarily the first installation completed.

Shortly before the arrival of the train at 6:00 P.M. each day, hacks and horse-drawn buses from the hotels scurried along the dirt and graveled streets to the depot hoping to pick up overnight guests among debarking passengers. And now, big city newspapers and mail arrived daily by train, and people began to feel a part of the larger world.[3]

Travelers were not staying at local hotels in large numbers. In fact, there were nights when the Ramona Hotel was empty except for the employees and an occasional permanent tenant. At the end of 1894, John L. Howard of the West Coast Land Company and Pacific Coast Railway Company sent word to close the Ramona until financial conditions improved. So, the new year of 1895 began with the doors of the great hotel closed.

For a time, the hotel loomed like a great ghost at the edge of town. The owners hoped to find someone to lease it and operate it. Finally, after six months, the doors opened for business again under lease management, but the Ramona was simply too large for the town, and it was never a financial success. Like so many wooden structures of the time, it met a tragic end. On November 10, 1905, it caught fire and burned to the ground.[4]

It is perhaps interesting to note here that the equally large El Paso de Robles Hotel in Paso Robles continued operation as a spa and health resort until the 1940s, but eventually this great wooden structure was also destroyed by fire. A new inn with motel units was built on the site soon after, and in 1980, it continues its role as a historic roadside stop for tired travelers.

The railroad did not change economic conditions nearly as much as was expected. No influx of immigrants arrived to purchase the great land tracts that had been opened.

When the census was taken at the beginning of the new century, it turned out that Paso Robles was the only community that had grown during the previous decade. The census for 1900 for the county was very disappointing to people who viewed growth as an important indicator of success.

The population of the county had scarcely changed. From 16,072 people in 1890, it had grown to 16,637 in 1900, an increase of only 565

people. The city of Paso Robles had had 827 people in 1890. By 1900, it had grown to 1,224. Poor San Luis Obispo, for all of its struggles, had grown from 2,995 to only 3,021, an increase of twenty-six people in ten years.

The *Tribune* tried to emphasize the good things that had happened during the previous decade. "Despite the fact that San Luis Obispo County has been 'shut in,'" the newspaper said, "it has witnessed considerable development and no little activity within its borders. During the past ten years a chrome mill was erected . . . The McClure seed ranch was started in the Arroyo Grande Valley. It covers several hundred acres of land, and many tons of seeds of all descriptions are now shipped annually to all sections of the country."

"In the Las Tablas hills," the *Tribune* continued, "within the last year there has been a great revival in quicksilver mining. The Dubost mine was only recently sold out to outside capitalists for $30,000. Many of the largest stock ranches of the county have been subdivided in the past ten years, and each year the acreage sown to grain has increased. This has occasioned the building of new flour mills at Paso Robles, Templeton and San Miguel.

"In the city of San Luis Obispo many of the old buildings on the business streets have given place to elegant brick structures."[5]

In September 1894 McMurtrie and Stone began cutting and scraping roadbed for track south of San Luis Obispo. The brick walls of the roundhouse in San Luis Obsipo were completed and accepted by Southern Pacific in November. Carloads of railroad ties and rails rolled through town in November 1895, and a work force of sixty men was brought in to lay track south of town. This work was followed by carloads of gravel used to fill in between ties and firm up the track.[6]

By January 14, 1895 track was completed to the edge of Pismo. Track construction proceeded toward Oceano, and on January 27, 1895 trains reached this developing town site. As part of their celebration, the new Oceano Townsite Company shipped a few sacks of potatoes to San Francisco.[7] R. E. Jack and others worked to make Oceano the new tourist beach community of the area. In an agreement with Southern

Turn table at San Luis Obispo.

Branding time on a ranch along the coastal rail line.

Pacific Company, the land development company paid for a spur track off the main line to the beach where Jack had arranged for the construction of a Victorian-styled pavilion to accommodate conferences, dances, and recreational activities. The new building was completed in August 1895.

Meantime, the main line was constructed in the direction of Guadalupe where in May 1895, piers for a railroad bridge had been placed across the Santa Maria River. By late summer, the bridge was completed and trains ran into the town.[8]

The next construction goal was the laying of track along the coast to the Santa Ynez River. This would bring tracks within fifty-five miles of Ellwood, near Santa Barbara, the terminus of track laid from the south. Then the gap between Los Angeles and San Francisco would be closed.

On Friday, October 11, 1895, Collis Hunt-ington and a party of Southern Pacific executives came to San Luis Obispo on an inspection trip. They stayed at the Ramona Hotel, and the next morning they traveled to Guadalupe. Huntington was optimistic during his visit. He allowed a *Tribune* reporter to interview him and was reassuring about plans for the completion of the line.[9]

Then on February 1, 1896 Southern Pacific began selling tickets in San Francisco to a new place eleven miles south of Guadalupe named Someo or Casmalia, with stage connections from there to Lompoc and Santa Barbara.[10]

Toward the end of 1896, work on the large railroad bridge across the Santa Ynez River was well underway. When it was completed in early 1897, another stop called Surf was added to the Southern Pacific schedule.[11]

With the end seemingly in sight in 1897, people found it nearly impossible to believe that the railroad company was again stopping all construction, but that is what was happening. It was late in 1899 before Huntington ordered work to begin again on the coastal line. This time he wrote to Ellwood Cooper in Santa Barbara to say that he expected to close the gap within a few months.[12] During those intervening years, passengers and freight between San Francisco and Los Angeles had continued to move through the San Joaquin Valley.[13]

In February 1900, Southern Pacific issued a folder describing the new coastal route. It included illustrations of the Paso Robles Hotel and bathhouses and a view of San Luis Obispo from San Luis Peak. "The Hotel Ramona," the folder read, "named for Helen Hunt Jackson's famous novel, shows by its size, its elegance, and its fine management that San Luis Obispo is already known to many outside the city."[14]

In February 1900, Southern Pacific did something it had not done for many years. The company began laying track from the south, beginning at Ellwood near Santa Barbara, toward the railroad terminus at Surf. At least forty men were at work. There was also activity outside of Surf. By March fourteen miles of track had been constructed. Along the remaining thirty-eight miles, the Southern Pacific built six more viaducts ranging from 650 to 850 feet in length.[15]

Even so, the first year of the new century ended without the gap's being closed. Finally, in March 1901, Passenger Traffic Manager E. O. McCormick of the Southern Pacific announced that regular trains would soon begin running.

Both a morning and an evening train were scheduled to make daily runs between Los Angeles and San Francisco in fifteen and a half hours. The Sunset Express Number 10 and the Daylight Express Number 2 were being transferred from the main line in the valley to the

Construction officials pose in 1896 for a picture at the site of the Santa Ynez railroad bridge. When the bridge was completed, a new Southern Pacific stop called Surf was added to the schedule. Completion of the bridge brought track within fifty-five miles of Ellwood, the coastal line terminus from the south. At this point, a spur track was constructed into Lompoc.

Stagecoach from Los Olivos and Santa Ynez headed for Santa Barbara.

new coast line. At Saugus, the coast line would connect with the valley line into Los Angeles.[16]

The Santa Barbara office of Southern Pacific received notice about the planned make-up of the first trains on the completed coast line. The notice read: "The daylight vestibuled train will be known as the Coast Line Limited and will run from Los Angeles to San Francisco. It will be composed of mail, baggage, smoker, coaches, tourist cars, cafe chair cars and parlor cars. The tourist cars will be the usual vestibule Pullman car of the very comfortable kind across the continent. They are really very handsome cars. The cafe will be one of the finest in the land, while the parlor cars will be Pullman's of the finest finish and equipment. This will be one of the most popular trains in the west. The number of cars will vary with the travel from 9 or 10 to 12."[17]

With the great day approaching, one San Luis Obispo resident sent a letter to the *Tribune* urging a celebration of the arrival of trains from both the north and the south, and he thought it appropriate that the depot be "festooned with flags and decorated with flowers."

"Let the band be engaged and the cannon be brought up and a salute fired," the writer urged.[18]

The first trains from both San Francisco and Los Angeles came through San Luis Obispo on Sunday, April 1, 1901. Many people gathered at the station to witness this remarkable event. Some of them had passed from the prime of life

into old age during the quarter-century of waiting for the gap to close. All were happy to see the trains, but the station was not "festooned with flags" and no one bothered to fire the cannon that had been heard so many times at San Luis Obispo celebrations.

One young lady's name should be recalled for her historic role that day. Miss Kate Cox organized the members of the Twentieth Century Club, a new group of young people, to go onto the trains while they were stopped and distribute bouquets to women passengers.

The *Tribune* said, "Probably our people have exhausted themselves by their efforts to bring about this great change, and now they are weary from the years of waiting, possibly not fully realizing that they are at last on one of the great train lines and that the 'gap' is at last really a thing of the past."[19]

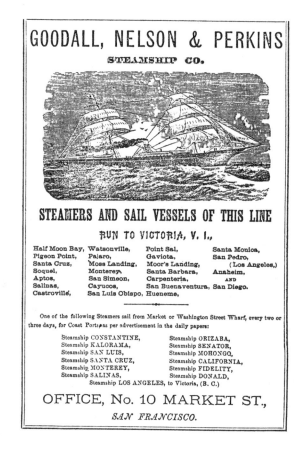

SAN LUIS OBISPO, SURF AND SANTA BARBARA LINE.
Time corrected to June 25, 1899.

No 53 Daily except Sun.	3 & 91 Daily except Sun.	No. 1 Daily.	Miles.	STATIONS. § Telegraph Offices.	Elev.	No. 2 Daily.	4 & 92 Daily except Sun.	No. 34 Daily except Sun.
P.M.	A.M.					P.M.	A.M.	
2 45	9 00		0	lv....San Fran.....§ar	6	4 10	10 36	
2 30	10 57		51	lv.....San Jose.....ar	51	2 35	9 07	
Mxd.								Mxd.
4 25	11 40		120	lv....Santa Cruz.....ar	15	1 45	8 50	
A.M.	3 29	11 45	125	lv.....Monterey.....ar	5	1 42	8 45	P.M.
7 25	6 05	11 25	110	lv....Castroville..§ar	17	12 10	7 10	5 00
8 20	6 25	1 39	118	......Salinas......§	44	11 56	6 50	4 35
8 33	P.M.		120	..Spreckels Junc.....			A.M.	3 45
8 50		1 52	125	......Spence......§	79	11 42		3 30
9 05		1 58	129	......Chualar......§	103	11 36		3 05
9 28		2 09	135	......Gonzales.....§	197	11 25		2 40
9 50		2 19	141	......Camphora......		11 15		2 19
10 10		2 25	144	......Soledad......§	182	11 10		1 55
12 30		3 04	164	.....Kings City.....§	332	10 30		12 15
1 05		3 20	173	.....San Lucas.....§	396	10 15		10 43
1 40		3 38	183	......San Ardo.....§	452	9 58		9 58
2 10		3 49	190	......Wunpost......	487	9 47		9 24
2 35		4 03	196	......Bradley......§	539	9 37		9 00
3 25		4 21	205	.....San Miguel.....§	616	9 18		8 22
3 45		4 30	211	......Wellsona......	671	9 07		8 02
4 10		4 40	217	....Paso Robles....§	723	8 55		7 43
4 50		4 50	222	.....Templeton.....§	773	8 44		7 18
5 15		4 55	226	.....Asuncion.....§	825	8 38		7 08
5 39		5 01	229	.....Atascadero.....	852	8 33		6 58
5 39		5 06	237	......Havel......§	879	8 29		6 50
6 00		5 13	236	...Santa Margarita.§	998	8 20		6 30
6 14		5 24	240	......Cuesta......	1290	8 11		6 16
6 30		5 37	244	......Serrano......	928	7 57		6 00
6 45		5 49	249	......Goldtree......	512	7 46		5 45
7 00		6 00	253	ar..San Luis Obispo.§lv	238	7 35		5 30
8 00		6 05	253	lv..San Luis Obispo.§ar	238	7 30		4 35
8 23		6 15	259	......Edna......§	225	7 20		4 08
8 47		6 28	265	......Grover......	12	7 07		3 45
8 54		6 32	267	......Oceano.....§	18	7 03		3 40
9 09		6 40	272	.....Callender......	92	6 55		3 75
9 18		6 45	273	......Bromela......	48	6 50		3 15
11 00		6 53	277	....Guadalupe....§	80	6 43		3 00
11 15		7 02	282	......Waldorf......	801	6 34		1 15
11 30		7 09	286	......Schumann......	401	6 27		1 00
11 38		7 13	292	......Casmalia.....§	244	6 22		12 48
11 46		7 17	295	......Antonio......		6 18		12 40
11 57		7 23	294	......Narlon......§	128	6 12		12 26
12 45		7 40	303	......Surf......§	46	5 55		11 45
1 30		8 00	313	ar.....Lompoc.....lv		5 39		11 00
A.M.		P.M.				A.M.		P.M.

SANTA BARBARA AND LOS ANGELES
COAST LINE.

Buffet				
	9 00	lv....San Fran....ar	4 10	Buffet
Drawing-Room	10 57	lv....San Jose....ar	2 35	Drawing-Room
	11 40	lv...Santa Cruz...ar	1 45	
Sleeper	11 45	lv...Monterey...ar	1 42	Sleeper
	6 05	lv..San Luis Obispo..ar	7 30	
	8 00	ar....Lompoc....lv	5 30	
DAILY	STAGE.			DAILY
BETWEEN	7 00	lv....Lompoc.....ar	ƒ5 30	BETWEEN
San Francisco	12 00	lv.....Honda.....ar	12 00	LOMPOC
AND	5 30	ar..Santa Barbara..lv	7 00	AND
	RAIL.			San Francisco
LOMPOC	8 15	lv..Santa Barbara..ar	8 40	
	12 40	ar...Los Angeles..lv	4 60	

d Remain in Sleeper over night. ƒ Take Sleeper for the night. § Meals

Light faced figures denote A.M.   Dark faced figures denote P.M.

Time table for the year 1899 shows stops between San Francisco and Lompoc. Stagecoaches met the train to transport passengers to Ellwood where they could continue there journey along the coast.

The newspaper writer wanted, somehow, to explain that the whole event was anticlimactic. People could not get excited. They had waited too long.

It must now also be emphasized that while it was possible to travel the coast line route all of the way between San Francisco and Los Angeles, the connection with the valley line at Saugus was only a temporary arrangement. Southern Pacific President Collis Huntington, the last of the Big Four and one of the world's outstanding industrial leaders, had given the order for the completion of the coastal gap, but he did not live to see the job done. He

died August 13, 1900. Mark Hopkins, the oldest of the four, had died March 29, 1878. Charles Crocker died August 14, 1888, and Leland Stanford on June 21, 1893, while serving his second term as a United States Senator. He and Mrs. Stanford had established Stanford University eight years earlier.

For years, E. H. Harriman of Union Pacific Railroad had sought to buy Southern Pacific, but even in the worst of times, Huntington had

1263 - LONGEST WHARF IN THE WORLD, SANTA MONICA, CALIFORNIA.

Santa Monica had the longest wharf in the world at the turn-of-the-century where trains met steamships to exchange freight.

resisted. Finally, through a series of skillful financial negotiations, Harriman succeeded in purchasing stock from the Huntington estate and through other sources until Union Pacific owned about thirty-seven and a half percent of the stock of the Southern Pacific. Later this interest was increased to forty-six percent.

The last great obstacles in completion of the coastal line were three tunnels through the Santa Susanna mountains, the longest of which was the one and a half mile Chatsworth Park tunnel.

With all members of the "Big Four" deceased, Harriman was elected chairman of the Southern Pacific executive committee in April 1901. Later that year, he became president of the company. His reorganization of the Southern Pacific provided an expenditure of $240 million to update the railroad during the next eight years.[20]

A part of this money was used to construct three tunnels through the Santa Susanna Mountains. The tunnel located at Chatsworth was nearly one and one-half miles long. These tunnels were necessary for the new and permanent routing of the coastal line. The final link in the coast line route was completed March 20, 1904, without fanfare. Rail traffic along the coast was routed south from Santa Barbara through Oxnard and Burbank and into Los Angeles.[21]

At last, the Southern Pacific Company's coast line was completed! Rails had fully replaced the stagecoach trails across the California ranchos.

This great coal burning engine, under the controls of Engineer J. J. Rockweel and Fireman William Bohrmeister, safely brought United States President William McKinley to San Luis Obispo on May 10, 1901, where the city hosted him at the Ramona Hotel, and he delivered a talk from the veranda of the hotel to an audience gathered on the lawn in front of the hotel.

Notes

Chapter I, THE GRAND PROMISE

1. San Luis Obispo Tribune (*hereafter referred to as Tribune*), June 19, 26 and July 3, 1885.
2. Tribune, April 23, 1886.
3. Myron Angel, *History of San Luis Obispo County, California*, Thompson & West, 1883 or Valley Publishers, Fresno, 1979, p. 361. (*hereafter referred to as Angel*)
4. La Vista, Vol. 2, No. 2, San Luis Obispo, California. (*hereafter referred to as La Vista*)
5. Tribune, May 22 and July 3, 1885.
6. Tribune, November 20, 1885, and Angel, p. 375.

Chapter II, MAKING LARGE RANCHOS INTO SMALLER ONES

1. Tribune, July 10, 1885 and May 21, 1886.
2. Angel, pp. 60A, B.
3. Angel, p. 320.
4. Erle Heath, *Seventy-five Years of Progress, Historical Sketch of the Southern Pacific Railroad Company*, published by Southern Pacific Bureau of News, San Francisco, California, December 1945, pp. 11 and 18. (*hereafter referred to as Heath*)
5. Angel, p. 320.
6. W. W. Robinson, *The Story of San Luis Obispo*, Title Insurance and Trust Company, San Luis Obispo, p. 53. (*hereafter referred to as Robinson*)
   Also Leonard Rudolph Bloomquist, "California in Transition, 1830-50," Master's thesis, University of California, October 1943, p. 98. (*hereafter referred to as Bloomquist*)
7. Carpenter Plate, volume on title transfers of Mexican land grants, Title Insurance and Trust Company, San Luis Obispo. This plate is a title transfer reference acquired from an early title company. (*hereafter referred to as Carpenter*)
8. Angel, p. 348.
9. Angel, pp. 341-42.
10. Angel, pp. 60A, B.
11. Angel, p. 320.
12. Angel, pp. 60A, B.
13. Angel, pp. 40A, B, C, D.
14. Bloomquist, U.S. Land Commission, Land Case 75, Southern District.
15. Ibid.
16. Angel, pp. 217-19.
17. Angel, p. 350.
18. Bloomquist, U.S. Land Commission, Land Case 365, Southern District.
19. Bloomquist, U.S. Land Commission, Land Case 45, Southern District.
20. Bloomquist, U.S. Land Commission, Land Case 120, Southern District.
21. Angel, p. 220.
22. Tribune, various issues including April 22, 1887.
23. Bloomquist, U.S. Land Commission, Land Case 196, Southern District.
24. Original letter, Mallagh to Stearns, Huntington Library, San Marino, California.
25. West Coast Land Company brochure, Bancroft Library, University of California, Berkeley; Tribune, August 27, 1886.

Chapter III, TRACKS FOR SAN MIGUEL

1. Tribune, May 7, 1886.
2. Heath, p. 18; and Southern Pacific Timetable, 1886, Huntington Library, San Marino, California.
3. Tribune, October 20, 1886.
4. Father Zephyrin Engelhardt (Charles A.), "San Miguel, Archangel, the Mission on the Highway." (*hereafter referred to as Engelhardt*)
5. James P. Beckwourth, "The Life and Adventures of James P. Beckwourth," unpublished manuscript, Bancroft Library, University of California, Berkeley.
6. Engelhardt.
7. Engelhardt.

Chapter IV, PASSING EL PASO DE ROBLES

1. Heath, p. 18.
2. Angel, pp. 372-74.
3. Robinson, p. 53.
4. Original letter, Thomas Larkin to Pedro Narvaez, dated September 4, 1844, Larkin Papers, Huntington Library, San Marino, California.
5. Larkin Papers, Vol. 4, p. 326.
6. Larkin Papers, Vol. 5, p. 134.
7. Robinson, p. 53.
8. Hubert Howe Bancroft, Vol. 3, pp. 71, 584, 672, 702; Vol. 4, p. 655; Vol. 5, pp. 375, 561, 637, 639-40.
9. Angel, pp. 372-73.
10. Edward Vischer, 1864 illustration, Pierce Collection items 9352, 9353, Huntington Library, San Marino, California.
11. Senator Chris N. Jesperson, *History of San Luis Obispo County*, Harold Meier, 1939.
12. La Vista, Vol. 1, Issue No. 4, p. 26.
13. La Vista, Vol. 1, Issue No. 2, inside jacket.
14. La Vista, Vol. 1, Issue No. 4, p. 26. For the most part, this chapter was taken from this issue of La Vista. However, I have tried to identify earlier sources. At every stage, newspapers of the time helped verify information. I wrote the earlier article in La Vista and feel that it is as factually sound as early written sources allow.

Chapter V, FIRE, TEARS AND MUSIC

1. Tribune, July 24, 1885.
2. Tribune, September 18, 1885.
3. Tribune, November 13, 1885.
4. Tribune, September 4, 1885.
5. Tribune, September 18, 1885.
6. Tribune, October 23, 1885.
7. Tribune, November 20, 1885.
8. Tribune, January 8, 1886.
9. Tribune, March 5, 1886.
10. Tribune, May 23, 1886.
11. Tribune, May 30, 1886.
12. Tribune, May 23, 1886.

Chapter VI, A NEW TOWN

1. Tribune, September 17, 1886.
2. Tribune, May 21, 1886.
3. Tribune, various issues, August and September, 1886.
4. Tribune, various issues, September through December, 1886.
5. Tribune, December 24, 1886.
6. Tribune, April 15, 1887.

Chapter VII, THE BOARD OF TRADE

1. Tribune, October 16, 1886.
2. Tribune, January 21, 1887.
3. Tribune, February 11 and 25, 1887.
4. Tribune, February 11 and 25, 1887.
5. Tribune, February 25, 1887, "For the Good of the County" (editorial).

6. Tribune, March 11 and 18, 1887.
7. Tribune, March 18, 1887.
8. Tribune, April 8, 1887.
9. Tribune, April 15, 1887.
10. Tribune, May 20, 1887.
11. Tribune, July 1, 1887.
12. Tribune, July 15, 1887.
13. Tribune, July 22, 1887.

Chapter VIII, THE HOTEL PROMOTERS

1. Tribune, March 4, 1887.
2. Tribune, March 4, 1887.
3. Tribune, April 22, 1887.
4. Tribune, June 10, 1887.
5. Tribune, August 8, 1887; August 19, 1887; September 30, 1887.

Chapter IX, ACTION ON THE SANTA MARGARITA

1. Tribune, June 24, July 1, 8, and 15, 1887.
2. Tribune, August 26, 1887.
3. Tribune, January 14 and 28, 1887.
4. Bloomquist, U.S. Land Commission, Land Case 149, Southern District.
5. Carpenter.
6. Bloomquist, U.S. Land Commission, Land Case 76, Southern District.
7. Carpenter.
8. Bloomquist, U.S. Land Commission, Land Case 113, Southern District.
9. Carpenter.
10. Angel, pp. 32A, B, C.
11. Tribune, January 6, 13, and 27, 1888.
12. Tribune, January 20, 1888.
13. Tribune, January 20 and March 9, 1888.
14. Tribune, March 9, April 6, 13, and 20, 1888.
15. Tribune, September 21, 1888.
16. October 26, 1888.
17. Tribune, November 9 and 30, 1888.
18. Tribune, December 28, 1888.
19. Carpenter.
20. Tribune, February 22, 1889.
21. Tribune, February 19, 1889.

Chapter X, NEW TOWNS TO THE SOUTH

1. Tribune, August 7, 1885.
2. Tribune, March 25, 1887.
3. Tribune, July 22 and 29, 1887.
4. Tribune, July 8, 1887.
5. Robinson, p. 53.
6. Angel, pp. 101-7.
7. Tribune, July 8 and August 5, 1887.
8. Tribune, July 5, 1887.
9. Tribune, July 5, 1887.
10. Angel, p. 350.
11. Angel, p. 351.
12. Tribune, September 16, 1887.
13. Tribune, December 2, 1887.
14. Tribune, December 16, 1887.

Chapter XI, TWO GREAT NEW HOTELS

1. Tribune, September 30, 1887.
2. Tribune, March 9, 1888.
3. Tribune, May 4, 1888.
4. Tribune, May 25 and December 14, 1888.
5. Tribune, June 8, 1888.
6. Tribune, July 20, 1888.
7. Tribune, October 5, 1888.
8. La Vista, Vol. 1, Issue No. 4, pp. 41-45.

Chapter XII, LAND SUBSCRIPTIONS

1. Tribune, January 6, 13, and 27, 1888.
2. Tribune, December 28, 1888.
3. Tribune, January 4, 1889.
4. Tribune, April 9, 1889.
5. Tribune, April 12 and 19, 1889.
6. Tribune, May 3, 1889.
7. Tribune, May 10, 1889.
8. Tribune, May 17, 1889.
9. Tribune, May 17, 1889.
10. Tribune, May 31, 1889.
11. Tribune, May 31, June 7 and 21, and July 26, 1889.
12. Tribune, May 24 and July 12, 1889.
13. Tribune, June 21, 1889.
14. Tribune, May 31, 1889.
15. Tribune, June 6 and 21, July 26, and August 9 and 16, 1889.
16. Tribune, July 26, 1889.
17. Tribune, June 6 and 21, July 26, and August 9 and 16, 1889.
18. Tribune, July 16, 1889.
19. Tribune, July 16, August 16 and 30, September 20, and November 15, 1889.

Chapter XIII, GATHERING NEW HOPE

1. Tribune, January 31, 1890.
2. Tribune, January 31, 1890.
3. Tribune, January 17 and February 7, 1890.
4. Tribune, March 14, 1890.
5. Tribune, April 25, 1890.
6. Tribune, April 25, 1890.
7. Tribune, May 23 and June 6, 1890.

Chapter XIV, THE SEARCH FOR OUTSIDE SUPPORT

1. Tribune, June 6 and 20, 1890.
2. Tribune, June 27, 1890.
3. Tribune, June 27 and July 11, 1890.
4. Tribune, August 4, 1890.
5. Tribune, July 4, and August 1, 8, 15, and 22, 1890.
6. Tribune, August 29, 1890.
7. Tribune, October 31, 1890.
8. Tribune, December 19, 1890.
9. Tribune, February 6, 1891.
10. Tribune, a composite of news items published during February 1891.

Chapter XV, RAILROAD WORK REALLY BEGINS

1. Tribune, December 11, 1891.
2. Tribune, December 19, 1891.
3. Tribune, December 19, 1891.
4. Tribune, January 1, 1892.
5. Tribune, various issues beginning in February 1892.
6. Tribune, February 5 and 12, 1892.
7. Tribune, April 12, 1892.
8. Tribune, April 12, 1892.
9. Tribune, April 1, 1892.
10. Tribune, May 13, 1892.
11. Tribune, May 13, 1892.
12. Tribune, May 13, 1892.
13. Tribune, May 13, 1892.
14. Tribune, July 1, 1892.
15. Tribune, July 1, 1892.
16. Tribune, August 12 and 26, 1892.
17. Tribune, September 30 and October 7, 1892.
18. Tribune, August 26, 1892.
19. Tribune, October 14, 1892.
20. Tribune, September 30, 1892.
21. Tribune, October 28, 1892.
22. Tribune, November 4, 1892.
23. Tribune, November 11, 1892.
24. Tribune, November 5 and 25, 1892.

Chapter XVI, TUNNEL BUILDING

1. San Francisco Chronicle, January 6, 1893.
2. Tribune, January 6, 1893.
3. Tribune, January 31, 1893.
4. Tribune, January 13, 1893.
5. Tribune, February 17, 1893.
6. Tribune, February 17, 1893.
7. Tribune, February 17, 1893.
8. Tribune, February 24, 1893.
9. Tribune, February 24, 1893.
10. Tribune, February 24, 1893.
11. Tribune, February 28, 1893.
12. Tribune, March 4, 1893.
13. Tribune, daily schedules published in March 1893.
14. Tribune, March 10, 1893.
15. Tribune, March 16, 1893.
16. Tribune, March 16, 1893.
17. Tribune, April 1, 1893.
18. Tribune, April 8, 1893.
19. Tribune, April 11, 1893.
20. Tribune, April 12, 1893.
21. Tribune, April 16, 1893.
22. Tribune, April 21, 1893.
23. Tribune, April 28, 1893
24. Tribune, April 29, 1893.
25. Tribune, May 2, 1893.
26. Tribune, May 4, 1893.
27. Tribune, May 18, 1893.
28. Tribune, May 18, 1893.
29. Tribune, May 21, 1893.
30. Tribune, May 26, 1893.
31. Tribune, May 26, 1893.

32. Tribune, May 28, 1893.
33. Tribune, June 1, 1893.
34. Tribune, June 10, 1893.
35. Tribune, June 10, 1893.
36. Tribune, July 6, 1893.
37. Tribune, July 9, 1893.
38. Tribune, July 18, 1893.
39. Tribune, July 19, 1893.
40. Tribune, July 20, 1893.
41. Tribune, July 20, 1893.
42. Tribune, July 23, 1893.
43. Tribune, July 25, 1893.
44. Tribune, July 28, 1893.
45. Tribune, August 1, 1893.
46. Tribune, August 8, 1893.
47. Tribune, August 8, 1893.
48. Tribune, August 17, 1893.
49. Tribune, August 20, 1893.
50. Tribune, August 24, 1893.

Chapter XVII, WORK ALL ALONG THE LINE
1. Tribune, August 25, 1893.
2. Angel, p. 361.
3. Tribune, August 27, 1893.
4. Tribune, August 25, 1893.
5. Tribune, September 9, 1893.
6. Tribune, September 17, 1893.
7. Tribune, September 17, 1893.
8. Tribune, October 18, 1893.
9. Tribune, October 8, 1893.
10. Tribune, October 8, 1893.
11. Tribune, October 20, 1893.
12. Tribune, October 29, 1893.
13. Tribune, November 2, 1893.
14. Tribune, October 25, 1893.
15. Tribune, October 25, 1893.
16. Tribune, November 7, 1893.
17. Tribune, November 17, 1893.
18. Tribune, November 15, 1893.
19. Tribune, November 18, 1893.
20. Tribune, November 21, 1893.
21. Tribune, November 30, 1893.
22. Tribune, December 2, 1893.
23. Tribune, December 8, 1893.
24. Tribune, December 9, 1893.
25. Tribune, December 10, 1893.
26. Tribune, January 3, 1893.
27. Tribune, December 12, 1893.
28. Tribune, December 13, 1893.
29. Tribune, December 14, 1893.

Chapter XVIII, OPENING THE TUNNELS
1. Tribune, January 2, 1894.
2. Tribune, January 11, 1894.
3. Tribune, January 23, 1894.
4. Tribune, January 23, 1894.
5. Tribune, January 23, 1894.
6. Tribune, February 1, 1894.

7. Tribune, February 3, 1894.
8. Tribune, February 7, 1894.
9. Tribune, February 16, 1894.
10. Tribune, February 22, 1894.
11. Tribune, February 23, 1894.
12. Tribune, February 25, 1894.
13. Tribune, February 28 and March 2, 1894.

Chapter XIX, THE STEEL BRIDGE ACROSS
STENNER CREEK
1. Tribune, March 3, 1894.
2. Tribune, March 11, 1894.
3. Tribune, March 12, 1894.
4. Tribune, March 12, 1894.
5. Tribune, March 15, 1894.
6. Tribune, March 15, 1894.
7. Tribune, March 21, 1894.
8. Tribune, March 21, 1894.
9. Tribune, March 22, 1894.
10. Tribune, March 25, 1894.
11. Tribune, March 28, 1894.
12. Tribune, March 29, 1894.
13. Tribune, January 24, 1894.
14. Tribune, March 29, 1894.
15. Tribune, March 30, 1894.
16. Tribune, March 31, 1894.
17. Tribune, April 7, 1894.
18. Tribune, April 5, 1894.
19. Tribune, April 12, 1894.
20. Tribune, April 10, 1894.
21. Tribune, April 10, 1894.
22. Tribune, April 13, 1894.
23. Tribune, April 13, 1894.
24. Tribune, April 12 and 14, 1894.
25. Tribune, April 14, 1894.
26. Tribune, April 15, 1894.
27. Tribune, April 24, 1894.

Chapter XX, THE TRAIN TO SAN LUIS OBISPO
1. Tribune, April 27, 1894.
2. Tribune, April 27, 1894.
3. Tribune, April 27 and 28, 1894.
4. Tribune, April 29, 1894.
5. Tribune, May 1, 1894.
6. Tribune, May 3 and 4, 1894.
7. Tribune, May 5, 1894.
8. Tribune, May 6, 1894.

Chapter XXI, EPILOGUE
1. Tribune, December 2, 1894.
2. Tribune, October 1, 8, and 15, 1897.
3. Tribune, May 13, 1894.
4. Tribune, November 11, 1905.
5. Tribune, February 22, 1901.
6. Tribune, various issues in September and November, 1894.
7. Tribune, January 27, 1895.

8. Tribune, August 17, 1895.
9. Tribune, October 13, 1895.
10. Tribune, February 1, 1896.
11. Tribune, November 21, 1896.
12. Tribune, February 4, 1900.
13. Tribune, February 23, 1900.
14. Tribune, Febraury 7, 1900.

15. Tribune, March 13, 1900.
16. Tribune, March 5, 1901.
17. Tribune, March 27, 1901.
18. Tribune, March 24, 1901.
19. Tribune, April 2, 1901.
20. Heath, pp. 20-21.
21. Heath, p. 21.

Index

Abella, Father Ramon, 23
Abbott, 53
Adams, Amos, 16, 17
Adams, Judge Frederick, 52, 53, 55, 96, 101
Adams, John, 139
Adams, Nichols & Co., 79
Adel, Captain W. T., 119
Ah Louis Chinese Labor Agency, 39
Ah Louis Store, 37, 39
Alamo Hotel (Los Alamos), 136
Alamo Pintado Creek, 82
Albion (steam schooner), 149
Alemany, the Rt. Rev. Joseph, 25
Alexander, George, 14
Allen (engineer), 165
Almada, Joaquin, 153
Alta Californian (San Francisco), 32, 71
Althano, Jacob, 26
Alum Rock Park, 119
Alvarado, Governor Juan Bautista, 9, 11-14, 16, 22, 23, 68, 80, 83, 84
Ambrose, Thomas, 16, 17
Amesti, Carmen, 10
Amesti, Prudenciana, 9
Amtrak, 134, 172
Andrews Bank, 3, 44, 148, 156, 158, 161
Andrews Hotel, 1, 2, 4, 5, 35, 37-40, 42-44, 52, 57, 87, 148
Andrews, John Pinkney, 2, 3, 5, 36, 40, 42-44, 51-53, 61, 71, 96, 100, 104, 145, 148, 149, 156, 175, 181
Andrews, Tennessee Amanda, 3
Angel, Myron, ix, 2, 3, 4, 23, 27, 28, 30, 31, 41, 52, 55, 77, 78, 96, 126, 128, 129, 164, 169, 181
Arabian Remedies Company, 149
Aranas Barbershop (Los Alamos), 136
Arce, Francisco, 18
Archer, Lawrence, 119
Arlington Hotel (Santa Barbara), 72
Armstrong, Mrs. J. D., 175
Arnold, 168
Arroyo Grande, 11, 12, 80, 81, 85, 96, 118, 120, 128, 135, 136, 138, 139, 146, 166, 179
Arroyo Grande Creek, 12
Arroyo Grande Herald, 153, 171
Arroyo Grande Land Grant (Rancho), 1, 11, 78
Arroyo Grande Valley, 183
Arroyo San Carpojoro, 55
Associated Press, 108
Asuncion Land Grant (Rancho), 1, 22, 66, 68
Atascadero Creek, 73
Atascadero Historical Society, vii
Atascadero Land Grant (Rancho), 1, 66, 68, 69
Atlantic and Pacific Railroad, 9
Atwood, E. A., 36
Aug. Spyer and Company, 139
Austin, A. S., 134-136, 138
Australia, 31

Avila, Catarina, 29
Avila, 2, 9, 17, 51, 54, 56, 78, 79, 83, 93, 101, 105, 110, 126, 127, 138, 145, 147, 149, 169
Avila, Jose, 22
Avila, Jose Camilo, 29
Avila, Juan, 79
Avila, Maria Lina, 29
Avila, Miguel, 15, 79
Avila, Ynocenta, 79
Ayala, Juan Pablo, 14

Babcock, William, 9
Backus, General S. W., 179
Bainbridge, Leslie, 38
Baker, J. C., 2
Bakersfield, 9, 20, 93, 126
Baldwin, Professor, 116
Ballard (community), 142
Ballard, Edward, 36, 38
Bancroft, 23, 30
Bancroft Scraps, 30
Bank of California (San Francisco), 162
Bank of Cayucos, 152
Barneburg, J. W., 167, 175, 181
Barnett family, 38
Barrett, J. H., 55
Barrett and Russell, Realtors, 61, 79
Bassett, A. C., 96
Batler (conductor), 166
Baumgartner, J. M., 168
Baywood Park (Moro), 129, 168
Bean family, 124
Bean, R. M., 2
Beckett, J. F., 36, 81
Beckwourth, James P., 23-25
Beebee, W. L., 14, 51, 89, 175
Bell, John S., 81, 82
Biddle, John, 3, 12
Biddle, Phillip, 3, 12, 14
"Big Four" (Huntington, Stanford, Crocker, Hopkins), 47, 187, 188
Black Canyon of the Gunnison, 142
Blackburn, Daniel, 18, 27, 28, 30, 31, 89, 91
Blackburn family, 27, 30, 32-34, 89, 181
Blackburn, Jacob, 28
Blackburn, James H., 2, 6, 18, 27-30, 33, 89
Blackburn, Margaret, 27
Blackburn, William, 28
Blockman and Son, 44
Bohrmeister, William, 188
Bolsa de Chamisal Land Grant (Rancho), 11, 12, 15, 78
Bonetti, E. M., 143
Bonilla, Jose Mariano, 14, 16, 17, 68
Bonilla, Patricio, 17
Borica, Governor Diego, 20
Boronda, Beatrice, 121
Boronda, Epifanio, 73, 119, 121, 124, 132

Boso, Frank, 3
Bosse, Henry, 156
Bowen (undertaker), 160
Branch, Francis (Francisco) Ziba, 11-17, 24
Branch, Frank, 13
Branch, Fredrico, 12
Branch, Jose F., 2, 181
Branch, Leandro, 13, 14
Branch, L. Ramon, 12-14
Breck, William, 69
Briggs, Fergusson & Company, 74, 76
Brizzolara Creek, 150
Broad Street (San Luis Obispo), 2, 5, 35, 37, 58, 121, 128
Broadway Wharf (San Francisco), 83
Bronson, 47
Brooks, Benjamin, ix, 52, 53, 56-59, 61, 71, 73-76, 78, 81-84, 88, 89, 93, 97, 98, 100, 103, 104, 106, 108, 110, 111, 113-115, 117-119, 122, 124-126, 129-132, 135, 137, 145, 151, 152, 166-168, 170, 173, 175-177, 179-181
Brooks, Mrs. Benjamin, 175
Brown, Arthur, 123
Brown, Jasper, 52
Brown, John, 14
Brumley, C. R., 2
Brunner, Henry, 122, 151, 161, 162, 175
Brunner, Mrs. Henry, 175
Buchanan, E. Y., 59
Buchon Street (San Luis Obispo), 121
Buckley, William, 2, 6
Buddhist Temple (San Luis Obispo), 7
Buena Addition (San Luis Obispo), 62
Buena Esperanza Land Grant (Rancho), 9
Buena Vista Lakes, 31
Burbank, 188
Burnett, George, 147
Burnett, Wesley, 157, 158
Burns, Frank J., 91, 94, 95, 173
Burns, Mrs. Frank J., 173
Burton, Lewis T., 12, 13

Cabot, Juan, 21, 22
Caledonia Adobe, 23, 29
California (magazine), 110
California Polytechnic State University (Cal Poly), 44
California Ranch, 54
California Southern Hotel Company, 61, 63.
California, vii, ix, 7, 9, 10-13, 15, 17, 18, 28, 29, 31, 50, 54, 65, 67-69, 82, 83, 93, 108, 129, 146, 148, 163, 169, 184, 188
California Supreme Court, 10
California, University of, 130
Call, Dr., 89
Callender, C. R., 61, 81, 85, 151, 181

Callender family, 49
Cambria, 32, 56, 102
Cameron, Hugh, 78
Canada De Los Pinos Rancho, 83, 84
Canon Perdido (Santa Barbara), 67, 69
Cappe, Juan, 6, 35
Carlon (Carlona), Zefarino, 11
Carlona, Manuela, 11, 12
Carnegie Library (Paso Robles), 89
Carnes (brakeman), 165
Carpinteria, 25, 66
Carrillo, Carlos Antonio, 80
Carrillo, Joaquin, 84
Carrisa Plains, 33, 131
Carter, 143, 144
Casmalia (Someo), 184
Cass, James, 2, 10
Cass, J. and Company, 10, 152
Castle Saloon (San Luis Obispo), 107
Castro, Jose C., 22, 29, 67, 98, 122, 177
Castroville, 74
Catholic Church, 25
Cayucos, 5, 9, 54, 56, 102, 152, 154
Central Addition, 62, 100, 134
Central California Hotel (San Miguel), 173
Central Coast Railroad Company, 9
Cerf, Moses, 11, 13-15
Chamblin, J. L., 38
Chatsworth Park, 188
Chile, 28
Chinatown (San Luis Obispo), 37
Chino Ranch (San Bernardino), 181
Chino Valley Railroad, 181
Cholome, 19, 120, 130
Chorro Creek, 136, 138, 150
Chorro flag stop. See Goldtree
Chorro Street (San Luis Obispo), 2, 35, 37, 58, 121, 126, 144, 147, 149-152, 159, 161, 166-168
Chorro Valley, 56, 150, 151, 155, 158, 165, 167, 169
Chumash Indians, ix, 12, 85
Cienaga Ranch, 139
Clark, Patricia, vii
Cleve, Dr. Van, 160
Coast Line Limited (Southern Pacific Railroad), 186
Coastline Stage Company, 6
Coburns, 19
Cohen, Morris, 14
Cojo Rancho, 69
Commercial and Savings Bank (San Jose), 120
Commercial and Savings Bank (San Luis Obispo), 151, 161, 162
Commercial Bank (Cayucos), 152
Commercial Hotel (San Luis Obispo), 129
Committee of Twenty-one, 106
Concord Stages, 138
Conference of California Historical Societies, 120
Congressional Harbor and River Committee, 169

Cook, Carol, 179
Cooper, Ellwood, 113, 114, 117, 181, 185
Cooper's Blacksmith Shop, 155
Corbet, John, 14
Corona (steamship), 138, 146
Coronado Beach, 65
Corral De Piedra Land Grant (Rancho), 11, 13-15
Corralitas Tract, 13
Cosmopolitan Hotel (Cayucos), 152
Cosmopolitan Hotel (San Luis Obispo), 6, 35, 36, 51, 61, 63, 94, 97, 104, 129, 135
Court Grammar School, 3
Court Street (San Luis Obispo), 2, 40, 41, 121, 155
Coward, W. M., 91
Cox, Dr. H., 53, 81
Cox, Kate, 186
Cox, the Reverend, 42, 44
Crawford Livery Stable, 77, 107
Creasy, Calvin J., 16, 17
Creston, ix, 16, 108, 167
Crittenden, T. T., 175
Crittenden, Mrs. T. T., 175
Crocker. *See* Templeton
Crocker Brothers, 151
Crocker, Charles F., 9, 45, 47, 71, 96, 98, 99, 102-104, 106, 111, 112, 115, 117, 118, 119, 122, 125, 140, 153, 160, 161, 181, 187
Crocker's General Store, 88, 94, 151
Crocker, J., 175
Cuesta (grade or pass), 1, 11, 51, 66, 73-75, 87, 95-97, 105, 119, 121, 123, 124, 127-35, 139, 140, 142, 143, 145, 146, 150-58, 160, 162, 165, 166, 168, 171, 173, 177, 178
Cullems, George, 107
Culverwell, R. S., 178
Cunningham, A. N., 124
Currier, Captain J. S., 179
Cushing (policeman), 127

Dahl, Charles, 14
Daisy Kimball (steam schooner), 149
Dallidet Adobe, 112
Dallidet, P. H., Jr., 2, 10, 36, 38, 96, 98, 181
Dana, Adelina, 84
Dana, Honorable Charles W., 2, 41
Dana, Mrs. C. W., 89
Dana, David A., 84
Dana, E. G., 81
Dana, Eliseo, 84
Dana family, 80, 181
Dana, Frank, 84, 170
Dana, Henry C., 84
Dana, John E., 83, 113
Dana, Josepha Carrillo, 80
Dana, Richard Henry, 80
Dana, Samuel, 84
Dana, William Goodwin, 80, 83, 84
Dart, A. E., 163
Dart, Louisiana Clayton, vii, 108
Davis, Charles, 95
Davis, Professor, 3
Davis, W. C., 107
Daylight Express No. 2 (Southern Pacific Railroad), 185
Dean's Barbershop, 152
Deer Creek, 28
Degelman, C. F., 179
De La Guerra family, 82
De La Guerra, Fred, 124
De La Guerra Street (Santa Barbara), 67
Del Monte Hotel, 66, 89, 139, 145
Dempsey, 25

Denman, Charles, 3
Denny, Captain, 24
Denver, Colorado, 126
Denver and Rio Grande Railroad, 131, 142
Diablo Canyon Nuclear Plant, 101
Dimond, General, 66
Dolliver, P. C., 78, 79
Dowe, Oscar, 38
Draper (conductor), 165
Drury, Mary, 31
Dubost Mine, 183
Dunn, Cecelia, 30, 31
Dunn, Louisa, 31, 32
Dunn, Mary Ann, 30
Dunn, Patrick, 30-32
Duran, Father Prefecto, 23
Durango, Mexico, 126

Eagle Ranch, 76
Easton family, 38, 42
Easton and Eldridge, 49
Easton, Wendell, 50
Echeandia, Governor, 22
Eddy, William L., 129-131
Edna Area, 149, 171
Egan, Judge M., 52, 162
Eight Mile House, 124
El Camino Real, 29
El Chorro Land Grant (Rancho), 89
Elliott, Van R., 89, 139
Ellwood, 75, 105, 111, 113, 114, 117, 121, 131, 140, 150, 154, 155, 162, 179, 186, 187
El Paso De Robles Hotel, 6, 27, 30-32, 34, 45, 48, 89-92, 183, 185
El Paso De Robles Land Grant (Rancho), 1, 18, 21, 22, 24, 25, 27-30, 33, 46, 53, 66, 113
El Pismo Land Grant (Rancho), 11-16, 30, 78
Emerson Elementary School, 39
Engelhardt, 23, 25, 26
Erickson, 135, 138, 143
Erickson's Construction Company, 138, 144, 154
Essex Street (San Luis Obispo), 121
Estabrook (Southern Pacific agent), 165
Estrada, A. R., 116, 122
Estrada family, 74
Estrada Gardens, 74, 142
Estrada, Joaquin, 67, 68, 74, 142
Estrada, Julian, 68
Estrada, Pedro, 68
Estrada, Ramon, 68
Estrella Creek, 20, 26
Estrella District, 19, 26
Estrella Plains, 26
Eureka (steamer), 5, 7, 138, 172
Eureka Ranch, 18, 54
Evans, William, 107, 108, 130, 181
Ewing, Judge W. G., 147
Exchange Hotel (Cayucos), 152

Fair Oaks, 15
Farnum, C. A., 161, 162, 174, 175
Farrely, the Rev. Phillip (Padre Felipe), 26
Faylor, George A., 105
Feliz, Felomena Valenzuela, 9
Feliz, Vicente, 9
Felts, J. M., 97-98, 145, 151-52, 175, 181
Fernandez Ranch, 154
Figueroa, Governor, 17
Fillmore, J. A., 178, 181
Fillmore, J. Millard, 88, 104, 105, 107, 175, 180

Fillmore, J. M., family of, 2, 5, 38, 63, 179
Fillmore, L., 178
Finley, Captain, 28
Finney, Fred, 3
First National Bank (San Luis Obispo), 117
First National Bank (Santa Barbara), 69
Fisher, I. K., 121
Fiske, Mrs. H. W., 89
Fleig, Dorothy, 112
Fleig, Robert, 112
Flickinger, J. H., 119, 121
Flint, Benjamin, 16
Flint, Bixby and Company, 6, 16, 17
Flint, R. G., 3
Fond De Lac, Wisconsin, 7
Fort Kearny, Nebraska, 31
Fourth Street (San Francisco), 49, 102, 104
Fox, A. A., 160
Fox, Michael, 84
Fredericks, Joseph, 147, 175
Fremont, Colonel John, 28, 67, 129
French Hotel (San Luis Obispo), 129, 153
Fresno, 9, 93, 118

Gallardo, F. F., 14
Garcia, Father, 23
Garcia, Inocente, 17, 67, 68
Garcia, Trifon, 68
Garden Street (San Luis Obispo), 102, 130
Garden Street Church, 160
Gates, 81
Gaviota Pass, 83, 105, 111, 119
Geiger, John, 95
Gillette, W. D., 119, 178
Gilroy, 74
Glass, Dr. J. H., 89
Godchaux, Lazarus, 18, 27, 28, 30, 32, 33
Godeys Ladies' Book, 2
Goldtree (Southern Pacific stop), 151, 173, 175, 176
Goldtree Brothers General Store, 2, 4, 56, 61, 63, 93, 117, 131, 151
Goldtree, Isaac, 14, 18, 51-53, 71, 151, 152, 181
Goldtree, Morris, 2, 63, 97, 98, 151, 152, 181
Goldtree, Nathan, 14, 122, 151-52, 181
Goldtree Tract, 152
Gomez, Father Miguel, 23
Goodall, Edwin, 53, 58, 59, 61-63, 89, 100, 101, 104, 109, 178, 179, 181
Goodall, Nelson and Perkins Steamship Company, 17
Goodall, Perkins and Company, 148
Goodman, T. H., 178, 179
Goodrich, J. A., 51, 175, 176, 181
Goodrich, Mrs. J. A., 175
Gorham, Eugene, 95
Gragg, George T., 97, 98, 145
Grand Hotel (San Francisco), 6
Grant, J. D., 38, 97
Grant, W. E., 89
Graves, Ernest, 63, 97, 98, 175
Graves, Madison, 87
Graves, William, 53, 61, 119
Gray, Colonel A. M., 35
Gray, Richard, 173
Greeley, Horace, 4
Gregg, W. A., 2, 97, 175
Grover, 81
Grover City, ix, 14, 15, 128, 146, 160, 166, 179
Groves Creek, 73

Guadalupe, 6, 78, 121, 156
Gulf of Mexico, 126

Haight, Fletcher M., 68
Haight, Henry H., 68, 69
Haight, Samuel W., 68, 69
Hale, O. A., 179
Haley, Captain W. D., 47, 82, 102
Haltier, Emil, 126
Hammond and Company, 137
Haydock, 123
Hamilton, Mount, 119
Hanford, John, 10
Hangtown (Placerville), 31
Hansen, Grant, 78, 94
Hansen, Hazel, 78, 94
Harkness, Frederick, 16
Harkness, Sally Sparks, 16
Harloe, Flora Sparks, 16
Harloe, Marcus, 16, 146
Harper's Ferry, Jefferson County, West Virginia, 27
Harriman, E. H., 187, 188
Harris, R. R., 45
Harris, Samuel, 38
Hasbrouck, A. B., 11
Hatch, E., 2, 18
Hathway (Southern Pacific stop), 173
Hathway, Dr., 55, 150
Hathway Street (San Luis Obispo), 98
Hawkins (fireman), 165
Hawley, W. G., 119
Hayes, Dr. W. W., 2, 36, 38, 53, 97, 98, 113, 175, 181
Hayes, Mrs. W. W., 175
Hazen, 55
Hearst Castle, 68, 148
Hearst, George, 9, 10, 121
Hearst, Phoebe Apperson, 122
Hearst, William Randolph, 10, 122, 148
Heath, Erle, *Seventy-five Years of Progress*, 46
Heister, Jacob, 159, 160
Henderson, W. A., 170, 175
Herrera, 53
Hersman, 97
Hewson House, 44
Hibernia Bank (San Francisco), 69
Higbee, C. E., 178
Higbee and Bernard Construction Company, 136, 138, 142, 154, 165-66
Higgins, John ("Black Jack"), 135
Highway 101, 23, 29
Higuera Street (San Luis Obispo), 2, 5, 35, 57, 58, 84, 102, 103, 108, 109, 120-22, 127-29, 132, 135, 137, 141, 147, 151, 152, 155, 156, 159, 166, 167, 171, 177, 179
Hinkle, W. S., 84
Hollister, 9, 89
Hollister family, 158, 181
Hollister, Honorable J. H., 2, 14
Hollister, Mrs. J. H., 88
Hollister, Joseph H., 2, 61, 97
Hollister, W. W., 2
Holt, L. L., 171
Hood, William, 74, 97, 100, 102, 122, 139, 140, 145, 153, 155, 160, 161, 166, 168, 178, 179, 181
Hopkins, Mark, 9, 47, 187
Hopkins, Timothy, 9
Horra, Antonio De La Conception, 20
Hosiner, Miss, 179
Hosiner, Mrs., 179
Hot Sulphur Wells (Avila), 101
Howard, John L., 18, 107, 178-81, 183
Huasna Land Grant (Rancho), 15, 16
Hubbard, A. F., 131

Huero Huero Land Grant (Rancho), 12, 16-18, 68
Huntington Beach, 128, 146
Huntington, Collis P., 9, 47, 70, 71, 96-99, 104, 110, 111, 114, 118, 122, 129-131, 139, 154, 162, 164, 175, 177-179, 181, 184-188
Huntington, Henry E., 139, 154, 178
Huntington Library, Museum and Art Gallery, 178
Huntington, Williard V., 53
Hutchinson, R., 156

Idaho, 30
Indian Valley Railroad, 20
Ingalls, Captain, 10
Ingleside (subdivision), 53, 101
Ionia, Michigan, 18
Iowa Point, Iowa, 28
Irish Hills, 88
Islay Street (San Luis Obispo), 121

Jack, Mrs. R. E., 89, 175
Jack, Robert E., 2, 18, 38, 51, 54, 57, 61, 63, 71, 89, 96, 100, 101, 103, 104, 107, 108, 110, 111, 113, 117, 118, 120-22, 126, 130, 131, 139-41, 145, 149, 152, 170, 173, 175-77, 179, 181, 183-84
Jackson, Andrew, 99
Jackson, Helen Hunt, 185
James, Drury Woodson, 2, 18, 31, 89-91, 113, 181
James family, 27, 32, 34
James, Louisa, 91
Jeffreys, W. M., 2
Jesperson, Senator Chris, 30
Jimeno, Governor Manuel, 14, 15, 67
Johnson Avenue (San Luis Obispo), 49, 57, 59, 100, 152, 155
Johnson, Captain, 57-59, 61
Johnson, Charles H., 7, 55, 96, 97, 111, 115, 164, 168, 181
Johnson, Charles O., 142, 173, 176
Jones, C. D. P., 2
Jones, Edward, 14
Jones Tract, 13
Jordon Bituminous Rock Mines, 171
Jordon, J. M., 2
Journal of Commerce (San Francisco), 53, 56

Kaiser, L. M., 2, 36, 38, 51, 52, 96, 104, 145, 161, 162, 173, 175, 181
Kaiser, Mrs. L. M., 175
Kansas City, Missouri, 56
Kemp, 174
Kern County, 52, 71, 118
Kiernan (policeman), 127
Kimball, Willard, 51
King City (Kings), 19, 74, 145
King, C. O., 55, 126, 139
King, G. L., 139
King Ranch, 19
Knight, Charles, 3
Knight, Mrs., 125
Knob Hill Subdivision (Arroyo Grande), 81, 85
Krampner, Jane, 9
Krebs, E., 35, 36, 130
Kurtz, 42
Kwitz, 52

La Fiesta (San Luis Obispo), 108
Laguna Lake, 159, 160
Laguna Largo, 78
La Panza District, 31
Larkin, Thomas, 29

Lasar, Mark I., 122, 131, 175
Las Tablas Hills, 183
Lasuen, Father Presidente Fermin de, 20
Lataillade, Cesario, 25
Latimer's Drug Store, 176
Laughery Hotel (San Luis Obispo), 157
La Vista, 94
Paso Robles Leader, 90, 92
Leadville, Colorado, 142
Lee, Charles, 73
Lee, R. E., 170
Leland, Captain, 172
Leland family, 38
Leland Stanford Jr. University, 116, 117, 187
Lenzen (architect), 90
Lester, Edward, 13
Lester, F. F., 13
Lewin, M., 126
Lewis Foundation Corporation, 67
Lewis, Frank, 38
"Life and Adventures of James P. Beckwourth," 23
Linnell (Southern Pacific agent), 165
Livingston family, 38
Logan County, Virginia, 27
Lompoc, 69, 119, 145, 148, 184, 185, 187
Lompoc Historical Society, vii
Long Beach, 78
Loobliners General Store, 2, 40, 41, 149
Loomis, R., 98, 127, 145, 181
Los Alamos, 2, 11, 36, 80-82, 135, 136, 138, 179
Los Angeles, ix, 6, 7, 9, 16, 18, 19, 28, 31, 43, 46, 52, 55, 60, 62, 65, 69, 73, 83, 93, 104, 110, 113, 114, 118, 119, 126, 133, 138, 139, 145, 148, 149, 154, 155, 168, 171, 172, 174, 184-88
Los Angeles (steamship), 7, 138, 172
Los Angeles Tribune, 104
Los Berro Area, 82, 138
Los Olivos, 81-85, 96, 106, 107, 109, 110, 135, 138, 142, 153
Los Olivos Hotel, 107
Los Olivos Stage, 110
Los Osos Land Grant (Rancho), 1
Los Osos Valley, 2, 100, 113, 151, 168
Los Tablas Creek, 26
Loughran, Bernice, vii
Louis, Ah, 37, 168, 181
Louis family, 37
Louis, Gon Ying, 38
Lucas, W. T., 2, 82
Ludington, George C., 50
Lynch, Joseph, 25
Lytton Theater, 3, 39

McBride, H. E., 96
McCabe, Leland, 160
McClure Seed Company, 183
McCoppin, 97
McCormick, E. O., 185
McCoy, Professor W. J., 3, 5, 37-39, 41
McCray, F. P., 89
McCullough, Captain, 28
McDougall, S. P., 12
McGreal, Thomas, 18
McKeen, David, 84
McKennon's Stable, 139
McKinley, Carmen Amesti, 9
McKinley, Elena, 9
McKinley, James, 9, 10
McKinley, President William, 188
McLaughlin's Drug Store (Los Alamos), 136
McLaughlin and Manns Stagecoach, 30
McLeod, Major A. C., 175

McMahon, Patrick, 165
McMurtrie, J. A., 131, 142, 153, 179
McMurtrie and Stone, 132, 134, 183
McShane, Edward W., 68

Maddux, 104
Madonna Road (San Luis Obispo), 137
Maenorchor Hall, 94, 130
Main Street (Arroyo Grande), 82
Mallagh, A., 38
Mallagh, David, 16, 17
Manderscheid, George, 144
Manderscheid, Mrs. George, 144
Manuel, Flora, 9
Markham, Governor, 148
Marre Hotel (Avila), 56, 94, 95
Marre, Luigi, 2, 94, 145, 151, 181
Marsh (construction engineer), 165
Marsh Street (San Luis Obispo), 58, 102, 121, 128, 130, 132, 135, 168
Marsh, W. F., 153
Marshall, Frank, 94
Marshall, Manuel, 3
Martin, Father Juan, 21, 22
Martin, William, 68
Martinez, Mr. and Mrs. D., 143
Mason, Colonel R. B. (governor of California), 24, 28
Masonic Temple (San Luis Obispo), 168
Mather, the Rev., 116
Maxwell, Charles, 2
Meherin, M., 78
Mehlman, 122
Menton, W. H., 26
Merced, 9, 118
Merritt, C. W., 2
Methener, 95
Mexican Army, 29
Mexico, ix, 15, 16, 28, 31
Mexico City, 16
Meyers, Jim, 124
Micheltorena, Manuel, 18, 28
Miguel Maria (Indian boy), 20
Miles, G. E., 96, 179
Miles Station, 7, 80, 138
Mill Street (San Luis Obispo), 2
Mills, D. O., 162
Mission La Purisima, 184
Mission San Antonio, 20
Mission San Juan Capistrano, 26
Mission San Luis Obispo de Tolosa, 1, 14, 17
Mission San Miguel, 16, 17, 19, 21-27, 30, 68, 181, 182
Mission Santa Ynez, 26
Mission School (San Luis Obispo), 39, 134
Mission Street (San Miguel), 94
Mission Vineyard Tract (San Luis Obispo), 169
Missouri River, 28
Missouri, 15, 31
Mitchell, F. C., 144, 162, 175
Modesto, 9
Mofras, Eugene de, 23
Monterey, 20, 24, 28, 29, 31, 58, 145
Monterey County, 30, 111, 114
Monterey Peninsula, 139
Monterey Street (San Luis Obispo), 1, 2, 4, 9, 31, 35, 37, 40, 41, 43, 44, 88, 96, 108, 109, 116, 120, 123, 128, 129, 134, 140, 141, 143, 146-50, 152-56, 163, 166-68, 170, 171, 177, 179, 181
Montgomery, Bishop, 181
Montgomery Street (San Francisco), 6
Moody, D. B., 119, 121, 122
Moore, Pat, 156
Moore, Patrick, 84
Moreno, Father, 23

McMahon, Patrick, 165
Morgan Hill Ranch, 126
Moro. See Baywood Park
Moro Y Cayucos Land Grant (Rancho), 1, 9, 10
Morris, E. B., 5, 38
Morris, T. B., 170
Morrison, J. C., 38
Morro Bay, 9, 51, 56, 169
Morro Street (San Luis Obispo), 2, 35, 40, 149, 155, 156
Morse's Detective Agency, 144
Motz, G. L., 131
Munoz, G., 171
Munras, Esteban, 22
Murdock, 123
Murphy, Bernard D., 68, 91, 119
Murphy, James T., 68
Murphy, Martin, 67, 68
Murphy, Mary Kate, 68, 69
Murphy, Patrick W., 2, 11, 51, 52, 61, 67-71, 74, 76, 97, 111, 116, 122, 142, 156, 168, 178, 179, 181
Murphy, Timothy, 156
Murray, Walter, 30
Muscio, Lillie, 43
Muscio, Miss, 116
Mut, the Rev. Jose, 26

Nacimiento River, 20
Napa County, 7
Narvaez, Pedro, 18, 24, 28, 29
National Bridge Company, 161
Neal's Drug Store (San Miguel), 95
Needles, 9
Nevada, 6, 30
Nevada House, 142
Never, Otto E., 34
Newhall, 43
Newsom, Anna, 12, 13
Newsom Springs, 136
New York Tribune, 4
Nichols, Dr. G. B., 125, 132, 139, 142, 160, 162, 167, 171, 172
Nichols family, 52
Nichols, Mrs. G. B., 175
Nicholson, Loren, vii, ix
Nicholson, Patricia Henley, vii
Nipomo, 80, 81, 83, 121, 128, 135, 138, 170
Nipomo Land Grant (Rancho), 1, 80, 83-85, 113
Nipomo News, 80, 81
Nipomo Street (San Luis Obispo), 2, 39
Noah (deputy collector), 38, 168
Nojoqui Falls, 83
Norton, Dr. T., 175
Norton, Mrs. T., 175
Noya (steam schooner), 149

Oakland, 172
O'Brien, Dr. P. M. family, 69
Occidental Bituminous Rock Company, 136
Ocean Street (Cayucos), 152
Oceano, ix, 13, 139-142, 156, 166, 183
Oceano Beach and Land Improvement Company, 142
Oceano Hotel, 143
Oceano Saloon, 143
Oceano Townsite Company, 183
Odd Fellows Hall (Cayucos), 152
Ohio River, 15
Olivera, Josepha Noriega de, 9
Olivera, Martin, 9
Oquawkee, Illinois, 27
Orcutt, J. H., 36, 97
Oregon, 30, 32
Oregon-California Line (Southern Pacific), 114

Oregon Improvement Company, 17, 18, 106
Orizaba (steamship), 7
Ormsby House (Carson City, Nevada), 38
Orra, Jose, 21
Orra, Josepha, 21
Ortega, Ernestine, 147
Ortega, Jose C., 6, 15, 169
Ortega Rancho, 25
Osos Street (San Luis Obispo), 1, 4, 31, 37, 40, 41, 43, 44, 58, 62, 98, 121, 128, 148, 155, 156
Otto, Richard, 168
Overland Monthly, 27, 32
Oxnard, 188

Pacific Coast, 2, 18, 34, 78, 129
Pacific Coast Petroleum, 11
Pacific Coast Railway, 1, 2, 4, 5, 11, 17, 37, 43, 51, 53, 55-58, 79-81, 83-85, 88, 89, 93, 95, 96, 101, 103, 106-10, 113, 115, 126, 127, 132, 135-38, 140, 142, 144, 147, 148, 153, 166, 168, 171, 176, 178, 179, 181, 183
Pacific Coast Stage, 123
Pacific Coast Steamship Company, 2, 5, 7, 17, 53-61, 93, 106, 109, 113, 137, 138, 144, 148, 149, 171, 181
Pacific Improvement Company, 67, 74, 76, 123, 127, 153
Pacific Ocean, 14
Pacific Street (San Luis Obispo), 121
Pajaro Junction, 9, 74
Palm Street (San Luis Obispo), 3, 36, 37, 58, 88, 130, 148
Panama, Isthmus of, 11
Parkfield, 20, 182
Parkhurst, W. A., 119, 121
Parsons, Levi, 11, 14
Paso Robles, 18, 20, 27, 31, 33, 34, 46, 48, 56, 71, 74, 75, 85, 89, 90, 92, 97, 98, 102, 120, 139, 144, 146, 178, 179, 182, 183
Paso Robles Board of Trustees, 89
Paso Robles Hot Springs. *See* El Paso De Robles Hotel.
Paso Robles Inn. *See* El Paso De Robles Hotel
Paso Robles Leader, 102
Paso Robles Moon, 105
Patterson, W. H., 14
Patton, J. R., 2
Peach Street (San Luis Obispo), 121
Pear Tree Ranch, 128
Perkins, Governor George, 17, 18, 148, 181
Pescadero Rancho, 11
Pettit, Benjamin F., 36, 84
Philips, A., 2
Phillips Addition, 134
Phillips, C. H. and Company, 10, 48, 62
Phillips, Chauncey Hatch, 2, 3, 6, 7, 9, 16-18, 36, 38, 41, 44-46, 49, 51, 52, 61, 63, 66, 82-85, 89, 108-11, 113, 114, 117-20, 123, 125, 126, 134, 139, 145, 151, 155, 164, 173, 176, 179, 181
Phillips, Jane Woods, 7, 11
Phillips, Jennie, 89
Phillips, Lyda, 89
Pickett, Mayor, 147
Pico, Governor Pio, 14, 16, 17, 23
Pirates Cove, 16, 67
Pismo Beach, 15, 77-80, 118, 146, 149, 156, 166, 179, 183
Pismo Hotel, 78
Pismo Inn, 80
Pismo Wharf, 149, 171

Point Reyes, 11
Point Sal, 146
Pollard, S. A., 84, 166
Pomeroy, A. E., 78
Port Harford (Port San Luis), 2, 5, 7, 17, 29, 53, 55, 60, 79, 80, 83-85, 93, 95, 101-3, 108, 110, 126, 137, 138, 144-47, 149, 151, 172, 174
Porter, Arza, 2, 16
Porter, Rosa Sparks, 16
Portland, 59
Potrero, 150
Potter, Arza, 36
Powers, Jack, 30
Pratt, R. H., 123
Prefumo, P. B., 84, 175, 181
Prefumo and Vollmers, 116
Price, Andrea Coloma, 15
Price, John, 15, 16, 24, 151, 181
Price, Margaret, vii
Pritchard, Captain, 157
Protection (steam schooner), 149
"Pueblo de San Luis Obispo de Tolosa" (painting), 129
Pujol, Domingo, 9, 10

Queen Pacific (steamship), 84, 95
Quijada, Francisco, 12, 15
Quijada, Leonora Manuela, 13
Quijada, Maria Dolores, 13
Quijada, Nasario, 12
Quinn, Peter, 25
Quintana Brothers, 116, 150, 175
Quintana, P., 181

Racliffe, L., 97, 104, 113, 123, 129, 145, 173, 175
Ramona Hotel (Hotel Del Montezuma), 59, 62, 87, 88, 94, 96, 100, 104-107, 109, 111, 112, 115, 117, 118, 123, 125, 139, 142, 147, 150, 153, 155-57, 166, 173, 174, 176-79, 183-85, 188
Rathbun, S. B., 88
Ready, Phillip, 74, 162
Reardon, Mat, 171
Redfield, Walter S., 168
Redlasbrook, A., 2
Redondo Beach, 147
Reed, C. H., 2, 122, 170, 175
Reed, Ralph, 95
Reed, William, 23-25, 29, 30
Refugio Ranch, 14
Reid, Whitelaw, 4
Remer (Raymond), Peter, 25
Remick, A. C., 109, 127, 144
Rice, Coffee, 139, 140
Rios, Catarina, 30
Rios, Petronillo, 18, 23, 24, 29, 32
Rockliffe, L., 2
Rockwell, J. J., 188
Rodriquez, Conception Villa de, 14
Rodriquez, Frank, 3, 129
Rodriquez, Rafaila, 14
Rodriquez, Ramon, 25
Rodriquez, Solano, 14
Rollins Company, 125
Roosevelt, President Theodore, 106
Rose Alley (San Luis Obispo), 35
Rosener, 81
Roth, Isaac, 14
Roundtree, Professor, 149
Rudy, Paul, 172
Russell, C. J., 2, 52, 61, 63, 98

Sacramento, 28, 104, 162
St. Charles Hotel (Santa Barbara), 66
Saint Louis, Missouri, 12, 15
Salinan Indians, ix

Salinas, 6, 9, 74
Salinas River, 6, 20, 128
Samuel's Store (Cayucos), 152
San Antonio Mission, 20-22
San Benito County, 9
San Buenaventura, 6
San Diego, 6, 62, 65, 83, 126, 146, 171
San Fernando Tunnel, 154
San Francisco, ix, 5-7, 9, 11, 16, 18, 19, 26, 29, 30, 32-34, 39, 46, 49-51, 53, 55, 60, 63, 65, 69, 73-75, 78, 81, 83, 84, 88, 90, 92, 93, 96, 98, 100-6, 110, 113-15, 117-20, 122, 123, 126, 128, 130, 131, 137-40, 143-45, 147-50, 154, 160, 164, 170-72, 174, 176, 178-80, 182-87
San Francisco Bulletin, 30, 105, 106, 140-42
San Francisco Call, 45, 98, 106, 182
San Francisco Chronicle, 120, 131-33, 140, 153, 155
San Francisco Examiner, 114, 120, 154, 163
San Francisco and San Jose Railroad, 7
San Joaquin County, 9
San Joaquin Valley, 49, 71, 75, 78, 80, 93, 126, 145, 185
San Jose, 7, 9, 30, 52, 69, 74, 96, 97, 113-15, 117-22
San Jose Board of Trade, 119, 121
San Jose Mercury, 114-16, 121, 126
San Jose News, 179
San Jose State University, 120
San Juan Bautista, 20
San Julian Pass, 119
San Luis Creek, 7, 35, 39, 55, 79, 101, 105, 108, 121, 150, 166, 171
San Luis Hot Sulphur Springs, 105
San Luis and San Joaquin Valley Railway Association, 126
San Luis Obispo, 1-3, 5, 6, 9, 11, 18, 24, 31, 32, 35-39, 42-44, 46-48, 51, 52, 54-62, 70-72, 74-77, 79-81, 84, 85, 87, 89, 92, 95-101, 104-12, 115, 117-20, 123, 125-33, 135-37, 140, 142-51, 153-60, 162, 163, 165, 166, 168-74, 176-86, 188
San Luis Obispo Agricultural Association, 61, 87
San Luis Obispo Bank, 2, 3, 7, 37, 40, 41, 69, 145
San Luis Obispo Bituminous Rock Company, 109, 136
San Luis Obispo Board of Health, 134
San Luis Obispo Board of Trade, 51-57, 61, 79, 93, 102, 109-11, 121, 132, 145, 170, 174
San Luis Obispo Building and Loan Association, 126
San Luis Obispo City Hall, 127, 129, 134, 173, 177
San Luis Obispo County, vii, ix, 7-12, 16-19, 23, 27, 29-31, 34, 36, 45, 49, 50, 52-56, 60, 65, 66, 68-71, 74, 77, 81, 82, 89, 92-94, 98, 106, 111, 113, 114, 116-18, 120, 121, 123, 126-28, 133, 149, 155, 168, 169, 174, 181, 183
San Luis Obispo County Bank, 3, 69, 151
San Luis Obispo County Courthouse, 43
San Luis Obispo County Historical Society, vii, 10, 108, 112
San Luis Obispo County Museum, vii
San Luis Obispo de Tolosa Mission, 1, 12-14, 17, 20, 23, 31, 35, 66-68, 76, 81, 113, 130, 144
San Luis Obispo Investment and Development Company, 145, 151, 152
San Luis Obispo Military Band, 3, 81, 84, 101, 147, 174

San Luis Obispo Mountain, 2, 88, 116, 154, 185
San Luis Obispo Public Library, vii, 161
San Luis Obispo Pavilion (also Agricultural Hall, Women's Civic Club), 87, 88, 129, 130
San Luis Obispo Railroad, 62
San Luis Obispo Railroad Committee, 120, 122
San Luis Obispo South County Historical Society, viii, 102
San Luis Obispo Tribune, ix, 2, 4-6, 19, 32, 36, 38, 40, 46, 48, 52, 55-57, 61, 65, 66, 69-74, 77-79, 85, 90-92, 94, 96, 100-102, 107, 108, 111, 118, 119, 124-26, 128, 131, 134-36, 138, 141, 142, 144-51, 153, 154, 156, 160, 161, 163-69, 171, 174, 181-84, 186
San Luis Obispo Twentieth Century Club, 186
San Luis Obispo Water Company, 69
San Marcos Hotel (Santa Barbara), 73, 110, 132
San Martin Ranch, 126
San Mateo County, 11
San Miguel, 6, 20, 27, 56, 93, 95, 118, 120, 128, 173, 182, 183
San Miguel Hall, 94
San Miguel Messenger, 94
San Miguelito Land Grant (Rancho), 1, 15, 79
San Pedro, 16, 105
Sanizal Rancho, 9
San Simeon Land Grant (Rancho), 17, 55, 68
San Simeon Wharf, 172
Sandercock, William, 61, 97, 98, 104, 123, 127, 128, 132, 151, 157, 167, 175, 181
Santa Barbara, ix, 6, 9, 12, 14, 16, 17, 25, 48, 53, 56, 58, 65-67, 69-71, 80, 82, 83, 85, 106, 110, 111, 113, 117, 119, 120, 122, 126, 129-32, 138, 142, 145, 148, 154, 173, 174, 184-86, 188
Santa Barbara County, 81, 82, 111, 113, 114, 121, 129
Santa Barbara Historical Society, vii
Santa Barbara Mission, 70
Santa Barbara Press, 65, 70, 111
Santa Barbara Street (San Luis Obispo), 37
Santa Clara College, 69
Santa Clara County, 9, 31, 111, 113-15, 120, 121
Santa Clara County Courthouse, 115
Santa Cruz, 52, 140
Santa Cruz Mountains, 28
Santa Fe Railroad, 9, 57
Santa Lucia Mountains, 51, 88
Santa Manuela Land Grant (Rancho), 1, 1, 12, 15
Santa Margarita, ix, 72, 74, 76, 87, 93, 95-98, 104, 106, 114, 118, 120, 121, 124, 126, 128, 131, 134-37, 139, 140, 143, 146, 147, 151, 153, 154, 157, 161, 164, 166, 173, 175, 176
Santa Margarita Land Grant (Rancho), 1, 11, 29, 30, 50, 51, 66-68, 70, 71, 73-75, 111, 113, 117, 122-24, 126, 127, 132, 142, 150, 168, 178
Santa Margarita Land and Cattle Company, 67
Santa Maria, 11, 56, 78, 80, 96, 119, 120, 138, 141, 145, 148, 156, 173, 178, 179
Santa Maria Historical Society, vii
Santa Maria Times, 156
Santa Monica, 155
Santa Monica Outlook, 154, 155
Santa Paula, 65
Santa Rosa (steamship), 7, 83, 138

Santa Rosa Land Grant (Rancho), 68
Santa Rosa Street (San Luis Obispo), 3, 31, 121, 128, 130
Santa Susanna Mountains, 188
Santa Ynez, 83, 84, 119, 142
Santa Ynez Land and Improvement Company, 84
Santa Ynez Mission, 83, 179
Santa Ynez River, 184, 185
Santa Ysabel (Isabel) Land Grant (Rancho), 18, 22, 54, 55, 66
Sastre, the Rev. Father, 31
Sauer Hall (San Luis Obispo), 94
Sauer, W. F., 53, 131
Sauer's Bakery, 4
Saugus, 65, 154, 186, 187
Schwartz, L., 9
Schwartz, W., 2
Scotia (steam schooner), 149
Scott, James, 10
Scott, John, 2
Seattle, Washington, 126
Seely, Colonel, 84
Serrano (Southern Pacific stop), 173
Serouf, C. C., 166
Seymour, Henry, 28
Shackelford, Hiram, 89, 91, 120, 121, 178
Shandon, 55, 112, 167
Sharp Brothers, 38, 42
Sharp, Henry W., 39, 41
Sharp, J. W., 38
Shea, John, 3
Shea, Mat, 3
Sheerin, 96
Shell Beach, 15
Shope, Judge, 147
Shortridge, C. M., 119, 121
Simas, John, 3
Sinsheimer, Mrs. A., 175
Sinsheimer, Benjamin, 2, 35, 51, 97, 98, 113, 175
Sinsheimer, Mrs. Benjamin, 175
Sinsheimer Brothers, 2, 35, 151
Sinton, Silas, 67
Siskiyou Mountains, 141
Sitjar, Father Buenaventure, 20
Skow, Smith, 175
Sloat, Commodore John Drake, 29
Small, H. J., 105
Smith, Frank, 125
Smith, Jedediah, 15
Smith, J. W., 81, 84, 85, 156
Sofar, Timothy, 21
Soledad, 9, 16, 19, 34, 43, 70, 145, 168
Solomon, W., 139
Someo. See Casmalia
South County Historical Society. See San Luis Obispo South County Historical Society
South Street (San Luis Obispo), 147
Southern California Immigration Company, 45
Southern Hotel Company. See California Southern Hotel Company
Southern Pacific Milling Company, 90, 96

Southern Pacific Railroad Company, 6, 9, 16, 18-20, 27, 34, 39, 43, 45-49, 51, 53, 55-57, 59-62, 65, 67, 69-74, 76, 78, 81, 85, 87, 93, 95-98, 100-106, 110, 111, 113-19, 121-35, 137, 139-42, 145, 146, 150-58, 160, 162, 163, 165-68, 170, 171, 173, 175-79, 181-88
Spain, ix
Sparks, Isaac, 15, 16
Spencer, W. H., 2
Sperry, H. A., 2, 12
Sperry, H. S., 12
Sperry, Louisa B., 12
Springfield, Ohio, 27
Spurrier, G. F., 89
Stanford, Leland, 9, 17, 47, 65, 102, 104, 110, 116-18, 148, 149, 187
Stanford, Mrs. Leland, 187
Staniford, G. B., 2, 123
Staniford, T., 38
Stanislaus County, 24
Stanley, Honorable H. Y., 2
Stanwood, E., 135
State Street (Santa Barbara), 65, 67, 69, 72
Stearns, Abel, 17
Steele, Delia, 11
Steele, Edgar W., 2, 11-14, 52, 53, 55, 57, 61, 63, 83, 96-99, 104, 119, 164, 175, 181
Steele family, 16
Steele, George, 2, 11-13, 41, 42, 44, 120, 121, 136, 146, 151, 175, 181
Steele, Mrs. George, 175
Steele, Isaac, 13, 14
Steele, Lewis, 11
Steele, Renseleur, 11, 14
Steele and Wheelan's Flour Mill, 40
Steele-Willey Syndicate, 83
Stenner Creek, 100, 102, 106, 147, 150, 155, 160, 161, 163, 165, 167, 169-75
Stephenson Brothers, 36
Stevens, W. F., 149
Stevenson, A. E. (Vice President of the United States), 147
Stevenson, Mrs. A. E., 147
Stewart, W. E., 2
Stockton, 120
Stokes, W. R., 89
Stone, George, 131, 132, 134, 178-80
Storni, Irene, 43
Stow, S. R., 61
Stow, W. W., 14, 158, 161
Stowe, J. M., 84
Stowell, 139
Stubbs, J. C., 178, 179
Stubbs, Mrs. J. C., 179
Sublet, Milton, 15
Sullivan, Joe, 3
Summers, J. D. E., 48
Sunset Express No. 10 (Southern Pacific Railroad), 185
Sunset Magazine, 34, 55, 91
Sunset Route (Southern Pacific Railroad), 9
Surf (Southern Pacific stop), 184-86
Sycamore Hot Springs, 127, 138

Taber (brakeman), 165
Taminelli, P. and Company General Store (Cayucos), 152
Tehachapi Mountains, 9, 49, 141
Templeton, Bank of, 73
Templeton (Crocker), ix, 18, 20, 29, 45, 46-48, 50, 51, 54-56, 60, 65, 66, 70-72, 74, 81, 89, 105, 108, 113, 118, 151, 167, 183
Templeton Hotel, 47
Templeton Institute, 47
Templeton Lutheran Church, 47
Templeton Times, 47, 82
Tennessee Pass, 142
Terrace Hill, 130, 134, 156
Terry, Frank, 3
Thayer, Colonel C. C., 81
Thompson, Francisca, 84
Thompson, Francisco A., 84
Thompson, J. D., 2
Thompson, John D., 31
Thompson, Tommy, 170
Tittle, H. S., 171
Tognazzini, A., 44
Toro Street (San Luis Obispo), 88
Towne, A. N., 102, 130, 131
Townsend Street (San Francisco), 49, 102, 104
Treat, Colonel R. B., 2, 55
Treat family, 38
Trimble, Alex, 160
Trousset, L., 129, 130
Tulare, 9, 31, 118
Tulare Indians, ix, 17, 21, 22
Turner, Jasper, 53, 55, 97

Unangst, Edwin P., 52, 97, 98, 104, 126, 130, 170, 175, 181
Union Pacific Railroad, 187, 188
United States Coast Guard, 102
United States Internal Revenue Department, 7
United States Land Commission, ix, 12, 14, 16, 18, 25, 29, 68, 84
United States Signal Service, 4
University of the Pacific, 120
Upchurch, Dillard, 157
Utah, 142

Vachell, Horace A., 38, 145, 164, 181
Vandoit, F. A., 175
Van Harreveld, Constance, 13, 15
Van Schaick, J. E., 3
Van Warmer, John M., 89
Vaughn, Charlie, 149
Vear, Joseph, 84
Venable, Judge McDowell R., 2, 97, 145, 147, 151, 152, 161, 162, 175
Venable, Mrs. McDowell R., 89, 175, 181
Vendome Hotel (San Jose), 113, 114

Ventura, 65, 105, 154, 174
Ventura County, 111, 113, 114, 155
Vetterline, F. W., 170
Villa, Fulgencio, 14
Villa, Jacinto, 14
Villa, Jose Ramona, 14
Villa, Menpeda Josepha, 14
Villavicencio, Jose Maria, 13-15, 22
Vischer, Edward, 30
Vollmer, August, 175, 181

Waite and Ryans, 177
Wallace, J. H., 105
Wallace, William, 143
Walker, J. H., 123
Warden, Mrs. H. M., 89
Warden, Horatio Moore, 2, 3, 7, 36, 97, 98, 104, 127, 145, 151, 181
Warden, Lew M., 2, 96, 100, 104, 113, 120, 123, 181
Warden, William, 38
Warner, E. L., 162
Warren, E. E., 152
Washington, D.C., 122
Waterman's Saloon (Cayucos), 152
Watson, H. B., 9
Watsonville, 9, 28
Waverly (brig), 80
Weber Creek, 31
Webster, J. V., 16, 17, 164
Weller, H. W., 84
Wells Fargo and Company, 3, 27, 34, 47, 146
West Coast Land Company, 17, 18, 45, 47-50, 54-56, 61, 63, 66, 68, 70, 71, 73, 82, 84, 97, 104, 108-11, 118, 134, 148, 151, 181, 183
Westerfield, James, 28
Wheeler, C. C., 72
Whippoorwill River, Logan County, Kentucky, 31
White, James, 14
Wilcoxon, J. M., 145, 175
Willey, Susie E., 9
William, T. W., 84
Williams, S. H., 142
Wilson, Captain John, 10
Wilson, S. W., 175
Winningstadt, O., 153
Wise, J. H., 126
Wittenberg, David, 11
Wright, Lillian, 89
Wurch, Dale, 3
Wyeth, John, 14

Ynocenta Subdivision, 79

Zaca Lake, 82
Zinman, Charles, 159, 160
Zoppi, Edward, 152